Cecil B. DeMille

CECIL B. DeMILLE

*a guide to references
and resources*

A
Reference
Publication
in
Film

Ronald Gottesman
Editor

CECIL B. DeMILLE

a guide to references and resources

SUMIKO HIGASHI

G.K. HALL &CO.

70 LINCOLN STREET, BOSTON, MASS.

Published by G.K. Hall & Co.
A publishing subsidiary of ITT
All Rights Reserved
Copyright © 1985 by Sumiko Higashi.

Library of Congress Cataloging in Publication Data

Higashi, Sumiko.
  Cecil B. DeMille : a guide to references and resources.

  (A Reference publication in film)
  Bibliography: p.
  Includes indexes.
  1. DeMille, Cecil Blount, 1881-1959 I. Title.
II. Series.
PN1993.A3D387 1985   791.43'0233'0924   85-2579
ISBN 0-8161-8533-6

This publication is printed on permanent/durable acid-free paper
MANUFACTURED IN THE UNITED STATES OF AMERICA

To
Satsuko, Setsuo, Bob,
Kim, Ted, and Pay

Contents

The Author

Sumiko Higashi received a PhD in history from UCLA. She is currently associate professor of history at the State University of New York College at Brockport and is the author of Virgins, Vamps and Flappers: The American Silent Movie Heroine.

Preface

    Since individual volumes in the Directors Series are shaped to some extent by idiosyncrasies concerning each director, the following should be noted about Cecil B. DeMille: for reasons discussed in the critical survey, film scholars have evinced little interest in DeMille. Consequently, the annotated bibliography is scant and contains references to a great deal of popular literature that does have value and in some instances proves to be more illuminating than scholarly books and articles. Standard works in film history have been omitted unless they elaborated on the usual, clichéd observations about DeMille's Jazz Age films and spectacles. Certain reference works have been included if the entries on DeMille were deemed useful. A few foreign language works, especially in French, are listed but, as would be expected, the availability of foreign film periodicals in the United States is limited to the better-known publications like Cahiers du cinéma. The Institut des Hautes Etudes Cinématographiques in Paris has a wide range of popular and scholarly French film periodicals. Like all researchers, I am indebted to the standard indexes: The Film Index, The New Film Index, Motion Picture Directors, Film Literature Index, Retrospective Index to Film Periodicals, Film Book Biography, and The Critical Index.

    Since DeMille's career as a filmmaker goes back to the early days of the motion picture industry, data about his films vary and cannot always be ascertained. Production credits, for example, were not completely listed in DeMille's films until the late thirties. Undoubtedly Wilfred Buckland worked as art director on practically all of the silent productions, but this cannot be substantiated by reference to the scripts or available research material. By contrast, all the names of DeMille's cameramen were scrupulously recorded on scripts during the silent era. Curiously the scripts for the silent films contain more information about the credits, however minimal, than the weighty tomes for the sound movies. Gene Ringgold and DeWitt Bodeen's The Films of Cecil B. DeMille has been a handy source though it contains some errors. Since the authors had access to the DeMille papers eventually donated to Brigham Young University, they are generally correct, but even the director's papers contain conflicting or inaccurate information or typographical errors. Film credits that bear a § mark were drawn from the French

publication, Présence du cinéma, which contains much data unavailable
in other works but is not always accurate and is difficult to verify.
Release dates and especially screening times cannot in some instances
be specified with exactness and are thus approximate. I have viewed
all but eleven of DeMille's seventy films but in varying conditions
and at different projection speeds.

Reviews for several of the silent films are most accessible in the
clipping files or early fan magazines and trade journals at the Academy
of Motion Picture Arts and Sciences in Los Angeles and the Library and
Museum of the Performing Arts at Lincoln Center in New York. The
DeMille Collection at Brigham Young University includes nearly five
hundred scrapbooks that contain reviews from American and foreign newspapers and periodicals for all of the director's films. Not surprisingly, The Index to Critical Film Reviews in British and American Film
Periodicals contains no mention of DeMille's films. A Guide to Critical
Reviews cites mostly popular literature; the more extensive or interesting reviews cited have been included in the annotated bibliography of
this work. Fortunately the collected New York Times reviews remain a
convenient source, and Variety reviews have not only been indexed but
are now available in a multivolume reference work.

With one exception, I have ascertained on the premises the nature
and availability of archival and library research material described in
the chapter on archives. DeMille proves to be a rich if untapped subject for film historians since his staff saved practically anything
having to do with his career and private life. A vast collection of
papers, photographs, artwork, and memorabilia is now housed at Brigham
Young University. As for films, an agreement between George Eastman
House and the DeMille Estate has led to the preservation of most of the
director's silent films. Fortunately, the UCLA Film Archive has most
of the DeMille sound films and thus complements the Eastman House collection. I have not listed the Cinémathèque Française for two reasons:
screening costs are prohibitive and the only DeMille film available
there but not in any American film archive, The Squaw Man (1931), is
rented by a film distributor. Since film scholars may eventually ex-
plore the rich sources detailing DeMille's career, I have described the
archival material in some detail.

Compilation of the name and film indexes proved unsatisfying since
there was no way to refer to material in the biography or critical essay
as these have no entry numbers. Names listed in the production credits
and casts for DeMille's films were too numerous to include even though
I attempted to minimize these, especially the cast listings that are
limited to the leads and important supporting characters. Given the
fact that DeMille made seventy films, minor characters are not even
mentioned in the plot summaries, which are as terse as possible. Gen-
erally names appearing in the index fall into four categories: persons
involved in DeMille's more important or better-known productions, which
tend to be the sound films; important stage or screen personalities;
actors and production staff who worked on a series of the director's

films; and all the authors listed in the annotated bibliography. The film index has been restricted to the seventy films that DeMille himself directed, films and miscellaneous footage in which he appeared as himself, and a few television programs.

Finally, a note of caution about the chapter on film distributors is necessary. Film rental companies and their catalogs are subject to the vicissitudes of business so that changes may occur before this work appears in print. Curiously, the DeMille film most available for rental is The King of Kings although The Ten Commandments (1956) is still the subject of the most bibliographical entries.

It is a pleasure to acknowledge the many debts I have accumulated while working on this project. First, I would like to thank Louis Giannetti for suggesting some time ago that I consider working on a volume for the Directors Series. I found the undertaking to be ideal since I could work in a discontinuous manner while engaged in both teaching and parenting. Second, I would like to acknowledge the assistance of the staff in the libraries and archives where I did my research: Ned Comstock at the University of Southern California; George Pratt, Allan Bobey, and Bob Ogie at George Eastman House; Samuel Gill at the Academy of Motion Picture Arts and Sciences; Emily Cohen at the Library of Congress; and Charles Silver at the Museum of Modern Art. I am especially indebted to James D'Arc at Brigham Young University for his assistance during various stages of this project and for his graciousness and enthusiasm. I would also like to thank the series editor, Ronald Gottesman, for helpful suggestions and Karin Kiewra and Mary Allen at G.K. Hall for being on the other end of the phone to answer numerous queries.

Lastly, I am grateful to friends and colleagues who assisted me with various parts of this book. James Card, who established the film collection at George Eastman House, encouraged my initial interest in DeMille and showed me some of the director's films. Eugene McCreary guided me through the Bibliothèque de l'Arsenal and wrote insightful criticisms about the critical survey. Arthur Nolletti, whose friendship has been a delightful consequence of an NEH summer seminar at the University of Iowa, commented on this project during all its stages in an incisive, thoughtful and encouraging manner. Robert J. Smith, my husband, helped me negotiate my way through French institutions and was a valuable critic. Roslyn Mass contributed helpful editing suggestions. Joseph Siracusa translated some articles in Italian journals. Robert Gilliam secured useful materials for me through the interlibrary loan service. Lastly, Brenda Peake typed sections of the final manuscript. I have concluded that anyone like myself who tackles a project of this nature without a computer and printer is excessively optimistic. A final word about the support of institutions: a one-semester sabbatical leave granted by the State University of New York enabled me to finish this work and an NEH summer seminar held at UCLA provided me with an opportunity to do additional research in the film archive. A born Angeleno, I always welcome the pleasure of returning to my favorite city.

I. Biographical Background

The life of Cecil Blount DeMille is no less astounding than the spectacles that became his trademark in the motion picture business. During an impressive career that paralleled the growth of the film industry, he was both pioneer and survivor in a revolutionary and powerful medium of mass entertainment. A particularly flamboyant, if not baroque, manifestation of the Horatio Alger Story, DeMille's life was a characteristically American fable in a nineteenth- as well as twentieth-century fashion. Although his values were basically Victorian, in his films and personal life he set a model for modern conspicuous consumption that profoundly affected American mores. In effect, DeMille straddled two centuries in a style that accounted for both his appeal and his rapid decline into obscurity soon after his death in 1959. While he lived, he was unequalled in the type of filmmaking that consistently drew large audiences and earned him the title "Mr. Hollywood."

DeMille was born in Ashfield, Massachusetts, on 12 August 1881. In his autobiography he notes without rancor that his father, Henry Churchill deMille, recorded the event in a diary with a simple sentence whereas the birth of his older brother, William, three years earlier had elicited a more detailed and joyous entry and an outburst of letters to relatives.[1] Schoolteaching during the summer had taken its toll. On his father's side, DeMille (deMil) was descended from Dutch immigrants who settled and prospered in American colonies in the Northeast during the seventeenth century. William Edward deMille, his grandfather, was a merchant and local politician in North Carolina, but his fortunes suffered a severe reversal after the Civil War. As a result, DeMille's father, Henry, grew up with relatives in the Northeast and attended Columbia College on a grant. Unfortunately Henry found himself socially ostracized at Columbia by students who scorned him for his poverty.[2] Upon graduation in 1875, he became a teacher at Lockwood's Academy in Brooklyn and married a colleague, Matilda Beatrice Samuel. Beatrice Samuel deMille was descended from an English Jewish family, but Cecil never acknowledged his Jewish ancestry and stressed instead his paternal and Protestant lineage. Always a social climber, DeMille dignified his father with the title "professor," so that later compilers of biographies incorrectly noted that deMille had taught at Columbia University, not at Lockwood's, and then at Columbia Grammar School in

Manhattan. Since DeMille had the mentality of an arriviste, his past had to accord with the lofty position he attained in the motion picture world.

Beatrice deMille exerted a paramount influence in the deMille family in that she persuaded her husband, Henry, to pursue his interest in the theater rather than enter the Episcopalian ministry. For later generations of deMilles who would earn their livelihood in the theater, this decision was of course a turning point. After a period of writing failures and acting in road shows, Henry deMille began a successful collaboration with David Belasco and later became a well-known playwright on his own. In 1891, he was prosperous enough to purchase some property at Pompton Lake in New Jersey and build a three-story house called Pamlico after a steamer that was once part of the family business. Unfortunately he died quite suddenly of typhoid in 1893.

At the time of his father's death, DeMille was twelve years old. Two years later his younger sister Agnes also died. Despite these family tragedies, his indomitable mother carried on by transforming their house into the Henry C. deMille School for girls. She arranged for his brother, William, to be educated in Germany and at Columbia and for him to attend Pennsylvania Military College. She never learned to manage finances, however, and the school fared badly. DeMille recalled that not a day passed when she did not worry about money, even in later years when she was secure.[3] As the school failed, she boldly decided upon another venture, became a theatrical agent in New York, and did a brisk business. Some time later, the DeMille Play Company was sold at a profit to the John W. Rumsey American Play Company.[4]

DeMille acknowledged that his mother played the most pivotal role in his life: "She remains the dominant figure, the strongest force, the greatest, the clearest and best experience."[5] Beatrice deMille seems to have been quite remarkable and rather formidable. "She was a strong character and a great soul, at once a driving power and an inspiration to us all. And when my father died it was she who taught her sons what it was to fight."[6] DeMille's famous niece, Agnes deMille, confirms that Beatrice, or "Bebe," was dominating, difficult, hard to please, and very proud of her son.[7] Cecil was his mother's favorite. She left him a curious and contradictory legacy. She had instilled in him enormous ambition, competitiveness, and a desire to dominate—attributes that made possible his success as an entrepreneur in the film industry. But she also contradicted the patriarchal order by emphasizing women's rights. A decade before the ratification of the woman's suffrage amendment, she stated in a newspaper interview, "This is the women's age. . . . Hereafter, no woman is going to be married without feeling that she is getting as much as she gives. This may sound . . . crude . . . but it expresses pretty clearly what I mean. . . . This theme—woman's equality—lies very close to my heart. . . ."[8] DeMille's relationships with women, as well as his portrayal of them on the screen, were understandably filled with ambiguities. Although he instinctively wished to dominate, he also admired strong-willed and independent women.

DeMille established an excellent record at the Pennsylvania Military College, but he followed in his father's and brother's footsteps by deciding upon a theatrical career and completed his education at the American Academy of Dramatic Arts. Upon his graduation in 1900, he acquired a small part in Charles Frohman's production, Hearts Are Trumps, and played in New York and on the road. Two years later, he married an actress named Constance Adams. During the next decade, as members of various troupes, they traveled together or separately through scores of towns and cities in the United States. DeMille's itinerary for the last ten days of September 1910 included the following: Chester, Lancaster, Lebanon, Reading, York, and Hanover in Pennsylvania; Havre de Grace in Maryland; Lynchburg and Clifton Forge in Virginia.[9] Actually DeMille's theatrical ambitions did not center so much on acting as on playwriting and producing. An initial writing assignment for David Belasco, The Return of Peter Grimm, became a bitter disappointment when he did not receive credit as coauthor. Joint writing ventures with his brother, William, who had already become a well-known playwright, and scattered efforts at producing plays were not very successful. DeMille also worked as manager for his mother's theatrical agency, the DeMille Play Company, but she retained control as president. Periodically he was forced to borrow from his brother to support his wife and a daughter, Cecilia, who was born at home to avoid hospital costs. For DeMille, the decade following his graduation from the American Academy of Dramatic Arts had yielded a series of professional disappointments.

DeMille's life changed dramatically in 1913. According to a story that has become legendary in motion picture history, in that year DeMille entered a partnership to make movies with Jesse L. Lasky, a vaudeville producer with whom he had collaborated on musicals; Samuel Goldfish, Lasky's brother-in-law and a glove salesman; and Arthur Friend, an attorney. Since his brother, William, disapproved of his dabbling in movies and declined to loan him $5,000, DeMille pawned the silver.[10] Undoubtedly his mother loaned him some money since she sold her theatrical agency that year.[11] Lasky later recalled that The Squaw Man, their first film, was budgeted at $25,000 and cost $43,000, but accounts vary. The total cost of production, the manner in which the sum was raised, and significant details about the picture remain unclear. For instance, DeMille claims that he shot two negatives to guard against fire and other losses, but his brother, William, recalls that the film had to be shot twice because the first print was sabotaged. Stories also differ about the nature of a projection problem solved by Sigmund Lubin, who repunched the sprocket holes, even though he was a member of the rival Patent Company.[12] At any rate, The Squaw Man, starring Broadway actor Dustin Farnum, eventually grossed $244,700 and launched the career of Cecil B. DeMille as well as the Jesse L. Lasky Feature Play Company.[13] The barn where the picture was shot remains standing in Los Angeles as a monument to early motion picture history.

DeMille assumed the title director-general in the Lasky Company, named after Lasky because he was the best-known partner, and cranked out films at the Lasky Studio in Los Angeles. Before the end of 1914, he had amassed a staff of five directors, five cameramen, including Alvin Wyckoff with whom he worked on several pictures, and eighty players. William deMille overcame his reluctance to traffic in film after he saw a print of The Squaw Man and left New York to organize the studio's scenario department. Beatrice deMille used her influence to recruit Wilfred Buckland, who did the lighting for Belasco's plays, to work as art director. Partly as a result of the talents of Wyckoff and Buckland, DeMille's early pictures were praised for their lighting effects or "Lasky lighting." Always in need of story material, the Lasky team accomplished a coup when David Belasco sold them the rights to ten of his plays for $100,000. Belasco's prestige as a Broadway producer and playwright was exploited in ads that featured his name more prominently than those of Lasky, Goldfish, or DeMille.[14] The Lasky Company also negotiated to release its films through a new distribution outlet, Paramount Pictures, organized on a national basis by W.W. Hodkinson.

In 1915, DeMille began a series of films with Metropolitan opera star Geraldine Farrar, and consolidated his growing prestige as a director with The Cheat, a society drama starring Fannie Ward and Sessue Hayakawa. According to William deMille, The Cheat became "the talk of the year."[15] Samuel Goldwyn wrote in his autobiography that The Cheat brought DeMille "to the front" and that it was "a first real 'knockout' after a number of moderate successes."[16] In Paris, The Cheat received even greater acclaim and its director immediately achieved unquestioned status as a great artist. Among its admirers was French director Louis Delluc, who wrote about the film in later years.[17] As DeMille began to streamline production during the teens, he made fewer films per year but at increased budgets. A total of thirteen films in 1915 dwindled to four in 1916. Certainly he was well on his way to success.

Yet almost from the beginning, the Lasky Company was plagued by rivalries that were intensified when a merger took place. Adolph Zukor's Famous Players was also under contract to release its productions through Paramount, but Zukor was intent on a vertical integration of the producing and distributing companies and outmaneuvered Hodkinson in a power struggle that left him in control. In 1916, Zukor's Famous Players merged with the Lasky Company to form the Famous Players-Lasky Corporation. Zukor became president while Lasky and Goldfish quarreled over the vice-presidency. A few months later, Goldfish was forced out after a struggle with Zukor but went on to form Goldwyn Pictures Corporation with several partners. Since DeMille was filming in Los Angeles, he avoided becoming too embroiled in the disputes of his colleagues in New York, but he conducted his own skirmishes with them about the manner in which the Los Angeles studio was run.

When Famous Players-Lasky was formed, DeMille signed a five-year contract at a salary of $1,000 a week. Significantly, his contract provided that his name, as director, would be "prominently displayed upon all motion pictures . . . produced under his personal direction. . . ."[18]

4

During the silent era, only DeMille rivalled D.W. Griffith in creating
a box-office name as director but unlike Griffith, he succeeded in ex-
tending his filmmaking career several decades before film critics
adopted the glamorous term "auteur."[19] DeMille established the cult of
the director through careful strategies that included a flamboyant and
well-publicized lifestyle. In 1916, he bought a hillside, Spanish
colonial house in Laughlin Park on a winding street that would later
be named DeMille Drive. For a weekend retreat he acquired several
hundred acres and built a ranch called Paradise. A yacht purchased in
1921 was christened the <u>Seaward</u>. Significantly, DeMille even managed
to infiltrate the Los Angeles social register, which to this day remains closed to most of the film colony.

DeMille's alleged advice to actress Paulette Goddard, "Never go
across the alley even to dump garbage unless you are dressed to the
teeth," reflected his awareness of the value of projecting a certain
image.[20] On the set, his costume included boots to support his weak
heels, puttees, jodhpurs, an open-throat shirt, a silver whistle, and
a Louis XV hat. He was supposedly the first director to use a mega-
phone and then a loudspeaker on the set.[21] As his productions became
more lavish and complicated, the retinue that accompanied him included
an associate producer, press agents, a secretary, script girls, at
least one assistant director, a microphone boy, and a chair boy.[22]
Any visitor to his office felt overwhelmed by the Gothic windows,
fur rugs, armor, cases of mementos, production sketches and paintings, and enormous carved desk.[23] Actors aspiring to play a part
might be subjected to scrutiny under a spotlight that the director
would kick on without warning.[24] DeMille intended to intimidate, so
he invented the proper costume and setting and provided himself with
the necessary accoutrements.

Always competitive about asserting the director's preeminence over
that of film stars, DeMille provided Zukor with a solution to an industry dilemma: though stars enhanced the audience appeal of a picture,
they were posing a threat with their enormous salary demands. Specifically, Mary Pickford had become the focal point of the industry during
the teens and her shrewd contract negotiations were a constant source
of worry to Paramount executives. DeMille, who had directed Pickford
in two films and found it not to his liking to compete for control, advised Zukor to allow her to sign with their competitor, First National.
Rather than paying bankrupting salaries to recognized stars, he pro-
posed "all-star" pictures that featured unknown players to be elevated
to stardom. In effect, DeMille's contribution to motion picture history at this juncture was to transfer the concept of a stock company
to filmmaking. Zukor decided to experiment with DeMille's idea but
was not ready to shelve the star system entirely.[25] DeMille went on
to acquire a reputation as a starmaker but he seldom worked with stars
who became too big. After discovering Gloria Swanson in a Mack Sennett
picture, he starred her in six out of seven productions scheduled for
1919-21 but advised her to pursue other options when she became queen
of the Paramount lot. The director did not enjoy sharing the limelight.

During the pre-World War I phase of his career in silent pictures, DeMille experimented widely and made several types of film: westerns, comedies, spectacles, society dramas, and war pictures. After the war, he began to produce a series of sex comedies and melodramas, stories about the rich geared to the rising expectations of the working and middle classes in a mass consumer economy. A number of these films contained spectacular flashbacks or fantasy sequences that contributed to soaring production costs but delighted the audience. As the "consumption ethic" replaced the Protestant ethic and the mood of the country became more hedonistic, sexual permissiveness, especially among the younger generation, also increased.[26] Although the so-called revolution in manners and morals began before the war and was at times exaggerated, there can be no doubt that its symbol was the "new woman." She was at the center of a materialistic society in pursuit of pleasure. William deMille recalled that shortly after the war "C.B. . . . discovered that the whole country was very much interested in 'sex appeal' . . . . He started a new era of stories--smart sophisticated comedy dramas."[27] DeMille wrote in his autobiography, however, that he made Old Wives for New, the first of his sex comedies, only after repeated urging from Jesse Lasky, who wired from New York: "You should get away from the spectacle stuff . . . and do modern stories of great human interest."[28] Whatever the impetus, this cycle of films was among the most popular and commercially successful of his entire career.

Straddling the nineteenth and twentieth centuries, DeMille was well-qualified to refurbish and update the Victorian image of woman for Jazz Age consumption. After all, his mother had been an extremely strong-willed and adventurous woman. Although he never relinquished Victorian sentiments about womanhood, he apparently had contradictory and more contemporary attitudes about sexuality. For instance, he dwelt excessively upon maternal love but boasted opinions about marriage reminiscent of pre-World War I, Greenwich Village espousals of free love. While planning a film about the Virgin Mary, he declared, "the love of mother for son and son for mother is perhaps the purest emotion of which our mortal consciousness is capable."[29] During an interview he stated, "woman's love that has not much of the maternal is only passion. And I know of no human emotion so entirely untrustworthy [sic], so disappointing, so certain to demonstrate its own mortality."[30] About a husband's philandering, he commented, "it's a matter of small importance, so far as his feeling for his wife is concerned," and pointed out that in eighteen years of marriage, he had never spent a single Saturday night at home.[31] But his wife, Constance, allegedly enjoyed the same privilege. Whether or not she absented herself as well is not clear. Further, DeMille also stated that sex "is the one thing that one is never free of. If the relations between a man and woman are not right, not harmonious, every other relation of their lives is affected."[32] Not surprisingly, DeMille's screen heroines were a hybrid version of the new woman, modern but with Victorian trappings.

DeMille's contradictory attitudes toward women surfaced in his personal and professional relationships with them. About his wife he simply declared in his autobiography that he was incapable of discussing her and resorted to quoting his niece, Agnes.[33] Constance, who was eight years older than DeMille, numbered him among her brood and supposedly ended their sexual relationship when she learned after Cecilia's birth that she could not bear any more children.[34] Two sons and another daughter were later adopted. DeMille struck up liaisons with his scenarist, Jeanie Macpherson, and actress Julia Faye, among other women. Not content with a loyal spouse and his share of mistresses, DeMille surrounded himself with a contingent of professional women including his scenarist; his editor, Anne Bauchens; his secretaries, notably Gladys Rosson; and his researchers. All these women never married, remained fiercely loyal to "the Chief," and spent day and night working at the studio or at the mansion. DeMille's professional association with women, a modern characteristic, was therefore compromised by his tendency to convert his female staff into a peculiar version of a harem.[35]

Controversy exists as to whether or not DeMille's post-World War I sex comedies and melodramas, produced in response to public demand, represented an artistic decline. During the teens and early twenties, DeMille's reputation as a director had become impressive. Peter Milne gave the following assessment in a work about film directing in 1922: [DeMille] early secured . . . superior results to those achieved by the general run of directors in the early days."[36] But Tamar Lane wrote the following year that DeMille was "the hokum merchant par excellence" who gave "if nothing else, a very enjoyable evening's entertainment."[37] In his work about the silent era, Kevin Brownlow stresses a point of view articulated by DeMille's niece, Agnes: After the disappointing failure of The Whispering Chorus at the box office in 1918, DeMille decided to lower his standards and cater to the masses. An artist thereby embarked upon his own ruin.[38]

The evidence does not altogether support Brownlow's speculation about DeMille's career. With respect to his attitude towards a mass audience, DeMille gave evidence of catering to its taste even before he made The Whispering Chorus. As he stated, "the very fact that we are reaching so many people makes it necessary for us to go slowly in our experiments towards more artistic pictures."[39] During World War I, DeMille made films vilifying Germans and even switched the ending of The Little American so that America's Sweetheart, Mary Pickford, would embrace a Frenchman; so much for artistic integrity.[40] Also debatable is the characterization of The Whispering Chorus as an artistic film ending in commercial failure. Although its photography was exceptional, the film was marred by the same tiresome moralizing that plagued later works. Further, DeMille's next picture, Old Wives for New, was not only au courant but witty and entertaining. It justifiably set a trend for moviemaking. Finally, the cycle of postwar sex comedies and melodramas included some of the director's better films, such as Why Change Your Wife? and The Affairs of Anatol. DeMille's point of view in these films was certainly less conventional than von Stroheim's in Blind Husbands and Foolish Wives. Certainly his touch was much less heavy-handed and is said to have influenced Ernst Lubitsch.[41] But the films made after this early cycle, such as Manslaughter, Adam's Rib, and The Ten Commandments, deservedly earned the label "hokum." Even so, the rest of DeMille's silent films cannot be consigned to the junk heap, for they included The Volga Boatman and the renowned King of Kings.

As a businessman, DeMille had remarkable entrepreneurial instincts and a compulsion to dominate and to be in control, two related characteristics. During the post-World War I period, a great deal of his energy was devoted to business details in filmmaking and other enterprises. For instance, he became interested in aviation. Always contemptuous of cowardice on the set, he was determined to conquer his own bouts with vertigo and join the air force as a pilot. Although his patriotic objective was unrealized, DeMille loved flying and realized its economic potential. With a group of associates, he founded the Mercury Aviation Company and became its president and board chairman. The airline provided passenger service to California cities between San Diego and San Francisco, engaged in stunts to attract publicity, and branched out into exports. Despite his enormous energy, DeMille was unable to give sufficient time to both the airline and movie business and opted for the latter, probably much to the relief of Zukor and Lasky. In 1921, the Mercury Aviation Company and the Mercury Export Corporation were disbanded.[42]

During the twenties, DeMille became as engrossed in complicated deals to finance film production as in filmmaking itself. When his contract with Famous Players-Lasky expired in 1920, he received attractive offers from both United Artists and First National. Since his loyalties lay with Famous Players-Lasky, he renegotiated his contract but bargained for a greater share of the profits by pointing out that only two of his thirty-seven films had been financial failures. A shrewd businessman, DeMille deemed it wise to form Cecil B. DeMille Productions, a partnership with his wife, Constance; his attorney, Neil McCarthy; and a relative, Ella King, to deal with Famous Players-Lasky in a more independent capacity. Since the departure of Sam Goldfish and Arthur Friend, two of the four founders of the Jesse L. Lasky Feature Play Company, intrastaff feuding had not ceased. DeMille argued constantly with corporation executives about budgets and control over his productions. According to his new contract, he received a weekly salary as a director for Productions, which contracted with Famous Players-Lasky for filmmaking costs, studio facilities, and actors against seventy percent of the net profits to be realized from distribution and rentals. In 1922, Cecil B. DeMille Productions branched out from the movies into business deals involving real estate, oil, securities, and other properties. But problems between Productions and Famous Players-Lasky regarding budget, accounting procedures, and division of profits led to a renegotiated contract in November of 1923.[43]

During the filming of The Ten Commandments in 1923, there was a great deal of acrimony between DeMille and Zukor. DeMille had spent a million

dollars on this, his first Biblical epic, filmed partly in color, but
the end was not yet in sight.[44] Zukor was not appeased by his director's offer to waive financial benefits guaranteed by his contract for
the picture, nor by the visit of his attorney, Neil McCarthy, to molli-
fy him. As a way out of the impasse that developed, DeMille offered
to buy the movie outright and quickly raised a million dollars through
his connection with A.P. Giannini of the Bank of America. DeMille had
earlier gauged the importance of banks in financing motion pictures
and held a number of offices in various banking corporations. Consequently he was able to outmaneuver Zukor, who backed down from his
ultimatum and allowed him to continue exceeding the budget, but their
dispute sowed the seeds of a final rupture.

Despite the great success of The Ten Commandments, Zukor sought to
renegotiate DeMille's contract and impose restrictions on his productions and the size of his staff.[45] At the beginning of 1925, DeMille
finally broke with Famous Players-Lasky, purchased the Ince Studio for
Productions, and contracted to release his films through Jeremiah
Milbank's Producers Distributing Corporation. The Cinema Corporation
of America was organized as a holding company that owned the stock of
PDC and a new subsidiary, Cecil B. DeMille Pictures Corporation, both
owned jointly by Milbank and DeMille. Cecil B. DeMille Productions
then contracted with Cinema for the service of DeMille as director in
exchange for production costs. Later that year, PDC merged with the
Keith Albee-Orpheum circuit of theaters. Unfortunately DeMille again
found himself in a large corporation in which his control over productions was challenged.[46]

In retrospect, DeMille claimed that Cinema failed to advance prompt-
ly the funds needed for production and to acquire the necessary theater
chains for distribution. But his position in the corporation was undoubtedly undermined by the fact that his films--both those directed
by him and those under his supervision at Productions--were earning
modest, if any, profits. Further, DeMille's two million dollar ex-
penditure for The King of Kings created a crisis that threatened bankruptcy and led to the merger of PDC, the Keith Albee-Orpheum chain, and
Pathe in 1927. DeMille was particularly unhappy about this move since
in his opinion, Pathe had always stood for cheap motion pictures as
opposed to his own high-budget, quality films. But even the success
of The King of Kings did not result in solvency. Consequently, Film
Booking Office under Joseph P. Kennedy and Keith Albee-Orpheum, renamed
Radio-Keith-Orpheum, were consolidated by the Radio Corporation of
America in 1928. Pathe passed under the control of RKO, but Cinema
was kept in existence for the purpose of continuing the distribution
of The King of Kings. DeMille saw little future for himself in the new
organization, signed a contract with MGM, and moved out of the DeMille
Studios.[47]

DeMille made three pictures for MGM: Dynamite, his first sound
film; Madam Satan, his only musical; and The Squaw Man, a third remake.
Although he made the transition to sound without difficulty, in essence

9

DeMille was recycling his silent films during the Depression and only
Dynamite made a profit. Not surprisingly, Louis B. Mayer did not renew
his contract with MGM upon its expiration in 1931. An attempt to establish a production company called the Directors Guild with Frank
Borzage, Lewis Milestone, and King Vidor came to naught. Curiously,
DeMille and his wife then embarked upon a lengthy and expensive trip
to Europe, Russia, and the Middle East though they were in the midst
of a professional and financial crisis. When they returned, Productions
had sustained further losses in addition to those incurred earlier as a
result of the introduction of sound. DeMille found himself on the verge
of bankruptcy and was forced to borrow on his life insurance, negotiate
additional loans, and mortgage his house and properties in Laughlin
Park. As a final blow, he learned that the Internal Revenue Bureau
had charged Productions with delinquency and faced a bill of almost
$1,700,000 in back taxes. Although the tax case was eventually re-
solved in DeMille's favor, it required six years of litigation.

DeMille decided upon The Sign of the Cross as his next picture, but
the industry had developed a dim view of his efforts since he left
Famous Players-Lasky and regarded him as box-office poison. According
to the director:

> I went around to all the companies. . . . Nobody would
> listen--I was through. I was dead. . . . Nobody said,
> "Yes, Mr. deMille, come on in." For the years that
> you had (done big things)--nothing. . . . You were
> completely dirt. Finally I went around to Mary Pickford
> and bought The Sign of the Cross from her, myself.[48]

Like a phoenix, DeMille emerged triumphant by returning to Famous
Players-Lasky, now Paramount, in 1932. Jesse Lasky, his former friend
and colleague, and Ben Schulberg prepared the way for his return.
Zukor placed him under severe budget constraints, however, and stipu-
lated that he finance fifty percent of the picture himself. Unfortunately Lasky and Schulberg were soon maneuvered out of the organization
in a power struggle that left even Zukor in a precarious position. But
The Sign of the Cross became a commercial success upon its general release and the first of several sound spectacles to follow. DeMille
not only recouped his reputation as a successful box-office director
but finally achieved what had been eluding him for years: during the
rest of his motion picture career, he was granted increasing and fairly
extensive control over his productions.[49]

Both in his personal and professional life, DeMille remained ob-
sessed with being dominant and in control. Agnes deMille, who has
written perceptively about her famous uncle, attributed this characteristic to sibling rivalry.[50] In the early days, William had become
a successful playwright in the footsteps of their father, while Cecil's
theatrical career had ended in failure. Cecil was thirty-two years
old when he left for California to film The Squaw Man and was painfully
conscious of his lack of achievement: "I was at an age when most men

have found their groove in life, even if the groove is a rut."[51] Significantly, the brothers engaged in a role reversal in the movie business. Cecil became a legendary producer and director whereas William's modest film career came to an end in the thirties when he was plagued by ill health and financial problems. It was William's turn to borrow money from his brother.[52] In later years the brothers seldom saw each other. But DeMille also held himself aloof from other members of his family and from his staff; he had no intimate friends. Agnes deMille recalled that his adopted sons, John and Richard, always called him "Mister;" to his staff, he was either "Mister" or "Boss." She observed that he was reluctant to associate with those whom he could not dominate and so eschewed the risks of close friendship.[53]

Since he prized his independence, DeMille's continuous battles with the front office or New York executives about control over his productions were understandable. As a director, he was incapable of delegating authority, left nothing to chance, and personally supervised details such as the selection of thousands of extras and animals for his spectacles. Unwilling to assign a script to a writer who would work alone in retreat, he stationed his writers in a studio bungalow and regularly harangued them.[54] Studio technicians were amazed by his grasp of mechanics. DeMille was well aware of his deficiencies as an administrator, especially his tendency to get bogged down in details.[55] Fortunately he required little sleep and had boundless energy. Even health problems were not enough to deter him. Although he had emergency prostate surgery when shooting Union Pacific, he continued to direct the film while flat on his back on a stretcher. A heart attack in the midst of filming The Ten Commandments remake on location in Egypt went unheeded despite a doctor's advice to the contrary. For DeMille, motion picture directing was an assertion of will that gave his very existence its meaning. As Agnes deMille has observed:

> . . . as a director of mass movement, this century has
> not seen his like. I have worked with many . . . and
> I know. . . . The power to dominate the mob came out
> of his guts, the very core of his nervous life. When
> I began to direct I recognized what went into these
> spectacular displays of endurance. . . . The strength
> for this domination came from an undeviating belief
> in what he was doing and from his enormous pride of
> position.[56]

Charles Higham contends in his biography of DeMille that as a result of facing bankruptcy and failure during the Depression, the director ceased to have any artistic aspirations and thereafter catered to the masses. Consequently the sound films represent "a very serious decline" in comparison with the silent pictures.[57] In effect, Higham restates Brownlow's thesis but establishes the moment of artistic decline later in DeMille's career. Critics confronted with the intriguing inconsistencies in the director's pictures persist in elevating him to the status of an artist and then tracing his fall. Undoubtedly DeMille

11

suffered a traumatic experience when faced with the possibility of the end of his filmmaking career during the thirties. A man with his ambitions and pretentions could not tolerate failure. As he wrote in his autobiography, "Almost the only time I feel physically weary and without energy, if my health is otherwise good, is when I am . . . not succeeding."[58] Precisely because DeMille enjoyed wealth, fame, and power, he understood from the beginning of his film career that he had to develop as broad an appeal to the audience as possible. If anything, he remained faithful to the concept of a commercial picture throughout his entire career. As for the sound spectacles that became his staple after his return to Paramount, they were the latest and most successful example of his brand of filmmaking. Further, the spectacles were hardly bereft of the usual artistic flourishes that so puzzle critics, nor did they represent a complete and dramatic break with the films of the silent era.

As he approached the end of his career, DeMille became engaged in political activities that embroiled him in controversy both before and during the Red-baiting years of the cold war. Controversy first arose as an indirect result of his lengthy association with the Lux Radio Theater. Approached by Lever Brothers in the mid-thirties with a lucrative contract to host and direct a weekly radio broadcast, DeMille took advantage of still another mass medium. At the height of its popularity, the radio program reached forty million persons who listened each week to dramatizations of films in distribution. DeMille stated in his autobiography that during a visit to the White House, he was informed that President Roosevelt gauged the size of his "fireside chat" audience by comparing their numbers to the listeners of the Lux program.[59] If his pictures had not already made his name a household word, the radio series accomplished that feat and undoubtedly boosted attendance at his films. But DeMille's increasing political conservatism led to a painful and costly exit from the program in 1944.

Although he was descended in part from a North Carolina family that had lost its fortune during the Civil War, DeMille became a conservative Republican and thereby contravened Southern Democrat traditions. His brother, William, not only remained a Democrat but became a liberal and married the daughter of reformist single-taxer, Henry George. Cecil was too much of an individualist, had strong entrepreneurial instincts, and was living proof of the Horatio Alger myth. He could have branched out into a political career that would have expressed the conservative and patriotic sentiments visible in his frontier epics. In 1936, he served as a delegate to the national Republican Party convention, and two years later refused the California State Republican Committee's nomination for senator.[60] Given his conservative, if not reactionary, political views, DeMille predictably became embroiled in a controversy involving his membership in the American Federation of Radio Artists.[61] In 1944, AFRA assessed each of its members one dollar to pay for a campaign against the so-called right-to-work proposition on the California state ballot. If passed, the proposition would have abolished the closed shop in the state of California. Characteristically, DeMille refused to pay the dollar levied by AFRA and was barred from any further radio (and subsequently television) appearances. Although he retaliated by initiating a series of lawsuits against AFRA and the American Federation of Labor, he lost decisions in the lower courts and an appeal to the California State Supreme Court. The United States Supreme Court declined to hear the case.[62]

Undeterred, DeMille organized the DeMille Foundation for Political Freedom in 1945 to campaign against right-to-work laws and communist infiltration. A supporter of the Taft-Hartley bill, which prohibited the closed shop and placed labor unions under restrictions, DeMille testified before the House Committee on Education and Labor in 1947 and also endorsed President Truman's executive order to establish standards of loyalty for federal employees.[63] In 1953, he became the chief consultant to the United States International Motion Picture Service, a State Department agency charged with producing "cold war films."[64] DeMille also sought to make his political position prevail within the motion picture industry, then wracked by divisiveness over the House Un-American Activities Committee hearings and the blacklist. While Joseph L. Mankiewicz, the liberal president of the Screen Directors Guild was abroad, DeMille led a Guild Board attempt to endorse a loyalty oath and to recall Mankiewicz as president. Upon Mankiewicz's return, a lengthy and acrimonious debate among the Guild's membership led to the ouster of the Board and defeat for DeMille.[65] Still, the director was recognized for his political activities during these postwar years. Among other awards, he received the American Legion's gold medal for Americanism and the Freedom Foundation Award, presented to actor Robert Montgomery, Bishop Fulton J. Sheen, and himself by Vice-President Richard Nixon.[66]

About this time, DeMille became involved in yet another attempt to capitalize upon the mass media, one that was again frustrated by his strong advocacy of a political viewpoint. A weekly syndicated newspaper column titled "Cecil B. DeMille Speaking" began to appear in papers across the country in 1950. Articles prepared by his staff, notably his publicist, Phil A. Koury, eventually reached twenty million readers each week. But DeMille was not satisfied with the columns and prevailed upon his writers to publicize his political beliefs. General Features Corporation, the syndicate, objected to the airing of his controversy with AFRA and his endorsement of the Taft-Hartley Act. Inability to resolve these differences led to the cancellation of the series in 1951. DeMille had by then become convinced that he himself was the target of a Red conspiracy.[67]

As a director, DeMille had long since become accustomed to negative criticism from those he bitterly labeled the "New Yorker crowd." In a lighter moment, he is said to have remarked, "Every time I make a picture the critics' estimation of the American public goes down ten degrees."[68] During the post-World War II years, DeMille's sensitivity about critical reaction to his pictures manifested itself in political paranoia. After the release of <u>Samson and Delilah</u> in 1949, he assigned a member of his staff to check the political convictions of every critic who expressed an opinion that the film was in bad taste. But the research did not validate the existence of a global critics' conspiracy against the director and showed moreover that the communist <u>Daily People's World</u> and <u>Daily Worker</u> had been more positive about <u>Samson and Delilah</u> than the highbrow magazines! When the Catholic Legion of Decency gave his next picture, <u>The Greatest Show on Earth</u>, a "B" rating (one step above "Condemned") for objectionable dialogue and costumes, DeMille compared the influence of the Catholic church to worldwide communism.[69]

During his last years, DeMille received the recognition due an elder statesman of the motion picture industry. In 1953, he accepted two statuettes at the Academy Awards ceremony: the Irving Thalberg Award "for consistent high quality of production" and a best picture Oscar the <u>The Greatest Show on Earth</u>. A founder of the Academy, DeMille had not been so honored previously. Also in that year, the Screen Directors Guild presented him with the first D.W. Griffith Award, a recognition to be given to directors who have made unique and outstanding contributions to the industry. The Hollywood Foreign Correspondents Association decided to present an annual Golden Globe named the Cecil B. DeMille Award for "outstanding contributions throughout the world" and named DeMille the first recipient. In 1956, the Screen Producers Guild honored DeMille with the Milestone Award for his "historic contribution to the American motion picture industry." In 1959, the nation's exhibitors voted DeMille the foremost producer-director of the industry in <u>Exhibitors Magazine</u> for the tenth consecutive year.[70] Further, the enormous success of <u>The Ten Commandments</u>, released at a time when the industry was ailing and attendance poor, brought DeMille awards and recognition in foreign countries as well.

DeMille, who had ignored a heart attack while filming his last picture, died three years later in 1959 at the age of seventy-seven after further heart complications. Not surprisingly, his death made front-page headlines all over the country and <u>Time</u> magazine announced the end of "DeMillenium." The Los Angeles papers reported in detail his request for a simple service and a private entombment in a family mausoleum at Hollywood Memorial Park. DeMille was survived by his ailing wife, Constance; his daughter, Cecilia; and three adopted children, John, Katherine, and Richard. Half an estate estimated at four million dollars worth of stocks and properties was left to his daughter, Cecilia, while the remaining half was set up in trust funds for his adopted children and grandchildren. DeMille also left seventeen individual bequests totaling $40,000, the largest to one of his former mistresses, actress Julia Faye. Constance, described as a "loyal, devoted and able helpmate," received no provision because she had controlled a separate source of income for several years. When she died the following year, she left the bulk of her estate valued at $750,850 to her daughter, Cecilia; $1,500 each to her three adopted children; and $1,000 each to her two maids, cook, and chauffeur.[71]

14

At the time of his death, DeMille was working on a picture about Baden-Powell and the Boy Scout movement, titled On My Honor. Perhaps his death in 1959 was fortuitous in that a film about scouting would hardly be the sort of film to appeal to the youth of the sixties. As a showman, DeMille knew well the audience of the small towns he had toured in theatrical companies at the turn of the century. For decades, he had captured a large segment of that audience with his stories of consumption and upward mobility, rugged individualism and empire-building, sexual titillation and religious uplift. But the basic values articulated in his pictures would be challenged in the sixties by political and countercultural dissidents, numerically a minority but vocal and influential. The motion picture audience would become fragmented. Already in the fifties, moviegoing patterns had been affected by the 1949 Paramount decision that forced the studios to divest themselves of theater chains, and by the impact of television. "The DeMillenium" was indeed at an end, for the studio system and the sociocultural context in which DeMille had flourished passed into eclipse with the director. Still, his concept of the blockbuster commercial film has prevailed among the young generation of directors who have made the big moneymakers of the seventies and eighties.

Notes

1. Cecil B. DeMille, The Autobiography of Cecil B. DeMille, ed. Donald Hayne (Englewood Cliffs, N.J.: Prentice-Hall, 1959), pp. 2-3. DeMille capitalized his name for business purposes, a practice not imitated by his brother, William, or his niece, Agnes.

2. Henry deMille Diary, Cecil B. DeMille Collection, Brigham Young University, Harold B. Lee Library, Provo, Utah (hereafter cited as BYU).

3. Mother-Character, Autobiography, Box 7, Cecil B. DeMille Collection, BYU.

4. New York Telegraph, 10 April 1913 in Cecil B. DeMille Scrapbook, Robinson Locke Collection, New York Public Library, Library and Museum of the Performing Arts at Lincoln Center (hereafter cited as NYPL LMPA).

5. Mother-Character, Autobiography, Box 7, Cecil B. DeMille Collection, BYU.

6. Ibid.

7. Agnes deMille, Dance to the Piper (Boston: Little, Brown & Co., 1952), p. 41.

8. New York Dramatic Mirror, 10 July 1912 in Cecil B. DeMille Scrapbook, Robinson Locke Collection, NYPL LMPA.

9. I am indebted to research by George Pratt for data about DeMille's itinerary.

10. DeMille, pp. 70-72; William to Cecil, 3 September 1913, William deMille Papers, New York Public Library, Manuscripts and Archives (hereafter cited as NYPL MA).

11. New York Dramatic Mirror, 4 August 1917 and New York Telegraph, 10 April 1913 in Cecil B. DeMille Scrapbook, Robinson Locke Collection, NYPL LMPA.

12. William deMille, Hollywood Saga (New York: E.P. Dutton, 1939), pp. 54-55; Terry Ramsay, A Million and One Nights (New York: Simon & Schuster, 1926), pp. 625-26; Charles Higham, Cecil B. DeMille (New York: Charles Scribners' Sons, 1973), p. 31; DeMille, pp. 90-91.

13. DeMille, p. 95.

14. See covers of the Fall 1914 issues of the trade magazine, Motion Picture News.

15. William deMille, p. 139.

16. Samuel Goldwyn, Behind the Screen (New York: George H. Doran, 1933), p. 82.

17. Stanley Hochman, ed., A Library of Film Criticism: American Film Directors (New York: Frederick Ungar, 1974), pp. 80-81; Louis Delluc, "Les cinéastes: Cecil B. DeMille" Cinéa, nos. 63-64 (21 July 1922):11.

18. Cecil B. DeMille with Famous Players-Lasky Corporation, Cecil B. DeMille Cage File, NYPL LMPA.

19. Benjamin B. Hampton, History of the American Film Industry (New York: Dover Publications, 1970), p. 218.

20. Phil Koury, Yes, Mr. DeMille (New York: G.P. Putnam's Sons, 1959), p. 180.

21. Lewis Jacobs, The Rise of the American Film (New York: Teachers College Press, 1968), p. 340.

22. Koury, p. 139; "Going Like Seventy," Time 65, no. 19 (9 May 1955):106.

23. Agnes deMille, Dance to the Piper, p. 36.

24. Jesse L. Lasky, Jr., Whatever Happened to Hollywood? (New York: Funk & Wagnalls, 1973), pp. 261-62.

25. Hampton, pp. 194-95.

26. See such works on the twenties as William Leuctenburg's The Perils of Prosperity (Chicago: University of Chicago Press, 1958) and Paul Carter's Another Part of the Twenties (New York: Columbia University Press, 1977).

27. William deMille, "Great Pictures and the Men Who Made Them" [October 1935], William deMille Papers, NYPL MA. Apparently this manuscript was a version of Hollywood Saga.

28. DeMille, p. 212.

29. Koury, p. 222. The film, The Queen of Queens was never made, partly due to protest from the Catholic Church.

30. "More About Marriage. As Told by Cecil B. DeMille to Adela Rogers St. Johns," Photoplay 19, no. 6 (May 1921):26.

31. "What Does Marriage Mean? As Told by Cecil B. DeMille to Adela Rogers St. Johns," Photoplay 19, no. 1 (December 1920):29-30; "More about Marriage," p. 25.

32. "More About Marriage," p. 26.

33. DeMille, pp. 51, 120-21.

34. Constance Adams DeMille, Autobiography, Box 7, Cecil B. DeMille Collection, BYU; Higham, pp. 35, 47.

35. Koury, pp. 35-39.

36. Peter Milne, Motion Picture Directing (New York: Falk Publishing Co., 1922), p. 48.

37. Tamar Lane, What's Wrong With The Movies? (Los Angeles: Waverly Co., 1923), p. 65.

38. Kevin Brownlow, The Parades Gone By (New York: Alfred P. Knopf, 1968), pp. 206-9.

39. Theater Magazine (January 1918) in Cecil B. DeMille Scrapbook, Robinson Locke Collection, NYPL LMPA.

40. James Card to Sumiko Higashi, 27 February 1983.

41. See Sumiko Higashi's Virgins, Vamps and Flappers (Montreal: Eden Press, 1978), pp. 132-53.

42. DeMille, pp. 193-203.

43. United States Circuit Court of Appeals for the Ninth Circuit. Commissioner of Internal Revenue, Petitioner vs Cecil B. DeMille Productions, Inc., Respondent. Transcript of the Record, 3 vols. (San Francisco: Parker Printing Co., 1936), pp. 89-95. Curiously, the content refers to Cecil B. DeMille Productions, Inc. as petitioner and the Commissioner of Internal Revenue as respondent, which makes more sense.

44. The final cost of The Ten Commandments was $1,475,836.93.

45. DeMille, pp. 264-65; Jesse L. Lasky, I Blow My Own Horn (Garden City, N.Y.: Doubleday Co., 1957), p. 169.

46. U.S. Circuit Court of Appeals, pp. 96-97; DeMille pp. 266-67.

47. U.S. Circuit Court of Appeals, pp. 97-101; DeMille, pp. 285-90; Hampton, pp. 319-20; Higham, pp. 170-72.

48. Personal Childhood, Autobiography, Box 7, Cecil B. DeMille Papers, BYU.

49. DeMille, p. 335.

50. Agnes deMille, "Goodnight, C.B.," Esquire 61, no. 1 (January 1964):124-25.

51. DeMille, p. 72.

52. William to Cecil, 2 February 1935, Personal Box D, Cecil B. DeMille Collection, BYU.

53. Agnes deMille, "Goodnight C.B.," p. 126.

54. Koury, p. 233.

55. DeMille, p. 120.

56. Agnes deMille, Dance to the Piper, pp. 35-36.

57. Higham, p. 221; Charles Higham interviewed by James V. D'Arc, 18 July 1977, Cecil B. DeMille Collection, BYU.

58. DeMille, p. 303.

59. DeMille, p. 347.

60. DeMille, pp. 352-53; Higham, pp. 252, 257.

61. During the twenties, DeMille had quarreled with Alvin Wyckoff, his photographer, about the formation of a cameramen's union and as president of the Association of Motion Picture Producers, he had fought the attempt of the Actors' Equity Association of New York to invade the film industry. Higham, p. 277; Unidentified article (21 August 1929), Cecil B. DeMille Clipping File, Margaret Herrick Library, Academy of Motion Picture Arts and Sciences, Beverly Hills, Calif. (hereafter cited as AMPAS).

62. Albert Woll and James A. Glenn, "DeMille Loses Again," American Federationist 52, no. 1 (January 1948):10-11; Koury, p. 296.

63. New York Herald Tribune, 23 February 1953, Cecil B. DeMille Clipping File, NYPL LMPA; Los Angeles Times, 26 March 1947, Cecil B. DeMille Clipping File, AMPAS.

64. Los Angeles Times, 24 April 1953, Cecil B. DeMille Clipping File, AMPAS.

65. Koury, pp. 300-302.

66. Motion Picture Herald, 29 September 1945 and Los Angeles Times, 24 April 1953, Cecil B. DeMille Clipping File, AMPAS; New York Herald Tribune, 23 February 1953, Cecil B. DeMille Clipping File, NYPL LMPA.

67. Motion Picture Herald, 25 November 1950, Cecil B. DeMille Clipping File AMPAS; Koury, pp. 303-6.

68. Koury, p. 13.

69. Koury, pp. 287-91, 275; Los Angeles Examiner, 29 December 1950, and Los Angeles Times, 25 January 1953, Cecil B. DeMille Clipping File, AMPAS.

70. <u>Los Angeles Times</u>, 28 January 1953 and <u>Times of India Publication</u> (undated), Cecil B. DeMille Clipping File, AMPAS; Unidentified article, 22 January 1956, Cecil B. DeMille Clipping File, NYPL LMPA; "Cecil B. DeMille, 77, Pioneer of Movies, Dead in Hollywood," <u>New York Times</u>, 1 January 1958, p. 31.

71. <u>Los Angeles Mirror</u>, 21 July 1960 and <u>Citizen News</u>, 5 June 1961, Cecil B. DeMille Clipping File, AMPAS.

II. Critical Survey

During most of his lengthy career as a film director, Cecil B. DeMille enjoyed a reputation as a showman who could attract vast audiences to his pictures year after year. As director Robert Parrish has observed, DeMille knew how to put something on the screen "that had more people looking at it than all the other members of the Directors Guild."[1] Such a phenomenon should have invited close scrutiny on the part of film scholars but has instead been overlooked. A few words about the reasons for this lack of interest are in order before moving on to a consideration of the director and his work.

Film studies is a recent discipline that thrived especially during the last decade. Within the field, theory and criticism have enjoyed more prestige and glamour than film history, whose scholars are still establishing the facts or requisite empirical data and debating the merits of various conceptual models. Despite some excellent studies, film history is still very much a developing field engaged in debate with the claims of film theory which has focused primarily upon the text and questions of intertextuality.[2] To the extent that the socio-historic aspect of filmmaking and viewing is considered, emphasis has been increasingly placed upon the interaction between text and spectator. And insofar as spectator refers to the Lacanian subject positioned within an ideological system, analysis about film and society has resulted in abstractions. Although feminist film theorists have been influential in stressing the concept of sexual difference with respect to the spectator, considerations about the audience in such concrete terms as class, enthnicity, region, historical period, and even gender have largely been ignored in favor of the audience construed as spectating subject or reader. Admittedly some film scholars have pointed out that abstractness of argument blocks more concrete analysis of sociohistoric context and have called for more specificity. Just exactly what is meant by specificity remains to be seen. Film historians who stress historiography based on empirical evidence are by no means predominant in the field.[3]

Significant studies of DeMille could be done in terms of the issues raised by auteurism even though it has been challenged or discredited since its vogue in the sixties. Andrew Sarris denied the director

21

admission to the celestial Pantheon but granted him status one rung
down on the Far Side of Paradise due to "fragmentation of . . . personal vision . . . or disruptive career patterns."[4] Actually DeMille
seems not to have exemplified either criterion for this second category,
nor was he an auteur in a doctrinaire sense. Auteurist critics focused
upon a director's style as a personal signature surviving the constraints of the industrial system but scarcely examined the specific
working conditions existing within a studio. Assumptions that a director somehow managed to preserve his artistic integrity despite the
hegemony of studio executives bent on profit create a false issue when
examining DeMille's career.

    As an auteur, DeMille deliberately courted commercial success but
nevertheless evolved a quintessentially personal style of filmmaking.
Certainly he was contentious about his productions but these disagree-
ments·were largely about financial affairs. For DeMille, interference
with his artistic vision quite often meant budgetary constraints imposed by the studio. Furthermore, he disliked being part of any hier-
archy which he himself did not control. At Paramount he acquired his
own studio gate and a table at the commissary that was for a time
elevated above the rest. Significantly, DeMille was on occasion more
astute than the front office at gauging the demands of the moviegoing
public. For instance, he quarreled with Adolph Zukor about his lavish
expenditures for The Ten Commandments (1923) but the film became a huge
commercial success. A scrutiny of DeMille's career should thus caution
film scholars about stereotyping the nature of conflict between directors and studios and of the resulting product, the commercial film.

    Aside from issues raised by auteurism, DeMille's significance as
a film director is best understood when his life and work are situated
in relation to the experience of the American public in a specific
socioeconomic and cultural context. After the turn of the century,
the American economy entered an early phase of high mass consumption
with an impressive surge of manufacturing output. The urban population,
swelled by migration from the countryside and abroad, comprised a
profitable market for recreational activities and consumer goods. With
the distribution of catalogs and the improvement of delivery systems,
even rural areas became a lucrative target for mass merchandising. The
events of World War I and its aftermath accelerated the trend towards
a consumer economy. During the twenties, mergers effected for wartime
purposes continued with the blessings of a Republican, pro-business
administration, and the scientific management of industry became the
province of a growing class of technocrats. Advertising and the availability of credit encouraged the masses, who were enjoying a relatively
increased standard of living and some leisure, to acquire spending
habits. But though it is difficult for us to imagine today, prospective
customers had to be weaned away from thrift to spendthrift habits.[5]
Benjamin Franklin's aphorism about a penny saved had to be vitiated
without discrediting the Protestant work ethic.

    Enter DeMille. Film's advent as a powerful and revolutionary mass

medium at a time when the American economy was shifting towards high
mass consumption proved to be especially meaningful. American employees,
both blue and white collar, had already become part of a regimented and
dehumanizing work system attuned to the demands of mass production, but
they had yet to learn thoroughly their role as consumers. As the leisure time counterpart of mass production, mass consumption would affect
human exchange so that a sense of community, specifically a sense of
class consciousness, would decline even further. American emphasis
upon outmoded but cherished ideals of rugged individualism would ration-
alize but also intensify the resulting isolation and powerlessness of
human beings. Within this context, film assumed critical functions.
According to Guy Debord, "The spectacle, as a tendency to make one see
the world by means of various specialized mediations (it can no longer
be grasped directly) naturally finds vision to be the privileged human
sense. . . ."[6] As part of the modern day phenomenon of spectacle, film,
especially in its silent phase, promoted the visual sense and the
preeminence of appearances over reality. Further, in its mediating
capacity in a mass consumer society, film became a showcase for the
display of commodities as desirable objects and thereby transformed
consumption into a pleasurable activity. Commodities endowed with the
illusion of magical properties thus provided substitutions or compensa-
tions for the estrangement inherent in a modern, capitalistic society.
As a consequence, the dynamics of class relations became opaque since
human relations were subject to reification. As Georg Lukacs has
pointed out:

> Reification requires that a society should learn to
> satisfy all its needs in terms of commodity exchange.
> The separation of the producer from his means of pro-
> duction, the dissolution and destruction of all "natural"
> production units, etc., and all the social and economic
> conditions necessary for the emergence of modern capi-
> talism tend to replace "natural" relations which ex-
> hibit human relations more plainly by rationally reified
> relations.[7]

Sexual as well as class relations were subject to reification, for
the role of the female in a mass consumer economy became essential.
Woman continued to serve as an object of exchange as in past economies;
further, her eroticization as spectacle on screen and in advertising
became central to commodity fetishism. Philip Slater, a provocative
critic of the American scene, has observed, "buying becomes a sexual
act. Indeed, we're approaching the point where it absorbs more interest than sex itself; when this happens people will be more comfortable
walking in the street nude with an unwrapped purchase."[8] Shulamith
Firestone has noted perceptively that reification "affects both men
and women alike, [but] in the case of women it is profoundly complicated by . . . forms of sexploitation" that result in all women becoming interchangeable commodities and thus requiring male validation.[9]
Significantly, the Jazz Age touted a revolution in manners and morals
based upon the "new woman" and commenced about the time when suffragists

finally accomplished ratification of the Nineteenth Amendment. Although the sexual revolution meant little more than higher divorce rates and increasing acceptance of birth control against a background that included the popularization of Freud, these represented advances for women at a time when their objectification as commodities became pervasive.

As a figure straddling late nineteenth century Victorian culture and the mass consumer society of early twentieth-century America, DeMille was singularly equipped to address an audience experiencing transition. A younger son who did not succeed in the theater as did his father and brother before him, he experienced privation as an actor and toured the small towns of America for several years. A firsthand acquaintance with the American public stood him in good stead for decades because he understood the nature of its desire for spectacle:

> Your poor person wants to see wealth colorful, interest-
> ing, exotic--he has an idea of it many times more brightly
> colored than the reality. How do I know? Because, when
> doing twenty weeks solid of one night stands, without
> baths, . . . or when broke and discouraged after three
> to six months layoff, my dreams of wealth . . . [had]
> color, lights, fun, things striking and unusual.[10]

The mass production and distribution of commodities meant not just the dream but the possibility of acquiring material goods to a greater degree by more classes of people than hitherto imagined. Consequently, not only the poor but the growing middle class experienced rising expectations and displayed a curiosity about how the rich lived. DeMille succeeded as a director of motion picture spectacles because he realized and disseminated his own fantasies on an extravagant enough scale. A point of confluence existed between the fulfillment of his own needs and desires and those of his audience via the celebration of materialistic values and consumption.

DeMille's hold on the public was based in part on his ability to adapt nineteenth-century sentiment and values to a twentieth-century mass medium that promoted consumerism and self-gratification. The director conceptualized spectacle within a didactic framework, for he retained toward film an attitude that harkened back to a past when his mother persuaded his father to turn from the ministry to the stage as an alternative calling. DeMille's emphasis on the moralizing function of film may be traced back not only to his father's religious sense of vocation but to his family's collaboration with David Belasco in various stage productions. As Charles Higham has observed, "DeMille came up out of the Belasco theater. . . . He thought in terms of major confrontations, collisions between good and evil on a very black and white basis, he set his scenes against spectacle which was the Belasco tradition. . . ."[11] Spectacle then served as the backdrop if not centerpiece for theatrical productions which had a significant moral dimension. According to David Robinson, Belasco's brand of spectacle theater

represented the pinnacle of stage developments transplanted to the
United States from England in the nineteenth century. Such productions
evolved in response to audience demand within the specific socioeconomic
context of urban and industrial growth.[12]

Significantly, DeMille's visual style, a result of his own theatrical career as well as his experimentation with film, enhanced the use
of spectacle for the purposes of didacticism. As early as 1917, the
director made a very telling statement: "the movie of the future will
resemble a series of paintings rather than a series of photographs."[13]
Although DeMille's perception of motion pictures as static and pictorial appeared to be noncinematic, especially to his later detractors,
it accorded with his vision of film as a medium with a didactic message
and was part of a tradition in painting that had existed for centuries.
Significantly, as his films became more spectacular, the preproduction
phase involved elaborate sketches and paintings of specific scenes,
characters, and costumes to be transferred on to celluloid. DeMille
characteristically employed a camera that was stationary and eschewed
excessive panning and tracking, even to take in the panorama of epic
scenes, as well as depth of field. Camera placement emphasized per-
pendicularity with respect to framing of the shot and resulted in a
rigorous frontality and shallow organization of space. Compositions
were symmetrically balanced and carefully lit to produce a sculptured
effect. A medium shot with characters in the foreground became standard, especially in the sound spectacles. Not surprisingly, DeMille's
flair for pictorial design resulted in the actors being reduced to objects. Critics have commented that even in his famous crowd scenes,
he gave the impression that every extra had been placed within the
frame with meticulous care. DeMille's editing style, perfected by Anne
Bauchens over a period of decades, was unobtrusive and rendered film
as a series of tableaux that expressed his painterly vision.[14]

As a producer and director of spectacles, DeMille was a visual
strategist who was intent on much more than the edification of his
viewers: he was determined to consolidate his own status and power
in the motion picture industry. Accordingly, his brand of spectacles
demanded hierarchical relations with him at the apex, a staff that
referred to him as God, and a childlike audience. Spectacles were
thus strategies in effecting the omnipotence of the director with respect to both the filmmaking process and the positioning of the audience that consumed the images. Audience complicity on the part of
the millions of viewers who flocked to see DeMille's didactic stories
or fables, not to mention familiar Biblical epics, cannot be under-
estimated. DeMille had established his authoritative persona with
great flair early in his filmmaking career. For instance, when he made
his famous cycle of sex comedies and melodramas in the teens and twenties, Photoplay solicited his views about marriage in a series of interviews. During the years of the Depression and World War II, audiences listened weekly to his reassuringly paternal and hypnotic voice
as he hosted the Lux Radio Theater. By the time he appeared as himself in Sunset Boulevard or the prologue to The Ten Commandments remake,

he had been an icon in the public's eye for decades. Consequently when his viewers attended his movies over the years, they were participating in a reenactment of a storytelling ritual in which a parental figure entertains and instructs his children. An interesting footnote to this history is the continuing appeal of The Ten Commandments as family viewing on television as evidenced by the Nielsen ratings.[15]

Since DeMille was intent on dominating both the filmmaking process and his audience, he established the concept of authorship long before it became fashionable in the sixties. In Call of the North, a frontier saga which was his second film but the first without a co-director, DeMille emerges on screen during the credits to present the actors. Decades later at the close of his career, he would appear on a curtained stage in a prologue to The Ten Commandments to address his audience directly about the import of the film. (Unfortunately this prologue has been deleted from repeated television broadcasts.) In the interim, DeMille always asserted his claims as filmmaker so that the credits of his films proved at times to comprise the most interesting footage. During the twenties, for instance, his head adorned a medallion in the shot preceding the credits since he ascribed to himself and his artifact an aristocratic status. With the advent of sound, trumpets blared on the soundtrack, as in Cleopatra, when the words, "Directed by Cecil B. DeMille," were superimposed over the Sphinx suffused with light.

Aside from asserting his rights to authorship during the credits of his films, DeMille retained control through visual strategies that enforced his dominance while minimizing spectator identification with the stars. For example, highly charged emotional scenes in Cleopatra, such as the rupture between Antony and his trusted general or the death of Antony in Cleopatra's arms, are photographed entirely in two shots as opposed to shot-reverse-shot or the use of close-ups and angles. Further, DeMille's objectification of characters resulted in their being utilized or eclipsed for the purpose of visual effects achieved by lavish costume and set design. Antony's seduction in Cleopatra is climaxed by a backtracking shot that reveals enticing slave girls offering incense as voluminous drapes enclose the bedchamber, four rows of ramheaded oars moving in unison to pull the Queen's barge down the Nile, and a drummer emerging in the foreground so that a steady, rhythmic beat blends with the exotic music. Spectacles after all were meant to inspire awe, especially for the director who had orchestrated the elaborate and stunning effects.[16] Furthermore, the prescription of a fixed distance between the spectators and the screen as a pictorial design meant for their edification was part of DeMille's concept of film as a medium with a message.

A closer analysis of DeMille's work within a chronological context should prove enlightening. Since periodization in film history has yet to be definitively established, this survey will rely to some extent upon periodization in American history. Such an approach is appropriate since DeMille produced and directed films within an industry which was not immune to the socioeconomic conditions affecting the rest of the country. DeMille's career will thus be considered in terms of three distinct and successive periods: 28 pictures from the pre-World War I era, 1913-17; 27 pictures dating back roughly to the Jazz Age decade, 1918-31; and 15 pictures completed during the Depression, World War II, and postwar years.

DeMille began his career with adaptations of westerns and costume dramas set in exotic locales; these pictures were based on popular novels and plays such as the works of his brother, William, and David Belasco. The director also began a productive collaboration with scenarist, Jeanie Macpherson, who wrote original scripts for his first spectacles, Joan the Woman and The Woman God Forgot, and for comedies and melodramas about the rich. Although this early period of filmmaking was marked by an initial reliance upon stage fare, a variety of genres, and experimentation with technique including a famous reference to Rembrandt lighting, characteristic themes began to surface. DeMille was preoccupied with the intersection of gender and class or cultural differences as these affected traditional sex roles and the relations of a romantic couple. Also significant was the attitude manifested towards the wealthy as a class and their accumulation of riches.

DeMille's portrayal of American manhood was typical of the silent era when "inner-directed" and "other-directed" male protagonists were relegated to different genres. In the westerns and costume dramas, such as The Squaw Man, The Virginian, Rose of the Rancho, The Unafraid, and The Arab, men defined themselves through heroic deeds. But in pictures with a then contemporary setting, male status became a reflection of such indexes as income, profession, class, dress, and etiquette. For example, the heroes of The Golden Chance, and The Dream Girl possess sufficient income to provide women with luxuries and access to leisure. Masculinity became a function of cash flow in an urban and industrial environment. Correspondingly, DeMille's characterization of women reflected both Victorian and more contemporary attitudes. Stereotypes of Pandora persisted, as did sirens betokening the collapse of male will as in Trail of the Lonesome Pine and The Woman God Forgot. But the evil temptress metamorphosed into a selfish and hedonistic, modern woman as evident in What's His Name, The Cheat, and The Heart of Nora Flynn. Always a counterpart to women who were no good were the guardian angels of civic, domestic, and private virtue. Significantly, DeMille's heroines were also strong-willed women who proved to be more than stereotypes. Geraldine Farrar, Blanche Sweet, and Mary Pickford were actresses who played compelling and courageous roles in his early pictures.

A critical aspect of heterosexual relations in these films was the socioeconomic status of the lovers, for these pictures implied that wealth constituted a barrier involving not only class structure but moral character. For instance, the heroine of What's His Name is negatively portrayed for abandoning her child and husband in straitened circumstances and desiring a sumptuous life that only an unprincipled, rich admirer can provide. In The Golden Chance, a woman who has married beneath her status suffers from poverty and ill treatment, covets a more luxurious and glamorous existence, and becomes a widow in time to marry a prosperous businessman. Well-heeled and powerful, older men in Temptation and The Devil Stone threaten virtuous and vulnerable, young women from humble origins. Should women themselves be endowed with riches, as in The Unafraid and The Man from Home, they become the prey of deceitful fortune hunters. Clearly wealth presents a problem which pits men against women and social classes against each other, a problem compounded by courtship across class lines. A Cinderella fantasy resolves these issues in The Dream Girl: an orphaned girl from the slums is adopted by a wealthy family and captures the heart of the frivolous, young heir, who will undoubtedly find marriage a sobering responsibility. But this resolution meant that upward mobility or movement across class barriers via marriage was permissible only for women.

Significantly DeMille's pre-World War I pictures expressed ambivalence towards the rich and their riches. Doubt surfaced about the moral effects of amassing worldly possessions. Consequently, sterling qualities characterized Bowery boys, Irish maids, small town folk, and struggling tenement dwellers, whereas the wealthy were often selfish and irresponsible. Class lines were rigorously delineated and upheld in films as different as Kindling, a realistic, urban drama about the haves and have-nots that reaffirmed the American safety-valve concept of westward migration; Chimmie Fadden and Chimmie Fadden Out West, both comedies that narrated a Bowery Boy's exploits among the unscrupulous rich; and The Heart of Nora Flynn, a melodrama that juxtaposed a domestic maid's selflessness and love for children against an upper class woman's philandering. Whatever the genre, the films of DeMille's first phase depict the pursuit of riches and the sudden acquisition of fortune as leading to individual or societal corruption. Although America had entered an early phase of high mass consumption around the turn of the century, attitudes towards money were still an expression of morality and congruent with an earlier economic stage when savings had been essential to capital formation and growth.

Undoubtedly the best-known work from this first phase of DeMille's career is The Cheat. Although in later decades his name became associated with gaudy, Biblical spectacles described at best as camp, DeMille enjoyed a reputation during the teens as a director whose productions were artistically and technically superior. Certainly before the premier of The Cheat, the prestige of his Lasky productions was established within the film industry and among the audience. With the release of The Cheat in 1915, DeMille became internationally acclaimed as well, for the picture created a sensation both at home and abroad. In Paris, the film was greeted with adulation and became a canon in French accounts about milestones in the history of the cinema.[17]

An original scenario by Hector Turnbull and Jeanie Macpherson, The Cheat exhibited characteristics typical of the early pictures but also

prefigured DeMille's most popular films of the late teens and twenties.
For instance, a triangular relationship in which male rivals vie for
a woman as trophy was a narrative ploy repeated in a compulsive if
varied manner in several plots. Also, the intersection of gender and
class or cultural differences animated and intensified conflict. An
extravagant and self-indulgent socialite flirts with a wealthy, oriental merchant to whom she becomes indebted when she loses charity
funds in a stock market gamble. Fortunately, her husband has amassed
a fortune in the same market so that she attempts to evade the merchant's
demand for her sexual favors as agreed upon. When he reacts by angrily
branding her shoulder with the mark he uses to stamp all his possessions, she retaliates by shooting and wounding him. Subsequently her
husband assumes blame for the incident and is tried, but an angry courtroom mob demands vindication and revenge when the socialite confesses
and bares the scar on her shoulder as proof of the merchant's bestial
nature.

In The Cheat, DeMille successfully and brilliantly created a filmic
style that was suited to the representation of wealth and consumption
as spectacle. Although it was unlikely that an oriental merchant
would circulate so freely as a respected member of the social elite
in America during the teens, the characterization was clever. Oriental-
ism lent a rich, mysterious, and depraved atmosphere to an illicit bargain involving woman as an object of exchange. During a sequence that
illustrates DeMille's use of mise-en-scène, Fannie Ward, a fabled beauty,
engages in a conscious form of self-theatricalization within the chambers of the merchant's estate. She admires the sensuousness of the
exotic and precious objets d'art which he exhibits to entice her, but
of course she is the most desired object on display both for the merchant and the film's spectators. DeMille's famous, Rembrandt lighting
was used to produce a sculptured and dramatic result that accorded with
his concept of the mise-en-scène. Further, the contrasting acting
styles of Fanny Ward and Sessue Hayakawa, the Japanese actor, reenforced the effects of the composition of the scenes. She engages in
histrionic behavior so that his subdued and impassive manner serves to
render her emotions, as well as her resplendent self, as part of the
display. Altogether, DeMille succeeded in composing a world in which
aesthetics, eroticism, and wealth were intertwined by manipulating the
visual imagery to create a spectacle.

During the second phase of DeMille's career, which corresponds
roughly to the Jazz Age, certain shifts in attitude occurred with respect to the issues articulated in the pre-World War I pictures. Ambivalence towards wealth gave way to endorsement of conspicuous consumption as an American ideal, even though the ideal was unattainable on a
luxurious scale for most moviegoers. Although in actuality the increase
in prosperity was relative, the availability of consumer goods enhanced
the public's sense of material well-being and contributed to the growth
of a mass psychology based upon economic abundance rather than scarcity.
Attitudes towards money underwent a transformation essential to mass
consumerism so that spending became pleasurable rather than guilt-
inducing. Consequently there developed a voyeuristic fascination about

the lives of the rich that endures even today. During the late teens
and twenties, the idle rich in DeMille's pictures were no longer questionable or morally defunct characters but served as models for consumption. Display, not in the sense of keeping up with but overawing
the Joneses, became de rigeur rather than merely vulgar. Self-indul-
gence and frivolousness became positive attributes to be encouraged.[18]

   Fittingly, spectacles became DeMille's trademark during a decade
when the construction of opulent movie palaces to attract crowds reached
its peak. As textbooks for consumption, the director's Jazz Age films
featured graphic illustrations of the sumptuous decor and wardrobe of
the smart set, fantasy or dream sequences that provided the plot ra-
tionale for extravaganzas, and flashbacks to bacchanalian revelries
that elevated quantity over quality. Fan magazines and trade journals
recapitulated for their readers the lavishness of the set and costume
designs in these pictures. Photoplay commented about Male and Female,
"a typical DeMille production," "Does Miss Swanson require a bed . . .?
It is such a bed, and such a boudoir, as we have hever seen before."[19]
Variety described one of Gloria Swanson's costumes in Don't Change Your
Husband as a "gold cloth and lace negligee trimmed with metallic fringe
. . . so loud it should have awakened her sleeping husband."[20] Ads for
Saturday Night featured a portrait of DeMille, a young woman wearing a
swimsuit and seated on a swing, and couples dancing in a swimming pool
dotted with balloons. The copy promised viewers every imaginable
thrill, including sensational romances that ignored class barriers:

     I. The Heiress Elopes With Her Handsome Chauffeur and the
         Young Millionaire Weds His Washerwoman's Daughter!
    II. The Chauffeur's Rescue of the Rich Society Girl
   III. The Collision Between Train and Auto Ninety Feet in Mid Air
    IV. The Coney Island Ferris Wheel Accident
     V. The Halloween Bathing Party With the Society Girls in
         Marvelous Creations in Bathing Suits!
    VI. The Tenement House Fire. Scenes that will dumbfound you!
   VII. The Most Gorgeous Gowns of Any DeMille Picture![21]

Always under constraint to exceed the elaborateness of his last spectacle, DeMille outdid himself in The Golden Bed. As his pièce de
résistance, a character who is a confections merchant decorates an entire ballroom with such concocted sweets as a gigantic heart serving
as a centerpiece, striped candy musicians, a peppermint candy pavillion,
female slaves festooned with candy chains, and women adorned from head
to foot with detachable lollipops.

   DeMille's impact upon the consumption of such commodities as
fashion apparel and furnishings, as well as a preoccupation with social
etiquette, was well-noted at the time. Theater Magazine concluded:
"It is without bounds to say that the taste of the masses have been
developed . . . by Cecil B. DeMille. . . ."[22] The director himself
commented, "I believe I have had an obvious effect upon American life.
I have brought a certain sense of beauty and luxury into everyday

existence, all jokes about ornate bathrooms and de luxe boudoirs
aside."[23] An integral part of educating moviegoers about the details
of consumption and etiquette was the persuasion that personal fulfillment could be obtained by gratifying materialistic urges. Surface
values prevailed. Consumerism meant that a preoccupation with appearances as against reality would be paramount. As illustrated by the
phenomenon of media personalities, a development boosted by the rise
of the star system and by the ascendancy of DeMille himself, packaging
became both style and substance.

Although mass consumption meant democratization in terms of the
distribution and availability of material goods, the intersection of
sexual and class differences remained problematic in DeMille's pictures.
Always alert to the didactic value of film, the director implied that
film had a function in terms of promoting understanding across class
barriers: "The screen has made good progress in teaching the lower
grades of society that every rich man is not purse-proud and heartless
and in disabusing the minds of the upper ten of the belief that every
laboring man goes home . . . and beats his wife and children."[24] Nevertheless, marriage involving persons from different socioeconomic back-
grounds was not often sanctioned in his own films. For instance, in
Male and Female, Forbidden Fruit, Saturday Night, and The Golden Bed,
class distinctions were violated but ultimately respected and upheld.
In Something To Think About, Triumph, Feet of Clay, The Volga Boatman,
and Dynamite, class differences posed an issue in courtship but were
levelled by the rise or fall of individual fortunes. Disparity in
wealth was resolved by women marrying into an upper class or relinquish-
ing comfort to live on a scale dictated by male status. Put another
way, women had to be schooled to adjust their consumption patterns
according to the means provided by men. Class disharmony threatened
to bring about sexual imbalance as well, but uniformity prevailed in
the end as did masculine superiority.

DeMille became a trend setter in the twenties by capitalizing upon
his observation that "the whole country was very much interested in
'sex appeal.'"[25] Class alignment may have been essential in the formation of a couple, but sexual attraction became the sine qua non for the
survival of matrimony. Requirements for a scintillating marriage à la
DeMille included wealth, leisure, and "the new woman."[26] DeMille show-
cased "the new woman" as spectacle in a series of popular sex comedies
and melodramas that detailed the marital exploits of the rich. Actress
Gloria Swanson, who starred in a number of these vehicles, came to
epitomize the well-dressed woman both on screen and off. Why Change
Your Wife? is typical of the films of this cycle. As Beth Gordon,
Swanson jeopardizes her marriage by clinging to decorous, Victorian
notions about her appearance and frowns upon frivolousness as evidenced
by a wine cellar and foxtrot records. Dissatisfied with his dowdy wife,
Robert Gordon (Thomas Meighan) is inspired to buy her a negligee which
is transparent, backless, décolleté, precariously suspended with beads,
and trimmed with fur. Beth is outraged by his "oriental" ideas and
thereupon loses him to Sally Clark (Babe Daniels), the enticing

mannequin who modeled the negligee in a boutique. Piqued by gossip,
however, she does a volte-face after her divorce and orders her new
gowns made "sleeveless, backless, transparent, indecent." Robert, meanwhile, has discovered that "wives will be wives" and finds matrimony
to Sally, who is petulant and selfish, is not without disadvantages.
Another round of divorce and re(marriage) occurs when the ex-spouses
meet at a luxurious resort hotel, and Robert is duly impressed with
Beth's transformation from a prim and proper, bespectacled housewife
to a seductive and playful fashionplate.

In Why Change Your Wife? sexual frigidity or incompatibility is
solved by a trip to the boutique to purchase a precariously constructed
swimsuit. Commodities invested with extraordinary powers could effect
magical transformations on screen and thus acquired a lure for the
spectators. Ironically the impact of mass consumption resulted in the
democratization and accessibility of sex appeal so that every woman became less individualistic and devalued at the same time that she became
the object of greater expense. DeMille's frivolous attitude towards
marriage and divorce may have been titillating but it certainly reenforced the notion that women (and sometimes men) were interchangeable
commodities. Since appearances became paramount, spouses functioned
as decorative objects or ornamentation. DeMille's predilection to
objectify his characters as part of a spectacle for the purposes of
mise-en-scène had the result of reducing human beings to decoration.
In effect, his cinematic style captured the essence of reification.

By effecting a reversal of the happily-ever-after narrative strategy
to focus on romantic life after the nuptial vows, DeMille succeeded in
creating a new genre of films that appealed to the Jazz Age audience.
Repeatedly in Old Wives for New, We Can't Have Everything, Don't Change
Your Husband, Why Change Your Wife?, Affairs of Anatol, Adam's Rib, and
Madam Satan, couples confronted the dilemma of a lackluster marriage.
Whether the offending spouse had been wandering from the hearth, im-
mersed in work, or lax about appearances, the deterioration of wedlock
into monotony was serious. The director's novel solution was to create
rivalry by means of triangular relationships that led to the transformation of the guilty spouse or the realignment of couples through
divorce and remarriage. DeMille found that in depicting the marital
misadventures of the leisured class, he could satisfy the public's
curiosity about the rich by creating spectacles in which marriage became the pivotal institution for the purposes of conspicuous consumption. Significantly the wealthy did not have children, for married
couples had to be unencumbered to pursue a frivolous, irresponsible,
and hedonistic life style.

Although DeMille easily made the transition to sound, his uncanny
ability to read the pulse of the audience failed momentarily after the
stock market crash. The director was not as quick to respond to the
changed circumstances of the Depression as he had been a decade earlier
to Jazz Age hullabaloo. A recycling of his silent films in sound version during a brief and unsuccessful stint at MGM proved disastrous.

But upon his return to Paramount in 1932, he changed strategy and began to concentrate almost exclusively upon spectacles set in the near or distant past. During the silent era, he had made a few historical and Biblical epics, especially The Ten Commandments, which would serve as prototypes. Since the ostentatious consumption of the rich was no longer suitable for an audience in the midst of an unprecedented and seemingly irreversible unemployment problem, DeMille cleverly transmuted the basis for extravagant display. Consumption was now associated with religious uplift or events enshrined in the American past.

With few exceptions, DeMille's pictures during the remainder of his career were either spectacles set in an historical period (The Sign of the Cross, Cleopatra, The Crusades, Samson and Delilah, and The Ten Commandments remake) or frontier epics featuring spectacular events (The Plainsman, The Buccanneer, Union Pacific, North West Mounted Police, Reap the Wild Wind, and Unconquered). The Greatest Show on Earth, the only DeMille film to win an Academy Award for best picture, may appear to be an exception but it too was a piece of Americana and dazzled the audience with colorful life under the big top. As the nation experienced depression, World War II, and the cold war, DeMille's formulaic movies reaffirmed the American system at a time when it was threatened from within and without. The religious and patriotic themes of these pictures were in effect endorsements of the American brand of modern capitalism and consumerism. Secular and religious critics both objected to the reification of the religious spirit in the Biblical films and protested against the resulting vulgarity.[27] But DeMille was simply exhibiting a characteristic of American Protestantism that fused the worldly and otherworldly in the valorization of material success. Since the evangelical revivals of the nineteenth century, dark Calvinist orthodoxy had yielded to an optimistic belief in enterprise more in keeping with the American dream. Faith in God, country, and prosperity became the cornerstone of the American way of life. As one historian explained, an important aspect of the economic spurt of the twenties fueled by consumerism was "the secularization of religion and the religiosity of business."[28] DeMille was not the first to equate Americanism with Christian dogma, Manifest Destiny, and the triumph of private enterprise.

DeMille's extravagant rendering of the past was not just a clever strategy to continue the production of films about consumption during the depressed thirties and stringent wartime forties. By recreating the past as lavish spectacle, the director cast history in contemporary terms and implied a linear continuity between our modern consumer society and distant and not-so-distant epochs. In so doing, he acquired for a mass consumption economy, thwarted by depression and then war, the endorsement of such empire builders as God, Biblical figures, Romans, Egyptians, and American frontier folk. During hard times, prodigality became a standard to be defended. Consequently, Nero fiddled while acres of Rome went up in flames, the Egyptians built mammoth cities and monuments with a cast of thousands, and Americans tamed a vast continent. As a director who produced sensational images

33

of excess to be consumed by the audience, DeMille proved to be pro-
phetic. When the United States emerged from World War II a superpower,
the country entered upon an even greater phase of consumerism spurred
by an unprecedented baby boom. Fittingly, DeMille culminated his career
in 1956 with the release of a colossal remake of The Ten Commandments.

   As DeMille's spectacles evolved, the didactic and ideological dimension of the narrative became increasingly formalized. Significantly
he dispensed with Jeanie Macpherson, the scenarist who wrote the scripts
for most of his silent movies about the "new woman," and began to recruit a team of male writers for his epics. Narrative titles superimposed over symbolic images in the silent pictures became elaborated
into a montage sequence with voice-over narration to function as a
preface. DeMille narrated some of these sequences himself and appeared
in the prologue to The Ten Commandments remake to impress the spectators
with the gravity of what they were about to see. Such introductions set
forth the terms of the moral and political contest dramatized in the
narrative. For example, the forces of slavery, fear, superstition,
idolatry, and tyranny were pitted against an unquenchable will for
freedom in Samson and Delilah. Underscored by violins and horns on the
musictrack, the loftiness of the narrator's tone was visually reenforced
by a montage of idol gods, marching armies, the heavens, and descent to
idyllic countryside. In effect, DeMille had devised yet another visual
strategy to assert his omnipotence as director and storyteller and to
emphasize the didactic nature of film.

   Reap the Wild Wind, one of DeMille's most popular pictures, is a
good example of the director at his best in creating a yarn about the
American past. Symbolically the picture begins with an eagle and the
stars and stripes on the prow of a ship while a lively rendition of
"Columbia, the Gem of the Ocean" plays on the soundtrack. With the
appearance of DeMille's name, the music becomes a rollicking sailor's
song. Credits are printed over shipboards punctuated by heavy, anchor
chains, while the music in turns becomes lively, dark, then lush and
romantic. During the credits, DeMille has artfully succeeded in con-
veying both the subject and emotional tone of the film: patriotic
sentiment, merriment, violent aggression, and romantic love. Further,
he has established the film as an artifact of his own construction.
Next, a typical DeMille prologue informs the audience that America's
lifeline in the nineteenth century, the vital sea lanes, became the
prey of unscrupulous cargo salvagers who threatened the nation's com-
merce. A succession of picture postcard shots of palm trees lining
scenic beaches, schooners off the Florida keys, and savage storms and
shipwrecks is erased by wipes and synchronized with narration. The
story which follows has all the ingredients that the audience had come
to expect from a DeMille film: heroic men cast as rivals for a pretty
but headstrong woman; despicable villains plotting to wreck the nation's
future; comic relief provided by a playful monkey; adventure and sus-
pense; and a fantastic ending with underwater special effects including
a giant squid. Like the rest of DeMille's sagas, the picture was calcu-
lated not only to entertain but to reaffirm audience belief in the

nation's future, especially its destiny as a great commercial power.

   Undoubtedly, DeMille's best-known movie today was his last, a remake of The Ten Commandments. The silent version consisted of two
parts: a Biblical prologue about the story of Moses, which featured
the spectacular parting of the Red Sea in tinted color and lasted about
a third of the entire footage, and a modern story about lovers caught
in a triangle, violating the commandments. Significantly, DeMille discarded the modern story in the remake and expanded the Biblical section
to a three hour, thirty-nine minute spectacular filmed in color and Vista
Vision. Critics dubbed the film "Sexodus" and worse, but DeMille
proved that he was still a consummate director who could create images
that enthralled the spectator. For example, he cast Charlton Heston
as an iconic representation of Moses and fictionalized the events of
the prophet's life from the moment of his discovery in the bulrushes
until the triumphal hour when the Hebrews are led out of captivity.
By focusing the first half of the picture upon Moses' early manhood,
DeMille was able to incorporate and augment the elements of the type
of spectacle he had been creating for years.

   As the adopted son of Pharaoh, Moses, laden with spoils and ac-
claimed by the people, becomes a dashing warrior who returns victorious
from foreign conquests. The Pharaoh's natural son, Rameses (Yul
Brynner), views him as a dangerous rival, for at stake are not only
the throne and the riches of empire but the beautiful Princess Nefretiri
(Anne Baxter) who claims, "I am Egypt." Among the Hebrew slaves, Joshua
(John Derek) admires Lilia (Debra Paget), but she is also eyed by Dathan
(Edward G. Robinson), a traitor to his people and Governor of Goshen.
Since both Rameses and Dathan eventually possess unwilling women be-
loved by hated rivals, DeMille's brand of sadistic sexuality becomes
part of the unfolding spectacle. Sexual conflict remains significant
in DeMille's ancient epics, but class differences are translated into
imperialistic and cultural terms with females representing the prize.
Unfortunately, DeMille's portrayal of women in the Biblical stories is
a throwback to the vamp and not so innovative as his "new woman" of the
silent era. As a siren, Princess Nefretiri is a cliché reminiscent of
both Delilah (Hedy Lamarr) in Samson and Delilah and Poppaea (Claudette
Colbert) in Sign of the Cross. She is also contrasted with an anti-
thetical stereotype, Sephora (Yvonne DeCarlo), the saintly shepherd
woman Moses marries during his exile.

   The Ten Commandments is very much a postwar, fifties film in that
its rhetoric and themes emphasize ideological conflict. As DeMille
himself informs us in the prologue, the film is a story about freedom
vs. slavery: whether men will live under the law of God (who is presumably on our side) or according to the whims of dictators as property
of the state. The film has a sanctimonious and self-righteous tone that
echoes the political debate of the cold war. It also celebrates
America's coming of age as a superpower. As Pharaoh's son, Moses was
a victorious warrior who conquered foreign peoples and built the massive city of Goshen with its monuments and vistas. But when he

discovers that he is Hebrew, he experiences a crisis of conscience and condemns the institution of slavery. Since Egypt has been founded on spurious principles, Moses relinquishes the possibility of inheriting its throne and becomes instead the architect of an empire based on God's law. At the end of the film, God's chosen people are within sight of the promised land where they will undoubtedly be fruitful and multiply and prosper. As dictated by the imperatives of God and Manifest Destiny, the land of milk and honey will be destined for expansion, the development of an internal market, and the benefits of a consumer economy.[29]

As a footnote, it is interesting to reconsider DeMille's spectacles today as an illustration of an aesthetic sensibility labeled camp by Susan Sontag. When viewed as expressions of camp, these spectacles provide a lesson unintended by the director, at least on a conscious level, and contrary to the overt message. As affirmations of the consumer culture, DeMille's spectacles celebrated plenitude and volume in a style appropriately theatrical. Visual style in fact became an end in itself and in the sound films conflicted with the soundtrack, carelessly marred by colloquialisms peppering the dialogue. As artifacts, spectacles were in themselves commodities to be consumed and thus provided an unwitting commentary about the orality of a consumer society. A feast for the eyes, spectacles lead to satiation despite the technological progression resulting in color, special effects, and widescreen. About Samson and Delilah, Bosley Crowther commented that the picture had "more chariots, more temples, more peacock plumes, more animals, more pillows, more spear-carriers, more bears, and more sex than ever before."[30] American consumerism had merely led to saturation. Significantly, Susan Sontag wrote in her well-known essay that "camp taste is by its nature possible only in affluent societies, in societies or circles capable of experiencing the psychopathology of affluence."[31]

During the teens, DeMille had secured artistic prestige for Lasky's productions, achieved status as a ranking director in American films, and won international acclaim. But his reputation suffered a decline in the early twenties when he was dubbed a showman who produced garish and tasteless spectacles. Although critics acknowledged the craftsmanship of his films, responded favorably to occasional pictures, and even confessed to being entertained, they did not for the most part take DeMille seriously. Further, they began to make invidious comparisons by labelling DeMille's older brother, William, who followed him to Hollywood and enjoyed a brief career as scenarist and director, as the more intellectual and serious filmmaker. DeMille's colleagues in the film industry conceded his power at the box office but never honored him with an Academy Award as best director. Conjectures about the reasons for DeMille's lapse from critical if not popular esteem remain speculative. Since the director lost his prestige among critics as he gained greater success at the box-office, some have concluded that as an artist he deliberately squandered his talents to court fame and fortune.[32] Such an explanation sounds romanticized and clichéd and further overlooks DeMille's roots and early career in the theater.

DeMille came from a theatrical family that was in business to entertain a mass audience, not a cultured elite, and he himself was by turns an actor, playwright, producer, and director who spent considerable time on the road and came to know his audience firsthand. After he made the transition to filmmaking, he never deviated from the concept of a commercial picture that would appeal to a wide audience. The movie industry was in its infancy, however, and DeMille made a reputation for himself because he paid scrupulous attention to scenarios, lighting, and set and costume designs. Since there was a constant exhibitor demand for pictures, DeMille worked at a breakneck pace and in an improvisational manner to turn out several films a year. For example, he directed both The Golden Chance and The Cheat in twelve days by shooting almost around the clock owing to scheduling constraints.[33] But as the studio production system became streamlined, DeMille made fewer pictures, became less experimental and certainly less spontaneous, and perfected a cinematic style that remained rather fixed for decades. As the director himself summed up late in his career, "Showmanship in movies is just telling an interesting story. That's all. There's love. Boy meets girl. There's conflict. Hero vs villain. Anything else is just the trimmings."[34] A typical DeMille film was constructed along just such lines with characters who functioned as sociological and ethical types. Given his extraordinary sense of the pictorial, however, DeMille found that in effect "the trimmings" intrigued him the most and he indulged his predilection for oversized spectacles. During his long career, his films received a number of Academy Awards and nominations for cinematography, art direction and set design, costumes, and of course, special effects.[35]

DeMille appeared dated long before the end of his career because his conception of film as a static pictorial design meant for the edification of spectators and his self-righteous, moralizing tone were Victorian legacies. Still, these legacies were based on a system of values that he shared with his audience, even the extent to which these values were shifting in a modern, consumer society. Significantly, DeMille fused together in his films reassuring, Victorian preachment and the "reification produced by commodity relations" that became so pervasive in a mass consumer economy. During the twenties, his sex comedies and melodramas emerged as a peculiar brand of baroque display, etiquette and consumption manual, and moral righteousness. After the Depression, the reification of religious and patriotic spirit in his spectacles served to endorse American materialism. As a film director and media personality, DeMille played an important role in coaching his audience to embrace a twentieth century consumer culture within the framework of nineteenth century ethical values.

The degree of DeMille's success according to the terms he most respected, attendance figures and box-office receipts, remains most impressive. A total of seventy pictures produced during the years 1913-56 had grossed $750,000,000 by the time of his death in 1959.[36]

<u>Variety</u> still lists such blockbusters as <u>Unconquered</u>, <u>Reap the Wild Wind</u>, <u>Samson and Delilah</u>, <u>The Greatest Show on Earth</u>, and <u>The Ten Commandments</u> on its list of "All-Time Film Rental Champs" though dollar figures have obviously not been adjusted for inflation.[37] And <u>The Ten Commandments</u> continues to attract higher Nielsen ratings than rival network counterprogramming on television. DeMille's conservative political and economic ideology, his didactic posture, and his filmmaking style would undoubtedly have appeared antiquated had he survived into the sixties. Curiously at the time of his death, he was contemplating a film about the Boy Scout movement projected for a decade to be marked by politicized and rebellious youth. But his concept of film as a spectacle targeted for the widest possible audience is still very operative in the film industry today. The real cinema descendants of DeMille are filmmakers like George Lucas and Steven Spielberg who have escalated special effects into space age wizardry and broken box-office records with commercial films that have extremely profitable tie-ins. Although his legacy is rarely acknowledged without ridicule, DeMille was certainly the father of the spectacle film as it evolved in the motion picture industry through the decades.

Notes

1. "Ready When You Are, Mr. DeMille," BBC television program, August 1981.

2. For recent works in film history that are based on empirical research about the film industry, see studies such as those done by Douglas Gomery, Robert Allen, Tino Balio, and Russell Merritt.

3. See Christine Gledhill, "Recent Developments in Feminist Criticism," <u>Quarterly Review of Film Studies</u> 3, no. 4 (Fall 1978):457-93 and Philip Rosen, "Screen and the Marxist Project in Film Criticism," <u>Quarterly Review of Film Studies</u> 2, no. 3 (August 1977):273-84. Reporting on the Asilomar Conference titled "Cinema Histories, Cinema Practices" held in 1981, Philip Rosen and Mary Ann Doane observed "the notion of specificity was reduced to the 'individual,' the 'unique,' or the 'local effect,' and no interrelationship between a theory of the cinematic apparatus in relation to the unconscious and an analysis of a historically specific instance was envisaged with a few exceptions. . . ." "Conference Reports," <u>Camera Obscura</u> 8-10 (Fall 1982):224-33. Some of the papers read at the conference have been published as an American Film Institute monograph, <u>Cinema Histories, Cinema Practices</u>, ed. Philip Rosen and Patricia Mellencamp (Frederick, Md.: University Publications of America, 1984).

4. Andrew Sarris, <u>The American Cinema</u> (New York: E.P. Dutton, 1968), pp. 83, 90-91. Sarris does not discuss DeMille's silent films at all! See also John Caughie, ed., <u>Theories of Authorship</u> (London: Routledge & Kegan Paul, 1981).

5. See William Ashdown, "Confessions of an Automobilist," in The Twenties: Fords, Flappers and Fanatics, ed. George Mowry (Englewood Cliffs, N.J.: Prentice-Hall, 1965), pp. 47-51.

6. Guy Debord, Society of the Spectacle (Detroit: Black and Red, 1977), no. 18. (Originally published as La société du spectacle [Paris: Editions Buchet-Chastel, 1967]).

7. Georg Lukacs, History and Class Consciousness (Cambridge, Mass.: MIT Press, 1971), p. 91.

8. Philip Slater, The Pursuit of Loneliness, rev. ed. (Boston: Beacon Press, 1970), p. 102.

9. Shulamith Firestone, The Dialectic of Sex (New York: Bantam Books, 1971), p. 153.

10. Motion Picture Classic (November 1925), Cecil B. DeMille Pamphlet File, UCLA Theater Arts Special Collections.

11. Charles Higham interviewed by James V. D'Arc, 18 July 1977, Cecil B. DeMille Collection, Brigham Young University, Harold B. Lee Library, Provo, Utah (hereafter cited as BYU).

12. David Robinson, "Spectacle," Sight and Sound 25, no. 1 (Summer 1955):22-27, 55-56.

13. Harry C. Carr, "What Next?" Photoplay (March 1917), Mother-Professional, Autobiography, Box 7, Cecil B. DeMille Collection, BYU.

14. For interesting discussions of DeMille's visual style see Ruth Perlmutter, "For God, Country and Whoppee," Film Comment 12, no. 1 (January-February 1976):27-28 and John Door, "The Griffith Tradition," Film Comment 10, no. 2 (March-April 1974):52.

15. At the time of this writing, The Ten Commandments was last shown on television by ABC on Palm Sunday, 15 April 1984. During its four-hour telecast, it beat the competition in every time slot except the first hour and finished seventh among all the programs for the week ending April 15. See "ABC-TV Wins Week 30; NBC Grabs 2d Spot," Variety 314, no. 13 (25 April 1984):70, 84.

16. For a psychoanalytic discussion of filmmaking, see Christian Metz, "The Imaginary Signifier," trans. Ben Brewster, Screen 16 (Summer 1975):14-76.

17. The Cheat was much admired by such French directors as Louis Delluc and Jean Cocteau.

18. For further discussions about DeMille, the movies, and mass consumption, see Charles Eckert, "The Carole Lombard in Macy's Window," Quarterly Review of Film Studies 3, no. 1 (Winter 1978): 1-23; Jeanne Allen, "The Film Viewer as Consumer," Quarterly Review of Film Studies 5, no. 4 (Fall 1980):481-99; Lary May, Screening Out the Past (New York: Oxford University Press, 1980), pp. 200-236. Also useful is Douglas Gomery's critical review of May's book in Wide Angle 5, no. 4 (1983):75-79. Also

see Stuart and Elizabeth Ewen, <u>Channels of Desire</u> (New York: McGraw-Hill, 1982), pp. 99–102.

19. <u>Photoplay</u> (December 1919) in Gloria Swanson scrapbook, Robinson Locke Collection, New York Public Library, Library and Museum of the Performing Arts at Lincoln Center (hereafter cited as NYPL LMPA).

20. <u>Variety</u> (7 February 1919) in Gloria Swanson scrapbook, Robinson Locke Collection, NYPL LMPA.

21. Ad for <u>Saturday Night</u>, George Eastman House, Rochester, New York.

22. <u>Theater Magazine</u> (undated) in Cecil B. DeMille scrapbook, Robinson Locke Collection, NYPL LMPA.

23. Frederick James Smith, "How Christ Came to Pictures," <u>Photoplay</u> 32, no. 2 (July 1927):118.

24. Edward Weitzel, "Talking It Over with DeMille," <u>Motion Picture World</u>, 21 December 1918, p. 18.

25. William deMille, "Great Pictures and the Men Who Made Them" (October 1935), William deMille Papers, New York Public Library, Manuscripts and Archives.

26. The sexes in middle class Victorian society had been segregated, and women turned to each other for emotional ties in sororital networks. Women in the Jazz Age, however, were encouraged to relate primarily to men. What their gains and losses were is an interesting matter of conjecture. See Caroll Smith-Rosenberg, "The Female World of Love and Ritual: Relations Between Women in Nineteenth Century America," <u>Signs</u> 1 (Autumn 1975):1–30; Nancy F. Cott, <u>The Bonds of Womanhood</u> (New Haven, Conn.: Yale University Press, 1977); and Lillian Faderman, <u>Surpassing the Love of Men</u> (New York: William Morrow, 1981).

27. See especially Malcolm Boyd, <u>Christ and Celebrity Gods</u> (Greenwich, Conn.: Seabury Press, 1958), pp. 51–79.

28. William E. Leuchtenburg, <u>The Perils of Prosperity 1914–32</u> (Chicago: University of Chicago Press, 1958), pp. 188–89.

29. See Michael Wood's discussion of spectacles in <u>America in the Movies</u> (New York: Basic Books, 1975), pp. 165–88.

30. Bosley Crowther, <u>New York Times</u>, 22 December 1949, in Gene Ringgold and DeWitt Bodeen, <u>The Films of Cecil B. DeMille</u> (Secaucus, N.J.: Citadel Press, 1969), pp. 346–47.

31. Susan Sontag, "Notes on Camp," <u>Against Interpretation</u> (New York: Delta, 1961), p. 289.

32. See discussions about Kevin Brownlow and Charles Higham in the biography.

33. <u>Variety</u> (17 May 1939), Cecil B. DeMille Pamphlet File, UCLA Theater Arts Special Collections.

34. Quick News Weekly (18 February 1952), Cecil B. DeMille Clipping
    File, Margaret Herrick Library, Academy of Motion Picture Arts
    and Sciences, Beverly Hills (hereafter cited as AMPAS).

35. Significantly, DeMille's spectacles and frontier epics garnered
    one Academy Award and six nominations for best cinematography,
    two awards and four nominations for special effects, one award
    and three nominations for art direction and set design, one award
    and two nominations for costumes. Further, DeMille's pictures
    won one award and two nominations for editing, one award and
    one nomination for best picture, two nominations for sound re-
    cording, and one nomination each for motion picture story and
    music. See Chapter III for details.

36. Variety (22 January 1959), Cecil B. DeMille Clipping File, AMPAS.

37. At the time of this writing, Variety's most recently published
    list appeared in Volume 315, no. 2 (2 May 1984):116, passim.

III. The Films:
Credits, Synopses, and Notes

1 THE SQUAW MAN

Credits

Directors:	Cecil B. DeMille and Oscar Apfel
Scenario:	Cecil B. DeMille and Oscar Apfel (based on the play by Edwin Milton Royle)
Photographer:	Alfred Gandolfi
Editor:	Mamie Wagner
Cast:	Dustin Farnum (James Wynnegate), Winifred Kingston (Lady Diana), Redwing (Nat-U-Rich), Monroe Salisbury (Sir Henry), Billy Elmer (Cash Hawkins)

Released by Jesse L. Lasky Feature Play Company, February 1914
Screening time: Approximately 50 minutes

Synopsis

Captain James Wynnegate and his cousin Henry, the Earl of Kerhill, are co-trustees of an orphan's fund. When Sir Henry embezzles the fund to cover racing debts, James takes the blame to save the honor of the Kerhill name and to shield his cousin's wife, Lady Diana, the woman whom he secretly loves. Escaping to America, James settles in the West and becomes a rancher. Nat-U-Rich, the daughter of an Indian chief, falls in love with him and saves his life on two occasions. When she becomes pregnant after a brief affair, James insists upon marrying her despite his love for Diana and the scorn accorded to squaw men. Some time later, a son is born and named Hal.

Meanwhile, Sir Henry has been fatally wounded during a mountain climbing accident and before his death, he discloses his guilt for the embezzlement. As a result, James becomes the heir to the Kerhill title and estate. Diana travels to America to bring James the news and arrives in the midst of dramatic events. James has been feuding for some time with an evil sheriff who now possesses evidence that Nat-U-Rich killed a man named Cash some years before. Actually, Nat-U-Rich had shot Cash from a hiding place to protect James during a confrontation

43

and is all too aware that she must now pay the penalty. But she is
even more dismayed by Diana's arrival and the disclosure that her son
will be taken to England to be educated as the Kerhill heir. In despair, Nat-U-Rich shoots herself and leaves James to face a lonely
life in America while their son seeks his destiny in England.

2   THE CALL OF THE NORTH

Credits

Director:	Cecil B. DeMille
Scenario:	Cecil B. DeMille (based on the play by George Broadhurst and the book, The Conjuror's House, by Steward Edward White)
Photographer:	Alvin Wyckoff
Art Director:	Wilfred Buckland
Editor:	Mamie Wagner
Cast:	Robert Edeson (Graehme Stewart, Ned Stewart), Theodore Roberts (Galen Albert), Winifred Kingston (Virginia), Horace B. Carpenter (Rand), Florence Dagmar (Elodie)

Released by Jesse L. Lasky Feature Play Company, August 1914
Screening time: Approximately 53 minutes

Synopsis

Galen Albert, the Factor of Hudson Bay Company, elopes with a young
woman named Elodie despite her being promised to another suitor. Rand,
the rejected suitor, later obtains revenge by convincing Galen that
Elodie has been unfaithful and implicates in the adultery a widower,
Ned Stewart. Galen exercises his power as Factor by condemning Ned to
take the Journey of Death, an unarmed trek through the frozen wilderness, and remains unmoved by pleas on behalf of Ned's young son.

Twenty years later, the tragedy is about to repeat itself when
Ned's son, Graehme, wins the affection of Galen's daughter, Virginia.
Graehme has been illegally trading in Galen's territory and becomes
even more defiant when he learns about the circumstances of his father's
death. Galen orders Ned to undertake the Journey of Death, but Virginia
disobeys the law by equipping him with a rifle and provisions. Meanwhile, Rand has been fatally wounded in an incident and, before he dies,
exonerates Ned Stewart from charges of adultery. Galen rescinds his
order to have Graehme put to death and the young lovers are reunited.

3 THE VIRGINIAN

Credits

Producer and Director:	Cecil B. DeMille
Scenario:	Cecil B. DeMille (based on the novel by Owen Wister and the play by Kirk LaShelle)

Photographer:	Alvin Wyckoff
Art Director:	Wilfred Buckland
Editors:	Mamie Wagner and Cecil B. DeMille
Cast:	Dustin Farnum (The Virginian), Jack Johnstone (Steve), Winifred Kingston (Molly Wood), Billy Elmer (Trampas)

Produced by Jesse L. Lasky Feature Play Company
Released by Paramount Pictures Corporation, September 1914
Screening time: Approximately 41 minutes

Synopsis

The Virginian and his best friend, Steve, participate in the horse-play and merriment of an all-male society until an Eastern school teacher named Molly Wood arrives on the scene. While the Virginian begins to acquire the rudiments of an education and to woo Molly, Steve becomes involved in the cattle rustling schemes of the local villain, Trampas. Despite his reluctance, the Virginian leads a posse that captures and hangs the rustlers, including Steve. But Trampas has escaped. The Virginian doggedly continues to trail him until he is attacked and wounded by Indians. During his convalescence, he wins Molly's affections. Unfortunately their wedding festivities in town are disrupted by the sudden reappearance of Trampas. A showdown results in the Virginian's triumph and his reunion with Molly.

4   WHAT'S HIS NAME

Credits

Producer and Director:	Cecil B. DeMille
Scenario:	Cecil B. DeMille (based on the novel by George Barr McCutcheon)
Photographer:	Alvin Wyckoff
Editor:	Cecil B. DeMille
Cast:	Max Figman (Harvey), Lolita Peterson (Nellie), Fred Montague (Fairfax), Cecilia Hoyt (Phoebe)

Produced by Jesse L. Lasky Feature Play Company
Released by Paramount Pictures Corporation, October 1914
Screening time: Approximately 56 minutes

Synopsis

Harvey, a soda jerk, marries his sweetheart Nellie and settles down in Blakeville, a small town. Some time later, Nellie becomes more enticed with the possibilities of a theatrical career rather than domestic life and the care of a young daughter. She persuades Harvey to move to New York, where she eventually becomes a successful actress. Since husband and daughter are in the way, Nellie installs them in a house in suburban Tarrytown and promises to see them on Sundays.

After Nellie becomes the toast of the town, she attracts the attention of a wealthy admirer named Fairfax and agrees to obtain a divorce.

Harvey, reduced to the status of What's-His-Name, is cruelly ejected from the Tarrytown house. Determined to return to Blakeville, he and his daughter Phoebe become a pair of ragged travelers and have a series of adventures on the road. When they return, Harvey's Uncle Peter, who has never had a good opinion about marriage, takes them in. Phoebe becomes ill and Harvey wires Nellie in Reno, where she has become disenchanted with Fairfax though in the midst of divorce proceedings. Nellie rushes to her daughter's bedside and the family is reunited.

5   THE MAN FROM HOME

Credits

Producer and Director:	Cecil B. DeMille
Scenario:	Cecil B. DeMille (based on the play by Booth Tarkington and Harry L. Wilson)
Photographer:	Alvin Wyckoff
Editor:	Cecil B. DeMille
Cast:	Charles Richman (Daniel Voorhees Pike), Mabel Van Buren (Ethel Simpson), Horace B. Carpenter (Ivanoff), Anita King (Helene), Fred Montague (Earl of Hawcastle), Monroe Salisbury (Almeric), Theodore Roberts (Grand Duke Vasili)

Produced by Jesse L. Lasky Feature Play Company
Released by Paramount Pictures Corporation, November 1914
Screening time: Approximately 54 minutes

Synopsis

Daniel Voorhees Pike wishes to wed a young girl named Ethel Simpson, but first she and her brothers are to be sent to Europe to complete their education. While Ethel is abroad, her father is fatally injured and appoints Daniel as her guardian and trustee of the family estate.

In Russia, Ivanoff, a government official, steals a considerable sum of money to aid a revolutionary society. Unexpectedly his wife Helene and her lover, a British aristocrat, decamp with the money and he is sentenced to prison in Serbia. Some time later, he escapes and makes his way to Italy.

At this time, Helene and Lord Newcastle are vacationing in Italy but their funds have been depleted. They decide to marry the Lord's son, Almeric, to Ethel Simpson since she is an heiress. Ethel is flattered to be courted by European royalty, but Daniel is dismayed to learn about her impending marriage and quickly appears in Italy. Upon his arrival, Daniel befriends Vasili, a Russian grand duke who is traveling incognito, and the escaped Ivanoff. From the latter he learns about the disreputable Hawcastles and Helene and foils their plot to trap Ethel in a marriage. Appraised of these events, Vasili pardons Ivanoff

and salutes Daniel as an American nobleman. Daniel once again resumes
his courtship of Ethel, presumably with greater success.

6   ROSE OF THE RANCHO

Credits

Producer and Director:	Cecil B. DeMille
Scenario:	Cecil B. DeMille (based on the play by David Belasco and Richard Walton Tully)
Photographer:	Alvin Wyckoff
Art Director:	Wilfred Buckland
Editor:	Cecil B. DeMille
Cast:	J.W. Johnstone (Kearney), Betsy Barriscale (Juanita), Dick LaReno (Kinkaid), Jane Darwell (Betsy's mother), Monroe Salisbury (Don Luis Torre)

Produced by Jesse L. Lasky Feature Play Company
Released by Paramount Pictures Corporation, November 1914
Screening time: Approximately 55 minutes

Synopsis

After the Mexican War, Spanish families in California are required
to register their land claims with the American government. Since the
Spanish are adamant in their refusal to recognize the "gringos," claim
jumpers are dispossessing them. A villain named Kinkaid is scheming
to assume control of various Spanish lands including the estate of the
Castro family. Authorities in Washington, D.C. assign Kearney, a government agent, to investigate the situation.

Upon his arrival, Kearney begins a flirtation with Juanita Castro,
a lovely but temperamental young woman, and solicits her aid to register
and save her family's estate. Juanita reciprocates Kearney's interest
and resists her mother's efforts to betroth her to a suitor, Don Luis
del Torre.

Not realizing that Kearney has managed to register the Castro lands,
Kinkaid has decided to evict the Castros by force. A group of men under
his command lay siege while Kearney, Juanita, and the Castros mount a
resistance inside the estate. Fortunately government troops arrive in
time to effect a rescue. In the aftermath, Juanita is disinherited by
her mother because she will not relinquish her "gringo" lover. She and
Kearney are married on the mission grounds by a priest before they leave
the region to begin a life together.

7   THE GIRL OF THE GOLDEN WEST

Credits

Producer and Director:	Cecil B. DeMille

Scenario:	Cecil B. DeMille (based on the play by David Belasco)
Photographer:	Alvin Wyckoff
Art Director:	Wilfred Buckland
Editor:	Cecil B. DeMille
Cast:	Mabel Van Buren (Mabel), House Peters (Ramerrez), Theodore Roberts (Sheriff Jack Rance), Jeanie Macpherson (Nina)

Produced by Jesse L. Lasky Feature Play Company
Released by Paramount Pictures Corporation, January 1915
Screening time: Approximately 50 minutes

Synopsis

Mabel, the spirited owner of the Polka saloon, is being courted by Sheriff Jack Rance, but she is more responsive to the attentions of a stranger who calls himself Dick Johnson. She is unaware that Johnson's real name is Ramerrez and that he is wanted as the leader of a group of Mexican bandits. Unenlightened, she shows Ramerrez where the miners hide their gold in her saloon. Ramerrez becomes captivated by her, accepts an invitation to dinner, and orders his men not to rob the Polka.

Meanwhile, Ramerrez's jealous, Mexican sweetheart, Nina, betrays him and reveals his identity to the Sheriff. Furthermore, his men have robbed the Polka in his absence and are being pursued by a posse. When the Sheriff reveals Ramerrez's true identity to Mabel, she is angered but remains enamored. She hides Ramerrez in her cabin after he is wounded by the posse and defies the Sheriff. Finally, she resorts to a ruse to save the man she loves. Challenging the Sheriff to a game of poker, she agrees to marry him if she loses, but Ramerrez is to go free if she wins. She triumphs by deceit and is not above publically labeling the Sheriff a card cheat when he later reverses himself and assents to Ramerrez's hanging. Faced with ignominy, the Sheriff relents, keeps his bargain, and permits Mabel and Ramerrez to leave together.

8   THE WARRENS OF VIRGINIA

Credits

Producer and Director:	Cecil B. DeMille
Scenario:	William deMille (based on his play of the same name)
Photographer:	Alvin Wyckoff
Art Director:	Wilfred Buckland
Editor:	Cecil B. DeMille
Cast:	Blanche Sweet (Agatha Warren), House Peters (Ned Burton), James Neill (General Warren)

Produced by Jesse L. Lasky Feature Play Company

Released by Paramount Pictures Corporation, February 1915
Screening time: Approximately 47 minutes

Synopsis

The outbreak of the Civil War separates Agatha Warren, the daughter
of a Southern general, and her sweetheart, Ned Burton, who chooses to
side with the North. During the fighting, however, the lovers are reunited by a Northern scheme to destroy a vital Confederate supply train.
Ned carries a misleading dispatch behind enemy lines and allows himself
to be arrested. Agatha now finds herself torn between affection for
her imprisoned lover and loyalty to her family and cause.

Unaware that the captured dispatch is a ruse, the Confederates lead
their supply train into an ambush and their cause is lost. General
Warren realizes that he has been tricked and orders Ned to be executed
as a spy, but the cessation of hostilities saves the young man from the
firing squad. Two years later, Ned returns to resume his courtship of
Agatha. Although General Warren has not forgotten the bitter events of
the war, he relents for his daughter's sake and consents to an eventual
marriage.

9   THE UNAFRAID

Credits

Producer and Director:	Cecil B. DeMille
Scenario:	Cecil B. DeMille (based on the novel by Eleanor M. Ingram)
Photographer:	Alvin Wyckoff
Art Director:	Wilfred Buckland
Editor:	Cecil B. DeMille
Cast:	House Peters (Stefan), Rita Jolivet (Delight Warren), Page Peters (Michael)

Produced by Jesse L. Lasky Feature Play Company
Released by Paramount Pictures Corporation, April 1915
Screening time: Approximately 45 minutes

Synopsis

In the kingdom of Montenegro, Michael conspires against his older
brother Stefan, the Grand Duke, and hopes to displace him. For this
purpose, he has secured a large sum of money from the agent of an enemy
kingdom but squanders it on a woman in Paris. Desperate for funds,
Michael woos an American heiress named Delight Warren and persuades her
to follow him to Montenegro where they shall be married.

Stefan learns about Michael's scheme, kidnaps Delight upon her
arrival, and forces her into a marriage with himself instead. But he
promises Delight that after Michael has been thwarted, the marriage
will be annulled and she will be permitted to return home. In the
weeks that follow, Delight learns more about the nature of Michael's

treachery and becomes concerned for Stefan's safety. Michael retaliates by abducting Delight and demanding a large sum of money, but Stefan
and his men come to her rescue. Aware that his schemes are lost, Michael
stabs himself. Later, Stefan informs Delight that she is free to leave
but she replies, "I _am_ home, Monsieur."

10   THE CAPTIVE

Credits

Producer and Director:	Cecil B. DeMille
Scenario:	Cecil B. DeMille and Jeanie Macpherson
Photographer:	Alvin Wyckoff
Art Director:	Wilfred Buckland
Editor:	Cecil B. DeMille
Cast:	Blanche Sweet (Sonia), House Peters (Mahmud Hassan), Gerald Ward (Milos)

Produced by Jesse L. Lasky Feature Play Company
Released by Paramount Pictures Corporation, April 1915
Screening time: Approximately 50 minutes

Synopsis

During the war between Turkey and the Balkan states, including
Montenegro, Sonia singlehandedly assumes responsibility for the family
farm and the care of a young brother, Milos. Since there is a severe
manpower shortage in Montenegro, the government assigns Turkish prisoners of war to till the fields. Sonia is unaware that Mahmud Hassan,
the prisoner assigned to her farm, is a Turkish nobleman. She is quite
tyrannical in her treatment of him and is displeased when he wins the
affection of young Milos. But after a period of time, she begins to
primp in the kitchen.

When Turkish soldiers overrun Montenegro, they harass Sonia and
Milos until Hassan reveals his identity to protect them. The Turkish
officer is intent upon molesting Sonia, however, and causes Hassan to
turn traitor and defend his Montenegran friends. A siege takes place
when Hassan, Sonia, and Milos barricade themselves inside the farm-
house, but Montenegran troops arrive in time for a rescue.

Hassan asks Sonia to return with him to Turkey as his wife, but
she points out irreconcilable differences in their nationalities and
their status. They sadly bid farewell. During the period of lawless-
ness which follows, Sonia and Milos are driven from their farm and become refugees. Upon his return to Turkey, Hassan is dispossessed and
banished for his misconduct during the war. Also reduced to the status
of a refugee, Hassan encounters Sonia and Milos on a road, and the
three of them are joyously reunited.

11   THE WILD GOOSE CHASE

Credits

Producer and Director:	Cecil B. DeMille
Scenario:	William deMille (based on his play)
Photographer:	Alvin Wyckoff
Editor:	Cecil B. DeMille
Cast:	Ina Claire (Betty Wright), Tom Forman (Bob Randall), Helen Marlborough (Mrs. Wright), Raymond Hatton (Mr. (Wright), Florence Smythe (Mrs. Randall), Ernest Joy (Mr. Randall)

Produced by Jesse L. Lasky Feature Play Company
Released by Paramount Pictures Corporation, May 1915
Screening time: Approximately 48 minutes

Synopsis

   Bob Randall and Betty Wright have never met, but they both have
wealthy grandfathers in France who wish to join their two families together through a marriage. When they are pressured by their parents
to marry each other to qualify for a large inheritance, both resort to
the same ruse and find an unattractive substitute to take their places.
As parental pressures increase, Betty runs away from home and Bob drops
out of college. Eventually they both join a theatrical company and
enact the roles of Romeo and Juliet, reluctantly at first and then with
greater enthusiasm. Unfortunately the company cannot pay its bills and
its members are jailed. Betty's parents trace her whereabouts and ar-
range to bail out the troupe provided she becomes more cooperative.
When Betty and Bob exchange their real names and addresses, they no
longer find the prospect of marriage to each other so objectionable.

12   THE ARAB

Credits

Producer and Director:	Cecil B. DeMille
Scenario:	Edgar Selwyn and Cecil B. DeMille (based on the play by Edgar Selwyn)
Photographer:	Alvin Wyckoff
Art Director:	Wilfred Buckland
Editor:	Cecil B. DeMille
Cast:	Edgar Selwyn (Jamil), Gertrude Robinson (Mary Hilbert), Horace B. Carpenter (The Sheik), Theodore Roberts (Turkish Governor), Syndey Deane (Dr. Hilbert)

Produced by Jesse L. Lasky Feature Play Company
Released by Paramount Pictures Corporation, June 1915
Screening time: Approximately 53 minutes

Synopsis

As a result of robbing an enemy caravan on a holy day, Jamil is punished by his father, the Bedouin Sheik, and loses his favorite horse. Embittered, Jamil leaves his tribe and becomes a tourist guide. In the meanwhile, his horse passes into the hands of the Turkish Governor, who bestows it upon Mary Hilbert, the attractive daughter of an American physician. When Jamil finds Mary astride his horse, he repossesses the animal during an unpleasant encounter. As time passes, however, he becomes enamored of Mary, returns the horse, and decides to become a Christian.

Mary becomes the focus of the attentions of the Turkish Governor, who intends to add her to his harem and detains her and her father by force. Jamil, aided by his father's men, comes to her rescue but is injured during the fighting. While recovering, he decides to go to America with the Hilberts but word arrives that his father is dead and that his people are leaderless. Assuming his sheikdom, Jamil renounces his love for Mary and returns to his tribe.

13   CHIMMIE FADDEN

Credits

Producer and Director:	Cecil B. DeMille
Scenarist:	Cecil B. DeMille (based on the book by E.W. Townsend and the play by Augustus Thomas)
Photographer:	Alvin Wyckoff
Editor:	Cecil B. DeMille
Cast:	Victor Moore (Chimmie Fadden), Camille Astor (Duchess), Raymond Hatton (Larry), Mrs. Lewis McCord (Mrs. Fadden), Anita King (Fanny Van Cortlandt), Tom Forman (Antoine)

Produced by Jesse L. Lasky Feature Play Company
Released by Paramount Pictures Corporation, June 1915
Screening time: Approximately 45 minutes

Synopsis

Chimmie Fadden, a well-mannered but clownish young man, rescues Fanny Van Cortlandt, a wealthy young woman who does charitable work in the tenements, from attack by a ruffian. As a result, he becomes employed as a footman in the Van Cortlandt uptown household. Although Chimmie is uncomfortable in formal dress, ignorant about the social conventions of the rich, and given to many hilarious faux pas, he enjoys the opportunity to court Fanny's maid, Duchess.

Meanwhile, Antoine, the household's French butler, interests Chimmie's disreputable brother Larry in a scheme to steal the Van Courtlandt silver. When the theft is discovered, Chimmie gallantly takes the blame, but his mother forces Larry to confess the truth. The

Van Cortlandts agree not to prosecute, and Chimmie is released from jail and reunited with Duchess.

14   KINDLING

Credits

Producer and Director: Cecil B. DeMille
Scenario: Cecil B. DeMille (based on the book by Charles Kenyon and Arthur Hornblow and the play by Charles Kenyon)
Photographer: Alvin Wyckoff
Art Director: Wilfred Buckland
Editor: Cecil B. DeMille
Cast: Charlotte Walker (Maggie Schultz), Thomas Meighan (Heine Schultz), Florence Dagmar (Miss Alice), Raymond Hatton (Steve), Billy Elmer (Rafferty), Lillian Langdon (Alice's aunt)

Produced by Jesse L. Lasky Feature Play Company
Released by Paramount Pictures Corporation, July 1915
Screening time: Approximately 51 minutes

Synopsis

Maggie Schultz has not informed her husband Heine that she is pregnant with their first child because he is pessimistic about the fate of children raised in tenement buildings. The situation worsens when Heine goes on strike and faces unemployment. Maggie thus agrees to do some sewing for a rich woman whose young niece, Miss Alice, visits the tenements to befriend the poor.

In the "House of Wealth," Maggie sadly contrasts the baby clothes she has sewn with the finery bestowed on her employer's dog. Embittered, she agrees to a robbery scheme devised by a crook named Steve, but she is dismayed when Steve steals Miss Alice's brooch. Nevertheless, she takes the brooch to a pawnbroker, explains to Heine that the money is a loan, and persuades him to move West in search of better opportunities.

Maggie is being followed as a suspect by a detective named Rafferty and is unaware that Steve has hidden the rest of the jewels in her bedroom. When Rafferty threatens her with arrest, she admits to the crime but erupts in a fiery speech protesting the condemnation of her unborn child to tenement life. Alice's aunt refuses to prosecute and Miss Alice herself gives Maggie and Heine a hundred dollars so that they may begin life anew in the West.

15   CARMEN

Credits

Producer and Director:	Cecil B. DeMille
Scenario:	William deMille (based on the book by Prosper Merimée)
Photographer:	Alvin Wyckoff
Art Director:	Wilfred Buckland
Editor:	Cecil B. DeMille
Cast:	Geraldine Farrar (Carmen), Wallace Reid (Don Jose), Pedro de Cordoba (Escamillo)

Produced by Jesse L. Lasky Feature Play Company
Released by Paramount Pictures Corporation, November 1915
Screening time: Approximately 51 minutes

Synopsis

Don Jose, a new officer on guard duty, refuses to accept a bribe and be impervious to the activities of gypsy smugglers. The smugglers try another tactic and appeal to Carmen, a tempestuous beauty who remarks with easy self-assurance, "Every man can be bought--by something. Leave him to me." Assuming the guise of a local factory worker, Carmen quickly attracts Don Jose's attention. When he sees her dancing alluringly at the neighborhood tavern, he becomes quite enraptured.

Carmen loses no time in convincing Don Jose to allow the smugglers to move their contraband goods. She involves him in even greater crimes when she is arrested for causing a fracas at the factory and is escorted to jail. En route, Don Jose becomes enraged by the taunts of one of her admirers and kills him. Carmen escapes amidst the confusion and Don Jose has no choice but to leave the military and join the smugglers. Assuming that Carmen now belongs to him, he feels angered and betrayed when she decamps for Seville with Escamillo, a toreador. When Carmen continues to assert her independence in a confrontation outside the bullfight arena, Don Jose stabs her to death.

16   CHIMMIE FADDEN OUT WEST

Credits

Producer and Director:	Cecil B. DeMille
Scenario:	Cecil B. DeMille and Jeanie Macpherson (based on the stories by E.W. Townsend)
Photographer:	Alvin Wyckoff
Art Director:	Wilfred Buckland
Editor:	Cecil B. DeMille
Assistant Director:	William Horwitz
Cast:	Victor Moore (Chimmie Fadden), Camille Astor (Duchess), Raymond Hatton (Larry), Ernest Joy (Mr. Van

Courtlandt), Harry Hadfield (Preston),
Florence Dagmar (Betty Van Courtlandt)
Produced by Jesse L. Lasky Feature Play Company
Released by Paramount Pictures Corporation, November 1915
Screening time: Approximately 58 minutes

Synopsis

Mr. Van Courtlandt and his business partner, Preston, engage Chimmie
Fadden to participate in a dishonest scheme that would create more
traffic on the Southwest Railroad. Chimmie is to journey to Death
Valley, strew gold nuggets around an abandoned mine, and create a stampede into the area. Since Chimmie's sweetheart, Duchess, is to travel
to Panama as Betty Van Courtlandt's maid, they are saddened by their
impending separation, and Chimmie wonders if he'll ever earn enough
money so they can be "spliced."

After a series of comic misadventures, Chimmie arrives in Death
Valley and succeeds in stimulating a gold rush. A host of people including Preston, his opportunistic brother, Larry, Betty Van Courtlandt
and Duchess, and a government mine inspector arrive on the scene.
Preston and Van Courtlandt decide to take advantage of the publicity
and sell shares of stock in the abandoned mine. Chimmie remains unaware of this latest development and is welcomed home in the East by
an enthusiastic crowd.

Since Van Courtlandt and Preston have rewarded him amply for his
efforts, Chimmie is now able to afford marriage. During the wedding
preparations, however, Larry reveals that the gold mine is a fake.
Duchess is horrified, points to a newspaper headline about the fraudu-
lent stock, and refuses to marry a thief. Considerably chastened,
Chimmie breaks off with Van Courtlandt and Preston, retrieves the life
savings of a deceived investor, and reconciles with Duchess.

17   THE CHEAT

Credits

Producer and Director:	Cecil B. DeMille
Story:	Hector Turnbull
Scenario:	Hector Turnbull and Jeanie Macpherson
Photography:	Alvin Wyckoff
Art Direction:	Wilfred Buckland
Editor:	Cecil B. DeMille
Cast:	Fanny Ward (Edith Hardy), Sessue Hayakawa (Haka Arakau), Jack Dean (Dick Hardy)

Produced by Jesse L. Lasky Feature Play Company
Released by Paramount Pictures Corporation, December 1915
Screening time: Approximately 55 minutes

Note

A change in the racial origin of the merchant from Japanese to
Burmese was dictated by World War I politics. Japan was then an ally.

Synopsis

Edith Hardy, an ambitious and extravagant socialite, quarrels with
her husband Dick about her spendthrift habits. She confides her plight
to Haka Arakau, a wealthy Burmese merchant who belongs to the smart set,
and flirts provocatively in response to his attentions. As treasurer
for a charity event, Edith is responsible for ten thousand dollars but
secretly gambles the sum on the stock market to gain funds for herself.
When the speculation fails, Edith agrees to enter a liaison with Haka
in exchange for the money to avoid ruinous exposure.

Meanwhile, Dick has been speculating himself but unlike Edith, he
has won a fortune. Pretending that she has gambling debts, Edith fi-
nagles ten thousand dollars from him and attempts to renege on her bargain with Haka. The Burmese merchant, dressed for the first time in
oriental clothes, refuses the check and remains impassive when Edith
threatens to kill herself. A struggle ensues during which Haka brands
Edith on the shoulder with the logo he uses to mark all his possessions.
Edith shoots and wounds him in retaliation. Arriving on the scene,
Dick protects Edith by confessing to the police that he is responsible
for the shooting. At the trial, Dick is pronounced guilty, whereupon
Edith makes a dramatic revelation of the truth and bares her scarred
shoulder as proof. The courtroom crowd surges forth and can hardly
restrain itself from attacking Haka while Edith and Dick embrace as
the case is dismissed.

18   THE GOLDEN CHANCE

Credits

Producer and Director:	Cecil B. DeMille
Scenario:	Cecil B. DeMille and Jeanie Macpherson
Photographer:	Alvin Wyckoff
Art Director:	Wilfred Buckland
Editor:	Cecil B. DeMille
Cast:	Cleo Ridgely (Mary Denby), Wallace Reid (Roger Manning), Horace B. Carpenter (Steve Denby), Edythe Chapman (Mrs. Hillary), Ernest Joy (Mr. Hillary), Raymond Hatton (Jimmy the Rat)

Produced by Jesse L. Lasky Feature Play Company
Released by Paramount Pictures Corporation, December 1915
Screening time: Approximately 58 minutes

Synopsis

Mr. and Mrs. Hillary are entertaining Roger Manning, a young mil-
lionaire whom they hope to interest in a business venture. Plotting
to delay his departure, Mrs. Hillary promises to introduce him to the
prettiest girl in the world at a dinner party. When the young woman
she has engaged becomes ill, Mrs. Hillary prevails upon her attractive
seamstress, Mary Denby, to dress up as a socialite and become the object

56

of Roger's attentions.

Mary grew up as the daughter of a judge but eloped with Steve
Denby, a man of questionable character. She has been living in poverty
and patiently enduring her husband's drunken and abusive behavior. Delighted by the opportunity to wear lovely gowns and jewels, Mary spends
the weekend as a guest in the Hillary household and entertains Roger.
She becomes distressed, however, when Roger becomes a persistent suitor.
She also finds herself entrapped in her husband's plot to steal Mrs.
Hillary's jewels. Caught, she entreats the Hillarys to allow Steve to
escape and discloses her true identity to Roger.

Steve and his accomplice, Jimmy the Rat, force Mary to cooperate
in a scheme to extort money from Roger. Concerned about Mary's safety,
Roger arrives at the Denby apartment but walks into a trap and is as-
saulted by Steve and Jimmy. When the police arrive, Steve is shot
while trying to escape. A few moments later, Roger conveys to Mary
the news that her husband has been killed.

19   TEMPTATION

Credits

Producer and Director:	Cecil B. DeMille
Scenario:	Cecil B. DeMille, Jeanie Macpherson, and Hector Turnbull (based on an original story by Hector Turnbull)
Photographer:	Alvin Wyckoff
Editor:	Cecil B. DeMille
Cast:	Geraldine Farrar (Renee), Pedro de Cordoba (Julien), Theodore Roberts (Otto Mueller), Elsie Jane Wilson (Madame Maroff)

Produced by Jesse L. Lasky Feature Play Company
Released by Paramount Pictures Corporation, January 1916
Screening time: Approximately 61 minutes

Synopsis

Julien, a young opera composer, and Renee, an aspiring soprano,
are in love but they are too impoverished to marry. While they await
success they both perform as entertainers in a restaurant. One night,
Renee's voice enchants an impressario named Otto Mueller and she receives an audition and contract. But when she realizes that Mueller
expects her to become his mistress as the price of her success, she
returns to Julien.

Since Mueller is a powerful figure in the world of music, Renee
and Julien both become unemployed and face poverty. Julien goes to
work in an iron foundry but his health is affected and he collapses.
Renee appeals to Mueller to finance the production of Julien's opera
and promises to become his mistress in return. Julien's opera becomes

a great success and Renee is saved from an ugly fate when a spurned prima donna, Madame Maroff, stabs Mueller in a jealous rage.

20   THE TRAIL OF THE LONESOME PINE

Credits

Producer and Director:	Cecil B. DeMille
Scenario:	Cecil B. DeMille (based on the play by Eugene Walter and the book by John Fox, Jr.)
Photographer:	Alvin Wyckoff
Art Director:	Wilfred Buckland
Editor:	Cecil B. DeMille
Cast:	Charlotte Walker (June Tolliver), Thomas Meighan (John Hale), Theodore Roberts (Judd Tolliver), Earle Foxe (Dave Tolliver)

Produced by Jesse L. Lasky Feature Play Company
Released by Paramount Pictures Corporation, February 1916
Screening time: Approximately 51 minutes

Synopsis

As the operators of an illegal whiskey distillery, Judd Tolliver and members of his clan find themselves in a battle with John Hale, a determined district revenue officer. Lured into a trap by Judd's winsome daughter, June, John becomes a prisoner of the Tollivers long enough to fall in love with his captor. After effecting an ingenious escape, he returns with armed men, but Judd and his clan escape through a secret tunnel. John trails them alone and is badly wounded in an ambush. June realizes that he will bleed to death and implores her father to send for help, but in vain. She then appeals to her cousin, Dave, who is in love with her and has regarded John as an unwelcome rival. Dave relents and brings help in the form of the sheriff and his posse. Judd is not arrested because he promises to relinquish "moonshining," but he and Dave have a violent quarrel that results in the latter's death. Some time later, John visits to inform Judd that he intends to marry June and offers his friendship, but the embittered old man refuses to shake his hand.

21   THE HEART OF NORA FLYNN

Credits

Producer and Director:	Cecil B. DeMille
Scenario:	Jeanie Macpherson (based on a story by Hector Turnbull)
Photographer:	Alvin Wyckoff
Art Director:	Wilfred Buckland
Editor:	Cecil B. DeMille
Cast:	Marie Doro (Nora Flynn), Elliott Dexter (Nolan), Lola May (Mrs.

Stone), Ernest Joy (Mr. Stone),
Charles West (Jack Murray)
Produced by Jesse L. Lasky Feature Play Company
Released by Paramount Pictures Corporation, April 1916
Screening time: Approximately 53 minutes

Synopsis

   Nora, a maid, and Nolan, a chauffeur, are in the employ of a wealthy
couple, Mr. and Mrs. Brantly Stone, and are saving their wages so that
they may be married. Unfortunately they become entangled in the ruinous
affairs of the Stone household. Neglected by a busy husband, Mrs. Stone
is involved in a flirtation with Jack Murray, a man-about-town, who is
urging her to decamp with him even though she has two young children.
Gossip about the frequent presence of Murray at the Stone estate irks
both Nolan, a hot-tempered and jealous lover, and Mr. Stone. In fact,
Mrs. Stone is on the verge of running away with Jack when Nolan unexpectedly drives her husband home one evening. Prevailing upon Nora's
affection for the children, Mrs. Stone convinces the maid to hide Jack
in her room and then implies that Nora is guilty of misconduct. Nolan
is so enraged that he breaks down the door to Nora's room and shoots
Jack as the latter tries to escape. Mr. Stone becomes irate about
Nora's moral character and discharges her, while Mrs. Stone refuses
to rescue her by disclosing the truth.

   Nolan is released from jail because Jack refuses to prosecute and,
upon learning the truth, threatens to release the whole story to the
newpapers. Nora is concerned about the welfare of the children, however, and pleads with him to remain silent. After extracting promises
from Mrs. Stone and Jack that they will not see each other again, she
bids a tearful farewell to the children and leaves the household with
Nolan.

22   MARIA ROSA

Credits

Producer and Director:	Cecil B. DeMille
Scenario:	William deMille (based on the play by Wallace Gilpatrick and Guido Marburg, which was in turn based on a play by Angel Guimera)
Photographer:	Alvin Wyckoff
Art Director:	Wilfred Buckland
Editor:	Cecil B. DeMille
Cast:	Geraldine Farrar (Maria Rosa), Wallace Reid (Andres), Pedro de Cordoba (Ramon), Horace B. Carpenter (Pedro), James Neill (Priest)

Produced by Jesse L. Lasky Feature Play Company
Released by Paramount Pictures Corporation, June 1916
Screening time: Approximately 46 minutes

Synopsis

Maria Rosa becomes the object of contention in a rivalry involving three men, Andres and Ramon, both vineyard workers, and Pedro, a fisherman. While she is being courted by Andres one night, Pedro stabs Ramon during a quarrel. Since Pedro used Andres's knife to murder Ramon, Andres is convicted and sentenced to a ten year prison term. Maria promises to wait for him and is determined to remain unwed. During the months which follow, Ramon tricks Maria into believing that Andres died while in jail, compromises her reputation among the men in the village, and enlists the aid of the priest in convincing her to marry him. Maria finally relents and yields to his wishes.

Meanwhile, Andres has been serving a sentence as a convict laborer. During the visit of a group of dignitaries including the prison inspector, he saves the life of a child endangered by a dynamite explosion. As a result, he is freed and returns to his village but arrives on the very day of Maria's marriage festivities. Maria is astonished to learn that Andres is still alive but her mood changes from elation to despair. Determined to elicit the truth from the man she has just married, she plies Ramon with quantities of wine and questions him. When Ramon admits that he is Pedro's murderer, she exacts her revenge by stabbing him and he dies while still clutching her hair. Disgusted, Maria shakes herself free and prepares to leave the village with Andres.

23   THE DREAM GIRL

Credits

Producer and Director:	Cecil B. DeMille
Scenario:	Jeanie Macpherson
Photographer:	Alvin Wyckoff
Art Director:	Wilfred Buckland
Editor:	Cecil B. DeMille
Cast:	Mae Murray (Meg Dugan), Earle Foxe (Tom Merton), Theodore Roberts (Dugan), James Neill (Mr. Merton), Mary Mersch (Alice Merton), Charles Welsh (English Hal)

Produced by Jesse L. Lasky Feature Play Company
Released by Paramount Pictures Corporation, July 1916
Screening time: Approximately 47 minutes

Synopsis

Meg Dugan, the daughter of a disreputable saloon owner, escapes from the sordidness of her existence by reading and daydreaming about medieval knights. When English Hal, a con man, kills her father during a quarrel, she becomes an orphan in an institution next to a great estate. The estate belongs to an elderly man named Merton, who is disenchanted with his self-indulgent granddaughter, Alice, and his spendthrift grandson, Tom. By climbing over the wall on occasion, Meg becomes a familiar figure to the Mertons and they adopt her. She begins to regard Tom as her Sir Galahad and he reciprocates her affection. Unfortunately, English Hal also becomes a frequent guest at the estate. Disguised as Lord Henry Trevor, he is successfully courting Alice and finds Meg's presence in the household a threat to his plans to marry an heiress.

During an excursion which takes her back to squalid neighborhoods, Meg is shocked to discover that her father is alive after all. She then finds herself in the midst of various schemes on the part of her father and Hal to extort money from the Mertons. Tom has Hal arrested but gives Dugan a sum of money as he is intent upon marrying his daughter. Meg is unwilling to abandon her father, however, and refuses to consider marrying Tom. Assuming responsibility as a parent at last, Dugan decides to slip away unnoticed so that his daughter may find happiness.

24   JOAN THE WOMAN

Credits

Producer and Director:	Cecil B. DeMille
Scenario:	Jeanie Macpherson
Photographer:	Alvin Wyckoff
Art Designer:	Wilfred Buckland
Editor:	Cecil B. DeMille
Second Unit Directors:	William deMille, George Melford, and Donald Crisp
Special Effects:	Max Handschiegel and Loren Taylor[§]
Music:	William Furst
Cast:	Geraldine Farrar (Joan), Wallace Reid (Eric Trent), Raymond Hatton (Charles VII), Hobart Bosworth (General La Hire), Theodore Roberts (Cauchon), Charles Clary (George de la Tremouille), Tully Marshall (L'Oiseleur)

Released by Paramount Pictures Corporation, December 1916
Screening time: Approximately 115 minutes

Synopsis

During World War I trench warfare in France, a soldier discovers an ancient sword lodged in a wall. Joan's apparition appears to him and the scene changes to that of the village of Domrémy in the fifteenth century. While the English and Burgundians attack the villagers, Joan hides a wounded enemy soldier named Eric Trent. Although a romantic attraction develops, Joan responds to apparitions that prophesy her destiny as the savior of France and proceeds to the court of the uncrowned Charles at Chinon.

Gaining the support of her king, Joan becomes the commander of the French army and leads her forces to a great victory. Eric is taken prisoner during the battle but Joan's intervention saves his life a second time. Despite his entreaties, she asserts that there is only room in her heart for France and departs for Compiègne. En route she is taken captive by the English and Burgundians, a plot in which Eric has unwillingly participated. Abandoned by her king, Joan is imprisoned and tried for witchcraft. Eric's attempt to free her from prison fails and she is burned at the stake.

Again, in France beseiged by Germans during World War I, the young soldier to whom Joan has appeared volunteers for a suicide mission. Later as he lies dying on the battlefield, Joan appears on the scene once again and she prays.

25   ROMANCE OF THE REDWOODS

Credits

Producer and Director:	Cecil B. DeMille
Scenario:	Cecil B. DeMille and Jeanie Macpherson
Photographer:	Alvin Wyckoff
Art Director:	Wilfred Buckland
Editor:	Cecil B. DeMille
Cast:	Mary Pickford (Jenny Lawrence), Elliott Dexter (Black Brown), Charles Ogle (Jim Lyn)

Produced by Artcraft Pictures Corporation
Released by Paramount Pictures Corporation, May 1917
Screening time: Approximately 73 minutes

Synopsis

In Boston, Jenny Lawrence prepares to journey west to live with her uncle John and is unaware that he has been killed by Indians and his identity assumed by an outlaw, Black Brown. Upon arrival in Strawberry Flats, Jenny is dismayed by the crude and dirty cabin where she is to reside and by her unpleasant encounter with Brown. She reluctantly agrees to pose as his niece but in the weeks that follow, she imposes her sense of cleanliness and order upon the household. When Brown finds her coquettishly entertaining a neighbor, Jim Lyn, he becomes jealous and possessive.

While mending Brown's clothes one day, Jenny discovers the bandana he wears as a masked bandit and guesses his true identity. She insists upon leaving but he declares his love for her and promises to reform. Brown attempts gold mining without success while Jenny supports them by taking in laundry. Before long, he reverts to robbing stage coaches and becomes the target of a vigilante committee intent upon hanging him. To save his life, Jenny sacrifices her reputation and uses doll clothes to convey to the posse the message that she is pregnant. Sentimental about motherhood, the men become witnesses to a wedding rather than a hanging.

26   THE LITTLE AMERICAN

Credits

Producer and Director:	Cecil B. DeMille
Scenario:	Jeanie Macpherson
Photographer:	Alvin Wyckoff
Art Director:	Wilfred Buckland
Editor:	Cecil B. DeMille
Cast:	Mary Pickford (Angela Moore), Raymond Hatton (Count Jules de Destin), Jack Holt (Karl von Austreim)

Produced by Artcraft Pictures Corporation
Released by Paramount Pictures Corporation, July 1917
Screening time: Approximately 65 minutes

Synopsis

Angela Moore, born on the Fourth of July, is being courted on her birthday by a Frenchman, Count Jules de Destin, and a German, Karl von Austreim. She is especially receptive to Karl though she disapproves when he teaches her young brother the goose step. The outbreak of war in Europe leads to the departure of both men to fight on opposite sides. Angela herself decides to go abroad and boards an ocean liner which is torpedoed in mid-passage by Germans. She is rescued and arrives at her aunt's chateau in Vangy only to find that German troops are advancing. She briefly encounters Jules, who has lost an arm but continues to serve, and decides to take charge of wounded soldiers rather than evacuate. Jules installs a secret phone in the chateau before he leaves and instructs Angela to report enemy positions.

German troops invade the chateau and behave like swine. Angela is at first shocked to discover that Karl is among them but involves him in a heroic effort to communicate German positions to the French. She and Karl are discovered and about to be executed, but they are saved by heavy bombardments that scatter the Germans. Karl is subsequently imprisoned by the French, but for Angela's sake Jules intervenes to obtain his release. Angela visits Karl in prison to inform him that he has been granted a passport to the United States in recognition for her service in the French cause.

27   THE WOMAN GOD FORGOT

Credits

Producer and Director:	Cecil B. DeMille
Scenario:	Jeanie Macpherson
Photographer:	Alvin Wyckoff
Art Director:	Wilfred Buckland
Editor:	Cecil B. DeMille
Assistant Director:	Charles Whittaker
Cast:	Geraldine Farrar (Tezca), Wallace Reid (Alvarado), Theodore Kosloff

(Guatemoc), Hobart Bosworth
(Montezuma)
Produced by Artcraft Pictures Corporation
Released by Paramount Pictures Corporation, October 1917
Screening time: Approximately 65 minutes

Synopsis

The arrival of Cortez, the "Fair God," and his men on the shores
of Montezuma's kingdom leads to the monarch issuing a decree that a
maiden will be sacrificed each day until the intruders leave. Tezca,
Montezuma's strong-willed daughter, defies the decree by shielding a
female slave and wishes to thwart her father even further by refusing
to marry Guatemoc, the man to whom she has been promised.

Cortez decides to exploit his reception as a god by sending Alvarado,
one of his men, into the Aztec fortress to demand tribute. Alvarado is
wounded during a fracas, however, and appeals to Tezca for protection.
The princess hides him in her chambers, nurses his wounds, and falls
in love with him. Informed about his daughter's betrayal, Montezuma
commands her to marry Guatemoc and orders Alvarado be sacrificed on
the wedding day.

To save her Spanish lover, Tezca further betrays her father and her
people by secretly conducting Cortez and his men inside the impenetrable
Aztec fortress. She has extracted a promise from the foreigners that
they will not use their arms, but glimpsing the riches inside, the
Spaniards decide upon conquest. Montezuma is captured and forced to
order his people to disarm, but Guatemoc slays him and leads a bloody
resistance. Tezca is horrified by the turn of events and joins her
people in battle against the Spanish. Gunpower prevails against bows
and arrows, however, and Guatemoc takes his own life. Cortez permits
Tezca to go free, and some time later she is joined by Alvarado who
pleads that love can conquer hate.

28   THE DEVIL STONE

Credits

Producer and Director:	Cecil B. DeMille
Scenario:	Jeanie Macpherson (based on a story by Beatrice deMille and Leighton Osmun)
Photographer:	Alvin Wyckoff
Editor:	Cecil B. DeMille
Assistant Director:	Charles Whittaker
Cast:	Geraldine Farrar (Marcia Manot, Griselda), Wallace Reid (Guy Sterling), Tully Marshall (Silas Martin), Hobart Bosworth (Robert Judson), Lillian Leighton (Marcia's mother)

Produced by Artcraft Pictures Corporation
Released by Paramount Pictures Corporation, December 1917
Screening time: Approximately 67 minutes

Synopsis

During a raging storm, Marcia Manot, a Breton fisherwoman, listens
to her grandmother recount the legend of the wicked Norse queen,
Griselda. A flashback depicts the queen ransacking a church and condemning to death a monk who places a curse on her. While praying amidst
the rocks, Marcia discovers in the sand a headband with a large emerald,
part of the treasure Griselda plundered from the church ages ago.
Against her better judgment, she decides to take possession of the
jewel, which bears an ancient curse, and becomes the focus of neighborhood gossip.

Marcia's mother wishes her to marry Silas Martin, an elderly but
rich American merchant, to improve their family's situation. Silas
courts Marcia because he wants to possess the emerald she has discovered and eventually marries and brings her to the United States.
Although Silas is rich, he is extremely miserly and Marcia quickly
finds her married life distressing. She arouses the sympathies of Guy
Sterling, one of her husband's employees and a man much closer to her
own age. She turns to him in a quandary when Silas deceives her into
thinking that she has lost the emerald. Sterling hires a detective
named Judson who uncovers the startling truth that Silas has in fact
stolen the jewel himself. During a violent encounter between husband
and wife, Marcia defends herself against Silas's attack and kills him
with a candlestick. Subsequently, Silas's death becomes an unsolved
mystery.

After she becomes a widow, Marcia rebuffs Sterling's attentions
until she is persuaded by a friend that she is entitled to happiness.
She eventually marries Sterling but is alarmed to discover that he has
hired Judson to discover Silas's murderer. Judson cleverly concludes
an investigation by implicating Marcia, but she pleads self defense.
As proof of her innocence, she returns to France and restores the
emerald to the church. Judson interprets Marcia's deed in a positive
light and permits her to be reunited with her husband.

29   WHISPERING CHORUS

Credits

Producer and Director:	Cecil B. DeMille
Scenario:	Jeanie Macpherson (based on the story by Perley Poore Sheehan)
Photographer:	Alvin Wyckoff
Art Director:	Wilfred Buckland
Editor:	Cecil B. DeMille
Cast:	Kathleen Williams (Jane), Elliott Dexter (George Coggeswell),

Raymond Hatton (John Tremble),
Edythe Chapman (John's mother)
Produced by Artcraft Pictures Corporation
Released by Famous Players-Lasky Corporation on the Paramount Program,
March 1918
Screening time: Approximately 73 minutes

Synopsis

John Tremble, a bookkeeper, is supporting a wife, Jane, and a frail, elderly mother but is unable to make ends meet. A weak-willed and self-pitying character, John finally capitulates to tempting voices and embezzles money from his firm. When he reads in the papers that the company books will be audited due to a government inquiry about graft, he panics and decides to disappear. During his peregrinations, he discovers a dead man floating in a river and assumes his identity, Edgar Smith, after dressing the corpse with his own clothes.

Jane believes that her husband is dead and becomes a clerk in the employ of Fighting George Coggeswell, a young reformer who successfully mounts a campaign to become governor. She and George eventually marry and have a child. John, in the meanwhile, has become crippled and disfigured and leads a dissolute life. A sudden impulse to see his mother, who has never believed him to be dead, leads him to her deathbed. Before expiring, she tells him about Jane's remarriage and extracts a promise that he will not destroy his former wife's happiness.

Ironically, John is arrested shortly thereafter as Edgar Smith and charged with the murder of John Tremble. Forgetting his promise to his mother, John reveals his story but is unconvincing and receives the death sentence upon conviction for murder. Jane is tormented by John's revelation and is prepared to sacrifice her family's welfare. She visits John in prison. Confronted by his wife, John finds the courage to deny the truth and goes to his death in the electric chair.

30   OLD WIVES FOR NEW

Credits

Producer and Director:	Cecil B. DeMille
Scenario:	Jeanie Macpherson (based on the book by David Graham Phillips)
Photographer:	Alvin Wyckoff
Editor:	Cecil B. DeMille
Cast:	Elliott Dexter (Charles Murdoch), Florence Vidor (Juliet Raeburn), Sylvia Ashton (Sophy Murdoch), Theodore Roberts (Berkeley), Julia Faye (Jess), Marcia Manon (Viola), Gustav von Seyffertitz (Blagden)

Produced by Artcraft Pictures Corporation
Released by Famous Players-Lasky Corporation on the Paramount Program,
May 1918

Screening time: Approximately 66 minutes

Synopsis

After several years of marriage, Charles Murdoch is still youthful
and dapper but his wife Sophy has become fat, unkempt, and indolent.
Claiming that it is degrading for a couple to live together when they
no longer love each other, Charles proposes a divorce and a generous
property settlement. When Sophy balks, he goes on a hunting trip with
their young son and meets an attractive dressmaker named Juliet Raeburn.
Charles and Juliet are drawn to each other but their budding romance is
disrupted by his frank revelation that he is a married man. Juliet decides that it would be improper for them to continue seeing each other
and she remains firm in her convictions.

Charles's business partner, Berkeley, is also married but he has
no qualms about pursuing younger women. One night he arouses the
jealousy of his mistress, Jess, and she retaliates by shooting him.
Charles attempts to save Berkeley's reputation by covering up the scandal, but he underestimates the fact that his own wife is an angry woman
scorned. Sophy informs reporters that she will be naming Juliet as
"the other woman" in her divorce proceedings. Finding herself wrongly
maligned but still in love with a married man, Juliet departs for
Europe. Since he wishes to salvage her reputation, Charles is seen
publicly as the ardent lover of a woman named Viola. Unfortunately
this ruse further diminishes his prospects for a reconciliation with
Juliet.

Meanwhile Sophy is being courted by Blagden, a young man who responds to her matronly appeal, and she undergoes a torturous beauty
regimen. Juliet is finally informed that Charles's relationship with
Viola was a ploy to deceive reporters and to protect her name. She
and Charles are reconciled and marry in Venice while back in the states,
Sophy also remarries.

31 WE CAN'T HAVE EVERYTHING

Credits

Producer and Director:	Cecil B. DeMille
Scenario:	William deMille (based on the novel by Rupert Hughes)
Photographer:	Alvin Wyckoff
Editor:	Cecil B. DeMille and Anne Bauchens
Cast:	Kathlyn Williams (Charity Cheever), Elliott Dexter (Jim Dyckman), Thurston Hall (Peter Cheever), Sylvia Breamer (Zada L'Etoile), Wanda Hawley (Kedzie Thropp), Raymond Hatton (Marquis of Strathdene)

Produced by Artcraft Pictures Corporation

Released by Famous Players-Lasky Corporation on the Paramount Program, July 1918
Screening time: Approximately 62 minutes

Synopsis

Charity Cheever is spending the evening alone at home when an old friend, Jim Dyckman, arrives and persuades her to dine with him. Jim has been in love with Charity for some time but she is married and remains faithful to her husband, Peter. Unfortunately Peter has been having an affair with a woman named Zada L'Etoile and capitulates to her demand that he obtain a divorce. Rebuffed by Charity, Jim becomes captivated by a young film star, Kedzie Thropp, whose interest in him has been motivated by rumors about his fortune. Charity suddenly discovers that not only has she been discarded by her husband, but her friend Jim has married Kedzie.

Jim's marriage to Kedzie quickly palls. Kedzie entertains herself by encouraging the interest of an English aviator, the Marquis of Strathdene, but she is unwilling to divorce Jim unless she has grounds to sue for alimony. Meanwhile, Jim encounters Charity in the country and they are forced to spend the night in a hotel due to torrential rains. Kedzie blackens Charity's reputation in a divorce suit and being assured of alimony, she decides to marry Strathdene. Discouraged by the turn of events, Jim goes off to fight in the French trenches and is wounded. Charity encounters him as a patient while she is working in a hospital. Jim proposes and they are married while surrounded by hospital ward well-wishers.

32   TILL I COME BACK TO YOU

Credits

Producer and Director:	Cecil B. DeMille
Scenario:	Jeanie Macpherson
Photographer:	Alvin Wyckoff and Charles Rosher
Art Director:	Wilfred Buckland
Editor:	Anne Bauchens
Cast:	Bryant Washburn (Jefferson Strong), Florence Vidor (Yvonne von Krutz), C. Butler Clonebough (Karl von Krutz), Winter Hall (King of Belgium)

Produced by Artcraft Pictures Corporation
Released by Famous Players-Lasky Corporation on the Paramount Program, September 1918
Screening time: Approximately 70 minutes

Synopsis

During World War I in Belgium, Yvonne von Krutz is the wife of a tyrannical and authoritarian German officer fanatically devoted to the Kaiser. She is helpless when he arrives home from the front and counters their son's devotion to the Belgian king by sending him to a strict orphanage. Returning to the front, von Krutz is captured and his identity assumed by an American engineer, Jefferson Strong. Jefferson arrives at the von Krutz home with the intention of destroying the nearby German Liquid Fire Chamber.

  At first, Jefferson and Yvonne are hostile and guarded but his kindness to her son, sent home from the orphanage for parental discipline, leads to a friendship and then a romance. With the aid of American doughboys, Jefferson constructs an underground tunnel from the von Krutz house to the Liquid Fire Chamber and he is preparing to explode German operations. Unfortunately Karl has escaped and arrives on the scene, as do several children who have run away from the orphanage. Jefferson scraps his plan to blow up the German chamber and uses the tunnel instead to lead the children to safety. An armed encounter with German troops in pursuit results in Karl's death. Although the orphaned children are saved, Jefferson's superiors order his court martial because he failed to execute plans to destroy the Liquid Fire Chamber. The Belgian king intervenes, however, and Jefferson is declared not guilty and reunited with Yvonne.

33   THE SQUAW MAN

Credits

Producer and Director:	Cecil B. DeMille
Scenario:	Beulah Marie Dix (based on the play by Edwin Milton Royle)
Photographer:	Alvin Wyckoff
Editor:	Anne Bauchens
Cast:	Elliott Dexter (Jim Wynnegate), Katherine McDonald (Lady Diana), Ann Little (Naturich), Theodore Roberts (Big Bill), Jack Holt (Cash Hawkins), Edwin Stevens (Sheriff)

Produced by Artcraft Pictures Corporation
Released by Famous Players–Lasky Corporation on the Paramount Program, December 1918
Screening time: Approximately 68 minutes

Note: A remake of DeMille's first film, the plot is essentially the same. See entry 1.

34   DON'T CHANGE YOUR HUSBAND

Credits

Producer and Director:	Cecil B. DeMille
Scenario:	Jeanie Macpherson
Photographer:	Alvin Wyckoff
Editor:	Anne Bauchens
Costumes:	Alpharelta Hoffman and Mitchell Leisen[§]

Cast:
                                Elliott Dexter (Jim Porter), Gloria
                                    Swanson (Leila Porter), Lew Cody
                                    (Schuyler van Sutpen)
Produced by Artcraft Pictures Corporation
Released by Famous Players-Lasky Corporation on the Paramount Program,
January 1919
Screening time: Approximately 71 minutes

Synopsis

After several years of married life, Jim Porter has developed an
expanded waistline, a fondness for onions, and a bad memory for anniversary dates. Leila Porter, on the other hand, is still a beautiful
and elegant woman susceptible to romantic sentiment. Dissatisfied with
her inattentive husband, she falls prey to the charms of Schuyler van
Sutpen, a ladies' man who pays no attention to her married status and
woos her with flowers and Shakespeare. Unaware of the extent of his
wife's discontent, Jim is stunned when Leila informs him that she is
tired of their "corned beef and cabbage" existence and would like a
divorce.

Some time later, Leila finds herself married to Schuyler and the
victim of déjà vu if not worse. Schuyler's table manners are displeas-
ing, his business acumen lacking, and his flirtations with other women
distressing. Leila has had to pawn her jewels and is unaware that
Schuyler is squandering huge sums of money on a golddigger named Toodles.
Meanwhile, Jim has recovered from his divorce by losing weight and acquiring a dapper, new wardrobe. A chance encounter with Leila, who
notices the change in her ex-husband, rekindles their former attachment
to each other. Subsequently, a lively squabble about money and morals
involving Leila, Schuyler, Jim, and Toodles leads to yet another divorce
and remarriage. In the end, Jim and Leila are together again but he
still falls asleep while reading the papers.

35   FOR BETTER, FOR WORSE

Credits

Producer and Director: Cecil B. DeMille
Scenario: Jeanie Macpherson (based upon William
                                 deMille's adaptation of the play by
                                 Edgar Selwyn)

Photographer: Alvin Wyckoff
Art Director: Wilfred Buckland
Editor: Anne Bauchens
Production Manager: Howard Higgin
Cast: Elliott Dexter (Ned Meade), Gloria
                                 Swanson (Sylvia Norcross), Tom
                                 Forman (Dick Burton), Wanda Hawley
                                 (Betty Hoyt)
Produced by Artcraft Pictures Corporation
Released by Famous Players-Lasky Corporation on the Paramount Program,
April 1919

Screening time: Approximately 76 minutes

Synopsis

At the outbreak of World War I, Dr. Ned Meade is prevailed upon to give up a commission and remain in the states as the physician of a children's ward. Ned's sweetheart, Sylvia, interprets his action as cowardice and impulsively marries another man, Dick Burton. Dick is too overjoyed to notice that Sylvia does not really love him or that Betty Hoyt, the woman who does care, has been cruelly disappointed. Shortly after the wedding, he leaves for France amidst cheering crowds. During the fighting, however, he is badly disfigured by injuries and instructs a friend to inform Sylvia that he has died in combat.

Sylvia is aiding the needy families of men at the front when her chauffeur accidentally injures and paralyzes a little girl. She is unable to find a qualified physician to help the child until she encounters Ned and begins to realize that braving public opinion to remain at home requires courage also. She and Ned resume their relationship and decide to announce their engagement at a party. Meanwhile, Dick's appearance has been improved by surgery and he returns to his wife on the very night of the engagement party. His sudden intrusion causes much consternation and only Betty is truly delighted to see him again. After Dick realizes that Sylvia and Ned are in love, he magnanimously steps aside and seeks consolation with Betty.

36   MALE AND FEMALE

Credits

Producer and Director:	Cecil B. DeMille
Scenario:	Jeanie Macpherson (based on the play The Admirable Crichton by James M. Barrie)
Photographer:	Alvin Wyckoff
Art Director:	Wilfred Buckland
Editor:	Anne Bauchens
Costumes:	Mitchell Leisen
Cast:	Gloria Swanson (Lady Mary), Thomas Meighan (Crichton), Lila Lee (Tweeny), Theodore Roberts (Earl of Loam), Robert Cain (Lord Brocklehurst), Rhy Darby (Lady Eileen)

Produced by Artcraft Pictures Corporation
Released by Famous Players-Lasky Corporation on the Paramount Program, November 1919
Screening time: Approximately 95 minutes

Synopsis

In fashionable Loam House in London, Lady Mary, the spoiled and willful daughter of the Earl of Loam, leads a luxurious life in contrast

to that of her maid, Tweeny, and her butler, Crichton. Mary is being
courted by Lord Brocklehurst and expects to become his bride according
to her family and class traditions. A friend, Lady Eileen Duncraigie,
has fallen in love with her chauffeur, however, and Mary disapproves
when the affair leads to a rash marriage.

The Earl of Loam takes his family on a South Seas cruise which becomes an altogether unexpected voyage. The ship crashes and the Earl's
family, together with Crichton and Tweeny, find themselves stranded on
a remote island. Crichton is the only person in the party capable of
ekeing out a survival and he assumes command. During the two years
spent on the tropical island, Crichton becomes a monarchical figure,
fantasizes romantically about the Babylonian past, and courts Mary to
Tweeny's dismay. But on the very day that Crichton and Mary are to wed,
a ship is sighted and they are all rescued.

Back in London, Mary is caught between her aristocratic status and
her love for Crichton, once again a butler. Sobered by her own experience, Eileen counsels that "love isn't everything" and speaks about
the importance of tradition. Crichton himself accepts the social
reality of class barriers and informs Mary that he is going to marry
Tweeny and emigrate to America. Reluctantly, Mary acknowledges her
destiny and once again receives the attentions of Lord Brocklehurst.

37   WHY CHANGE YOUR WIFE?

Credits

Producer and Director:	Cecil B. DeMille
Story:	William C. deMille
Scenario:	Olga Printzlau and Sada Cowan (from the story by William deMille)
Photographer:	Alvin Wyckoff
Editor:	Anne Bauchens
Cast:	Gloria Swanson (Beth Gordon), Thomas Meighan (Robert Gordon), Bebe Daniels (Sally Clark), Theodore Kosloff (Radinoff), Sylvia Ashton (Aunt Kate)

Produced by Artcraft Pictures Corporation
Released by Famous Players-Lasky Corporation on the Paramount Program,
May 1920
Screening time: Approximately 70 minutes

Synopsis

Robert Gordon, a married man, feels oppressed by his virtuous and
dowdy wife, Beth. Hoping to inject some excitement into his marriage,
he purchases a sexy negligee in a boutique. But when the negligee is
delivered, Beth is angered by his "Oriental" ideas and rebuffs his advances. Increasingly bored, Robert proves vulnerable to the attentions
of Sally Clark, the boutique model on whom the negligee had originally

looked so enticing. Beth is outraged by his flirtation with Sally, sues for divorce, and is about to devote her life to charity. While shopping however, she overhears some gossip about her frumpy appearance and in a dramatic volte-face, orders her gowns "sleeveless, backless, transparent, indecent. . . ."

Robert, meanwhile, marries Sally only to discover that "wives will be wives." If Beth was too prim and proper, Sally proves petulant and demanding. Accommodating her wish for a vacation at a resort hotel, Robert is surprised to discover that one of the hotel guests is Beth. She has delightfully transformed herself into a very fashionable woman. The former spouses are so attracted to each other that they both leave town but end up on the same train. When they disembark, Robert slips on a banana peel, sustains a serious head injury, and becomes a patient in Beth's house.

Sally, who has remained at the hotel to enjoy a flirtation with a European violinist named Radinoff, arrives at Beth's home to claim her husband. She insists, against doctor's orders, upon moving Robert to her house. When Beth objects, the two women engage in a physical brawl while Robert remains helpless and barely conscious. Beth cows Sally with a threat to ruin her beauty with acid and keeps an anxious, all-night vigil by Robert's bedside. In the morning, the doctor announces that Robert may be safely moved. But by then Sally has opted for alimony and leaves the former spouses to be reconciled.

38   SOMETHING TO THINK ABOUT

Credits

Producer and Director:	Cecil B. DeMille
Scenario:	Jeanie Macpherson
Photographer:	Alvin Wyckoff and Karl Struss
Art Director:	Wilfred Buckland
Editor:	Anne Bauchens
Production Manager:	Howard Higgin
Cast:	Gloria Swanson (Ruth Anderson),
	Elliott Dexter (David Markley),
	Theodore Roberts (Luke Anderson),
	Monte Blue (Jim Dirk)

Produced by Artcraft Pictures Corporation
Released by Famous Players-Lasky Corporation on the Paramount Program, October 1920
Screening time: Approximately 78 minutes

Synopsis

David Markley is a wealthy, small town philosopher who takes an interest in the village blacksmith's daughter, Ruth, and finances her education. When "Ruth the Woman" returns home after three years in boarding school, David restrains his impulse to propose marriage because he is a cripple. But Ruth's father, Luke, intervenes because he approves of the match and prevails upon her to accept. David cannot believe his good fortune and anticipates the marriage with joy. Neither he nor Luke is prepared, however, for Ruth's impulsive actions once she falls in love with a young farmer named Jim Dirk. Forced to choose, Ruth suddenly elopes with Jim and leaves her engagement ring behind. Although David is grieved about his loss, he remains philosophical while Luke is so angered that he disowns his daughter.

Ruth and Jim as newlyweds have settled in New York and are happily expecting a child. Unfortunately, Jim is killed in an accident and Ruth is unable to support herself. She returns to her father's house only to discover that he has been blinded and is unremitting in his bitterness about her. In despair, Ruth decides to commit suicide but David saves her and offers her a refuge. Ruth marries David to give her child a name and a home and eventually grows to love her husband. David at first confuses her affection with gratitude and remains aloof but gradually learns to trust her and even recovers the use of his legs. As for Luke, he has become a resident of the Poor House as he is too proud to accept help, but a chance encounter with his young grandson finally brings some joy to his life.

39   FORBIDDEN FRUIT

Credits

Producer and Director:	Cecil B. DeMille
Scenario:	Jeanie Macpherson (based on Cecil B. DeMille's film, The Golden Chance)
Photographers:	Alvin Wyckoff and Karl Struss
Editor:	Anne Bauchens
Production Manager:	Howard Higgin
Cast:	Agnes Ayres (Mary Maddock), Forrest Stanley (Nelson Rogers), Clarence Burton (Steve Maddock), Kathlyn Williams (Mrs. Mallory), Theodore Roberts (Mr. Mallory), Theodore Kosloff (Guiseppe, the butler)

Released by Famous Players-Lasky Corporation on the Paramount Program, February 1921
Screening time: Approximately 88 minutes
Note
A remake of The Golden Chance, the plot is basically the same but has been embroidered and contains two lavish flashback sequences that depict the Cinderella fairy tale. See entry 18.

40   THE AFFAIRS OF ANATOL

Credits

Producer and Director:	Cecil B. DeMille
Scenario:	Jeanie Macpherson, Beulah Marie Dix, Lorna Moon, and Elmer Harris (based

	on the play, <u>Anatol</u>, by Arthur Schnitzler)
Photographers:	Alvin Wyckoff and Karl Struss
Art Director:	Paul Iribe
Editor:	Anne Bauchens
Production Manager:	Howard Higgin
Cast:	Wallace Reid (Anatol deWitt Spencer), Gloria Swanson (Vivian), Elliott Dexter (Max Runyon), Wanda Hawley (Emilie Dixon), Theodore Roberts (Gordon Bronson), Agnes Ayres (Annie Elliott), Monte Blue (Abner Elliott), Bebe Daniels (Satan Synne), Theodore Kosloff (Nazzer Singh)

Released by Famous Players-Lasky Corporation as a DeMille-Paramount Special, September 1921
Screening time: Approximately 98 minutes

Synopsis

Recently married, Anatol deWitt Spencer is already tiring of his wife Vivian's childish ways and under the pretense of philanthropic interest, he embarks upon a series of misadventures with other women. Anatol's first humanitarian case is named Emilie, a former school chum who has become a "Jazz Girl" and the mistress of a cynical, middle-aged philanderer, Gordon Bronson. Distressed by her fast and immoral life style, Anatol provides Emilie with the means to leave Bronson and to refine herself by taking music lessons. But as the title reads, "we wonder if He would be quite so eager to save her Soul--if her Face were less pretty. . . ." Emilie becomes chagrined, however, when Anatol refuses to leave his wife and reverts to her "Jazz Girl" ways and her relationship with Bronson.

Disillusioned but undeterred, Anatol next falls prey to a farmer's wife named Annie, whom he rescues from a suicide attempt. Foolishly, his ministrations on her behalf become rather sensual and Vivian departs in anger. Annie revives and decamps with Anatol's money, for it was her extravagance that led to a rupture with her husband Abner and her attempted suicide. She now possesses the means to effect a reconciliation.

Vivian, in the meanwhile, has decided upon a divorce and Anatol returns home to find his own marriage in danger. Angered by Vivian's unforgiving behavior, he drops pretenses and decides to console himself with the notorious Satan Synne. Ironically, Satan is really the devoted wife of a wounded soldier in need of costly surgery and once again, Anatol's checkbook is in demand. Deciding that "a bird in hand" may be best after all, Anatol returns to Vivian only to find that in a fit of pique, she has spent the entire night out with his friend Max. Suspicion torments him and he goes so far as to have Vivian hypnotized by a swami to question her fidelity. But at the last moment he decides to have faith in his wife and is reconciled with her.

41   FOOL'S PARADISE

Credits

Producer and Director:	Cecil B. DeMille
Scenario:	Beulah Marie Dix and Sada Cowan (based on the story, "The Laurels and the Lady," by Leonard Merrick)
Photographers:	Alvin Wyckoff and Karl Struss
Editor:	Anne Bauchens
Cast:	Conrad Nagel (Arthur Phelps), Dorothy Dalton (Poll Patchouli), Mildred Harris (Rosa Duchene), Theodore Kosloff (Rodriguez), John Davidson (Talat Noi)

Released by Famous Players-Lasky Corporation on the Paramount Program, March 1922
Screening time: Approximately 98 minutes

Synopsis

In an oil town near the Mexican border, aspiring poet Arthur Phelps dreams about a French ballerina, Rosa Duchene, whom he met on the continent during the war. Arthur is so entranced by his memories of her that he is completely unresponsive to Poll Patchouli, a woman who pursues him as energetically as she rejects the unwanted attentions of Rodriguez, the owner of a cantina. When Rosa arrives in town as part of a dance troupe, Arthur is enthralled to meet her again. Piqued by his indifference, Poll gives Arthur a trick cigar that blows up in his face and blinds him. She is so appalled by the harm done that she impersonates Rosa and marries Arthur in order to care for him.

During the months that follow, Poll creates an illusory world in which she poses as the French dancer and leads Arthur to believe that his poems have finally been published. Rodriguez scornfully regards her existence with amusement and promises to be waiting when she tires of it. One day a famous surgeon arrives in El Paso, and Poll asks him to cure Arthur's blindness though she realizes she may lose him. When he recovers his eyesight, Arthur learns about her impersonation and angrily spurns her.

Arthur becomes a wealthy man when oil is discovered on his land and he divorces Poll in order to pursue Rosa on the other side of the globe. The French ballerina is studying ancient dance in Siam and flirting dangerously with the Siamese prince, Talat Noi. She also dallies with Arthur and thoughtlessly risks the lives of both men by pitting them against each other in an alligator pit. Arthur finally comes to his senses and returns to the states to search for Poll. She is now working in Rodriguez's cantina and her Latin lover is unwilling to relinquish her. Poll is shot while attempting to prevent a gunfight between the two men, but Arthur nurses her back to health and happiness.

42 SATURDAY NIGHT

Credits

Producer and Director:	Cecil B. DeMille
Scenario:	Jeanie Macpherson
Photographers:	Alvin Wyckoff
Editor:	Anne Bauchens
Art Director:	Mitchell Leisen§
Costumes:	Claire West§
Cast:	Leatrice Joy (Iris van Suydam), Conrad Nagel (Richard Prentiss), Edith Roberts (Shamrock O'Day), Jack Mower (Tom McGuire)

Released by Famous Players-Lasky Corporation on the Paramount Program, January 1922
Screening time: Approximately 95 minutes

Synopsis

Shamrock O'Day daydreams about silks and perfume to escape from her dreary existence as a washerwoman. While delivering the laundry, she captures the attention of a wealthy young man, Richard Prentiss, who responds to her sprightly and amusing manner. Richard is bored with his sweetheart, a spoiled and willful heiress named Iris van Suydam, and delays announcing their engagement. Iris is piqued by Richard's flirtation with his laundress and retaliates by going on an excursion with her chauffeur, Tom McGuire. When Tom saves her life during a spectacular accident on a railroad bridge, she becomes enamored of him.

Although Richard's engagement to Iris is formally announced by his sister Elsie, both parties are having second thoughts. Iris is disinherited by her uncle when she insists on marrying Tom, and Richard is equally impulsive in deciding to wed Shamrock. While Iris attempts to set up housekeeping in a dilapidated apartment and to entertain Tom's raucous friends, Richard finds that his mother and sister both disapprove of his uneducated and unrefined wife. When Elsie suggests that she refrain from joining a lavish entertainment, Shamrock persuades Tom, who has become her chauffeur, to spend the evening at Coney Island. During the outing, the two of them are trapped on a ferris wheel for several hours and decide that they prefer each other to their social register spouses. Several years later, the discarded spouses, Iris and Richard, decide to forget the past and renew their engagement.

43 MANSLAUGHTER

Credits

Producer and Director:	Cecil B. DeMille
Scenario:	Jeanie Macpherson (based on the novel by Alice Duer Miller)
Photographer:	Alvin Wyckoff

Editor: Anne Bauchens
Art Director: Paul Iribe
Costumes: Paul Iribe
Choreography: Theodore Kosloff[§]
Cast: Leatrice Joy (Lydia Thorpe), Thomas
                           Meighan (Dan O'Bannon), Lois Wilson
                           (Evans)
Released by Famous Players-Lasky Corporation on the Paramount Program,
September 1922
Screening time: Approximately 102 minutes

Synopsis

    Lydia Thorpe is a spoiled and reckless socialite who lives a fast
life and has always bought her way out of scrapes. By contrast, her
maid, Evans, is desperate for funds to send a sick child to convalesce
in California. When Lydia refuses to loan her money, Evans steals her
mistress's jewels and is arrested by the district attorney, Dan O'Bannon.
A puritanical character, Dan sternly disapproves of Lydia's careless
and frivolous ways but he is in love with her. By advising Lydia to
appear in court and plead for mercy, he hopes to save Evans from a
prison term, but Lydia oversleeps after a night of gin and jazz. Consequently, Evans is sentenced to prison and separated from her sick child.

    Fate catches up with Lydia, however. She is driving too fast (as
usual) when she becomes responsible for the death of a motorcycle police officer. Despite the requests of influential friends and a plea
from Lydia herself, Dan seeks and obtains a conviction for manslaughter.
Lydia finds herself serving a prison term in the same institution where
her former maid, Evans, has been jailed. At first, Evans is unsympa-
thetic when Lydia has difficulties adjusting to prison life but the
two women eventually become friends. After serving two years, Lydia
emerges a reformed woman and very unlike her former self.

    Meanwhile, Dan has felt so tortured about his role in sending Lydia
to jail that he has become an alcoholic and a bum. Lydia encounters
him in a soup line while working as a volunteer in the slums. When
she convinces him that he helped save her soul, he vows to reform himself, resumes his law career, and makes a successful bid for political
office. Later, he realizes that marriage to Lydia would be incompatible
with politics because she has a criminal record, but he thinks nothing
of sacrificing his ambitions to marry her.

    44   ADAM'S RIB

Credits

Producer and Director: Cecil B. DeMille
Scenario: Jeanie Macpherson
Photographer: Alvin Wyckoff
Art Director: Wilfred Buckland
Editor: Anne Bauchens

Cast: Anna Q. Nilsson (Marian Ramsay),
                                         Milton Sills (Michael Ramsay),
                                         Theodore Kosloff (Jaromir), Pauline
                                         Garon (Matilda Ramsay), Elliott
                                         Dexter (Professor Nathan Reade)
Released by Famous Players-Lasky Corporation on the Paramount Program,
March 1923
Screening time: Approximately 105 minutes

Synopsis

Marian Ramsay is approaching forty but still craves romance while
her husband Michael is absorbed day and night with his business deals.
Feeling neglected, Marian responds to the artful flattery of Jaromir,
former king of Morania, who has always thought too much of romance and
not enough about politics. When Michael realizes that his wife is becoming infatuated with Jaromir, he liquidates his business holdings
to purchase Moranian wheat and thus finance the ex-king's return to
the throne. As a result, Jaromir's ministers are able to prevail upon
him to fulfill his obligations, including marriage to an appropriate
princess.

Meanwhile the Ramsays' seventeen year old daughter, Tillie, is
energetically pursuing Nathan Reade, a bookish professor. She grows
alarmed, however, when she observes her mother ardently wooed by Jaromir
and proposes to disrupt their romance by enticing the ex-king herself.
She follows her mother to Jaromir's apartment but both women must con-
ceal themselves when Michael and a delegation of Moranians arrive.
Jaromir reluctantly agrees to perform his duty and return to Morania,
but Michael's suspicions are aroused and he demands to see his wife.
Alarmed about her mother, Tillie suddenly reveals her presence and pre-
tends that she has been having a secret rendezvous with Jaromir. Although her father declares that no self-respecting man would now want
to marry her, Nathan volunteers to save her reputation. Tillie becomes
distressed, however, when Nathan continues to mistrust her and leaves
for an expedition in Honduras. Marian later confesses the truth to
her husband, who has recouped his fortune, and they reconcile, but their
daughter is bitter and claims that "Romance and Business" have ruined
her life. Determined to win Nathan back, Tillie pursues him in Honduras
and they are happily reunited.

45   THE TEN COMMANDMENTS

Credits

Producer and Director: Cecil B. DeMille
Scenario: Jeanie Macpherson
Photographers: Bert Glennon, J. Peverell Marley,
                                  Edward S. Curtis, Fred Westerberg,
                                  and Archibald J. Stout
Editor: Anne Bauchens
Color photography (Biblical
    story):   Ray Rennahan

Art Director: Paul Iribe
Special Effects: Roy Pomeroy
Assistant Director: Cullen Tate
Cast: The Biblical Story: Theodore Roberts
                        (Moses), Charles de Rochefort
                        (Rameses), Estelle Taylor (Miriam),
                        James Neill (Aaron), Lawson Butt
                        (Dathan), Julia Faye (Pharaoh's
                        wife). The Modern Story: Rod
                        LaRocque (Dan McTavish), Leatrice
                        Joy (Mary Leigh), Richard Dix (John
                        McTavish), Edythe Chapman (Mrs.
                        McTavish), Nita Naldi (Sally Lung)
Released by Famous Players-Lasky Corporation as a DeMille-Paramount
special, December 1923
Screening time: Approximately 125 minutes

Synopsis

In ancient Egypt, enslaved Hebrews are brutally forced to labor on
the Pharaoh's massive construction projects. During a series of encounters with Moses and his brother Aaron, the Pharaoh, Rameses, refuses to free the Hebrews until a plague causes the death of his son.
On an appointed day, Moses finally leads multitudes of his people out
of Egypt, but the Pharaoh and his chariots follow in pursuit. As the
Hebrews watch in fear and amazement, their Egyptian pursuers are swal-
lowed up by the Red Sea. Subsequently, Moses ascends Mount Sinai and
receives the ten commandments, but during his absence, the Hebrews wor-
ship a golden calf and engage in bacchanalian revels. When he returns,
Moses vents his rage upon his people and destroys the stone tablets in-
scribed with the commandments.

Mrs. McTavish, a pious, elderly woman, has been reading the story
of Moses to her two grown sons, Dan and John. Dan and his bride-to-be,
Mary Leigh, think the ten commandments are outmoded and intend to lead
exhilarating lives but John, who also loves Mary, adheres to his mother's
religious beliefs. While John pursues his trade as a carpenter, Dan
becomes wealthy by practicing fraud in the construction business and
engages in an adulterous relationship with Sally Lung, a "combination
of French perfume and Oriental incense."

Dan's crooked world begins to unravel when his own mother is killed
by the collapse of a church wall built with diluted concrete. In order
to buy off a scandal sheet, he insists that Sally return an expensive
pearl necklace, but she retaliates by revealing her escape from the
leper colony of Molokai. Sally gloats momentarily. Dan is so horrified that he shoots her and confesses the whole story to his wife, who
shields him from the police. Mary is plunged into despair by the
thought of having contracted leprosy and decides to leave town to face
death alone, but John comforts her by reading the Biblical story of the
leper. With John at her side, Mary finds consolation in religious belief while Dan is killed in a boat crash in a futile escape attempt.

46   TRIUMPH

Credits

Producer and Director:	Cecil B. DeMille
Scenario:	Jeanie Macpherson (based on the novel by May Edington)
Photographer:	J. Peverell Marley
Editor:	Anne Bauchens
Music:	James C. Bradford
Cast:	Leatrice Joy (Anna Land), Rod La Rocque (King Garnet), Victor Varconi (William Silver)

Released by Famous Players-Lasky Corporation on the Paramount Program, April 1924
Screening time: Approximately 93 minutes

Synopsis

    Anna Land, a factory worker at Garnet Can Works, is being courted by the foreman, William Silver, and the boss's son, King Garnet. Anna prefers Garnet to Silver but she has decided upon an operatic career rather than marriage and refuses the proposals of both men. Garnet's elderly father has long been disappointed by his extravagant and indolent ways and intends to teach him a lesson. After he dies, his entire estate goes to Silver, an unacknowledged son by a secret marriage, because King refuses to take life seriously and to work. Silver quickly discards his anarchist principles and begins to squander the Garnet fortune while King is unable to support himself and ends up a tramp.

    Anna becomes a celebrated opera singer but her voice is damaged during a fire in Paris. She is disconsolate and returns to her home town to find that Silver is also in desperate straits as he has lost both his mansion and his factory. She promises to marry him because she feels sympathy but is thrown into a quandary when she returns to her former job at the plant. During her absence, King has worked his way up from a menial job to the presidency and he willingly restores Silver to his former position as foreman. When Silver realizes that Anna is still in love with King, he generously releases her from their engagement to be married. King reciprocates by offering to share the management of the factory with him and the two rivals finally become friends.

47   FEET OF CLAY

Credits

Producer and Director:	Cecil B. DeMille
Scenario:	Beulah Marie Dix and Bertram Milhauser (based on the novel by Margaretta Tuttle and the play, Across the Border, by Beulah Marie Dix)
Photographers:	J. Peverell Marley and Archibald J. Stout

81

Editor: Anne Bauchens
Art Directors: Paul Iribe and Norman Bel Geddes[§]
Special Effects: Roy Pomeroy[§]
Assistant Director: Frank Urson[§]
Cast: Vera Reynolds (Amy Loring), Rod
                           LaRocque (Kerry Harlan), Julia Faye
                           Bertha Lansell), Richard Cortez
                           (Tony Channing), Robert Edeson (Dr.
                           Lansell)
Released by Famous Players-Lasky Corporation on the Paramount Program,
September 1924
Screening time: Approximately 107 minutes

Synopsis

Kerry Harlan and Tony Channing are engaging in water sports with
Amy Loring, the woman whom they both love, and her stepsister, Bertha
Lansell. Kerry is forced to abandon his boat when it catches fire and
before he can be rescued, he is attacked by a shark. While recuperating, Kerry is reluctant to court Amy because she receives a generous
allowance from Bertha, whereas he makes a rather modest salary as an
engineer. Also, his foot has been badly injured and he is uncertain
about recovery. Amy insists that they marry, however, and the announce-
ment of their engagement stuns not only Tony but Bertha, who is unhappily married and secretly in love with Kerry. Amy declares that she
will no longer accept an allowance from Bertha and becomes a model to
support Kerry while he convalesces. But she is quickly depressed by
married life in a Harlem flat and angers Kerry by accepting a luncheon
invitation from Tony.

Bertha is still intent on pursuing Kerry and surprises him with a
visit to his apartment. An unexpected appearance by her husband, who
is Kerry's physician, causes her to panic and while hiding outside the
bedroom window, she plunges to her death. Subsequently Kerry quarrels
with Amy and is in such despair that he decides to turn on the gas and
kill himself. Amy returns to the apartment and is so appalled that
she too decides to commit suicide. During an afterworld sequence, Amy
and Kerry are both dead and find themselves traveling on a road with
other despondent persons who have taken their own lives. After an encounter with Bertha, who encourages them to return to life, they decide
to march back against hordes of dead swarming from the opposite direction. Dr. Lansell, who has arrived at the apartment with the intention
of killing Kerry, discovers them in time and the revived couple decide
to live their future together.

48   THE GOLDEN BED

Credits

Producer and Director: Cecil B. DeMille
Scenario: Jeanie Macpherson (based on the novel,
                           Tomorrow's Bread, by Wallace Irwin)

Photographer:	J. Peverell Marley
Editor:	Anne Bauchens
Art Director:	Paul Iribe
Assistant Director:	Frank Urson
Cast:	Lillian Rich (Flora Lee Peake), Rod LaRocque (Admah Holtz), Vera Reynolds (Margaret Peake), Theodore Kosloff (Marquis de San Pilar), Warner Baxter (Bunny O'Neill)

Released by Famous Players-Lasky Corporation on the Paramount Program, January 1925
Screening time: Approximately 92 minutes

Synopsis

When her wealthy family becomes bankrupt, Flora Lee Peake, a golden-haired girl, marries the Marquis de San Pilar, a rich nobleman, while her brunette sister Margaret finds employment in a candy store. With Margaret's advice and encouragement, Admah Holtz, the candy store proprietor, succeeds in making his business quite a profitable venture. Flora, in the meanwhile, has caused a fatal argument between a lover and her husband and she has become a penniless widow. She returns home and entices Admah away from Margaret in order to marry him for his money. Admah quickly finds himself debt-ridden as Flora squanders huge sums to compete with a banker's wife for leadership of the smart set. Flora's coup de grace is a magnificent ball with a candy motif, but in order to finance such an extravaganza, Admah embezzles funds from his own company. After the guests depart, Admah is imprisoned while Flora accepts the jewels of a new lover, Bunny O'Neill.

During several years in prison, Admah has been corresponding with the ever faithful Margaret and is looking forward to beginning life anew. Upon his release, he walks by the former Peake mansion, now a boarding house, and asks to see an ornate golden bed. When he goes upstairs into the bedroom, he is startled to find that Flora has returned to her room to live out her life. She has been abandoned by her lover and has become ill and impoverished. She dies towards morning and Admah sadly brings Margaret the news that her sister is dead. As a new day dawns, Admah and Margaret resolve to rebuild their lives together.

49   THE ROAD TO YESTERDAY

Credits

Producer and Director:	Cecil B. DeMille
Scenario:	Jeanie Macpherson and Beulah Marie Dix (based on the play by Beulah Marie Dix and Evelyn Greenleaf Sutherland)
Photographer:	J. Peverell Marley
Editor:	Anne Bauchens
Art Directors:	Paul Iribe, Mitchell Leisen, and Anton Grot

Costumes: Claire West
Assistant Director: Frank Urson[§]
Cast: Joseph Schildkraut (Kenneth Paulton,
                               Lord Strangevon), Jetta Goudal
                               (Malena Paulton), William Boyd
                               (Jack Moreland), Vera Reynolds
                               (Bess Tyrell), Casson Ferguson
                               (Rady Tompkins)
Released by Producers Distributing Corporation, November 1925
Screening time: Approximately 110 minutes

Synopsis

Ken Paulton is honeymooning with his bride Malena, but he senses a strange fear in her and becomes embittered because he thinks she is repulsed by his crippled arm. At a wedding reception for the Paultons, Bess Tyrell, a decided "modern" who approves of trial marriages, is unenthusiastic about a "lounge lizard" named Rady Tompkins and much more attracted to Jack Moreland. Jack is a minister, however, and he refuses her demand that he give up his calling and accept a position in the business world. As a result, Bess promises to marry Rady and they are to board a train that very night.

After consulting a physician about his arm, Ken is advised to leave immediately to have surgery in San Francisco. Still angered by his wife's terrified response to him, Ken finally forces himself upon her and causes her to run away. Unwittingly, Ken and Malena, as well as Bess, Rady, and Jack, all become passengers on board the Western Limited to San Francisco. En route, their train becomes involved in a spectacular crash and momentarily they all become unconscious.

In a flashback sequence that occurs in the seventeenth century, Ken as Lord Strangevon desires to marry Bess, a runaway heiress, but first he must discard both his wife, Malena, and Bess's lover, Jack. Ken forces Bess to marry him, declares Malena a sorceress to be burnt at the stake, and tortures Jack to death. As he observes from the window, the smoke and flames of the fire devouring Malena dissolve into the smoke and flames of the train wreck. Ken prays to God for strength in his crippled arm and rescues Malena, who has been trapped by a fallen beam, while Jack saves Bess and is reconciled with her.

50   THE VOLGA BOATMAN

Credits

Producer and Director: Cecil B. DeMille
Scenario: Lenore J. Coffee (based on the novel
                               by Konrad Bercovici)
Photographers: J. Peverell Marley, Arthur Miller, and
                               Fred Westerberg
Editor: Anne Bauchens
Art Directors: Mitchell Leisen and Anton Grot

Costumes: Adrian
Special Effects: Gordon Jennings[§]
Assistant Director: Frank Urson[§]
Cast: Elinor Fair (Princess Vera), William
                                 Boyd (Feodor), Victor Varconi
                                 (Prince Dimitri Orloff), Julia
                                 Faye (Maruisha)
Released by Producers Distributing Corporation, May 1926
Screening time: Approximately 106 minutes
Note
    A disclaimer in the opening title emphasizes that the film pleads
no political causes.

Synopsis

    In Russia, Princess Vera and Prince Dimitri are having their for-
tunes read when they hear the singing of the Volga boatmen who are
resting from their labors. The Princess is especially moved when she
hears the voice of Feodor, but Dimitri wishes to prove to her that the
boatman is merely a filthy body. She witnesses a hostile exchange between the Prince and Feodor, who is proud and rebellious, and muses
about the boatman even after her betrothal to Dimitri is celebrated.
Suddenly, Dimitri is called to active duty to suppress a rebellion
while Feodor, who has risen to a position of leadership in the Red
Army, recruits followers among the people of the Volga.

    Feodor leads a rabble that attacks the estate where Princess Vera
resides and the crowd clamors for her death. Although he is especially
goaded by a jealous peasant woman named Maruisha, Feodor cannot help
but admire the Princess's courage and spirit. Impulsively, he decides
to save her life and help her escape, but they soon fall into the
clutches of Prince Dimitri and the opposing White Army. Dimitri orders
Feodor's execution but Vera thwarts the firing squad long enough for
the Red Army to effect a rescue. When the Princess and Dimitri are
yoked to a boat, Feodor joins them and the other aristocrats who are
forced to pull the vehicle upstream. Later, Feodor pleads before a
tribunal for the lives of Vera and Dimitri and is granted his request.
The Princess elects to join him to build a new Russia while Dimitri
chooses exile.

51   THE KING OF KINGS

Credits

Producer and Director: Cecil B. DeMille
Scenario: Jeanie Macpherson
Photographers: J. Peverell Marley and Fred Westerberg
Editors: Anne Bauchens and Harold McLernon
Art Directors: Mitchell Leisen, Paul Iribe, Anton
                                 Grot, Wilfred Buckland, and J.
                                 Harrison
Costumes: Adrian, Gwen Wakeling, and Earl Luick[§]

Music: Hugo Riesenfeld[§]
Assistant Director: Frank Urson[§]
Advisors: Bruce Barton, Dr. William E. Barton,
                                    Reverend George Reid Andrews,
                                    Father Daniel A. Lord, Father G.G.
                                    Fox, and Rabbi Alkow[§]
Cast: H.B. Warner (Jesus), Dorothy Cumming
                                    (Mary), Jacqueline Logan (Mary
                                    Magdalene), Joseph Schildkraut
                                    (Judas), Ernest Torrence (Peter),
                                    Joseph Striker (John), Rudolph
                                    Schildkraut (Caiaphas), Victor
                                    Varconi (Pontius Pilate)
Produced by Cinema Corporation of America
Released by Pathe Exchange, Incorporated, April 1927
Screening time: Approximately 140 minutes for the silent version,
115 with sound

Synopsis

In the Hall of Magdala in Judaea, Mary Magdalene, "the wickedest and most beautiful Woman of her time," is courted by an Egyptian pharaoh, a Persian shah, Roman noblemen, and Jewish merchants. Displeased by the absence of her favorite, Judas Iscariot, Mary Magdalene drives her zebra-drawn chariot to the house of Jesus. She arrives while Jesus, surrounded by his mother and disciples, is healing the sick and becomes the subject of another miracle when the seven deadly sins are driven from her body. A woman reformed, Mary Magdalene becomes a devout follower and now spurns the attentions of Judas, who has joined Jesus only to profit.

While Caiaphas, the High Priest, schemes to have him arrested by the Romans, Jesus goes about his business: paying tribute to the Romans, saving an adulterous woman from being stoned, driving the moneychangers out of the temple, resisting the temptations of Satan, and raising Lazarus from the dead. After Jesus bids farewell to his apostles at the last supper, Judas betrays him with a kiss and has him arrested. Pontius Pilate, the Roman governor, accedes to the demands of the crowd that Jesus be crucified while Barabbas, a thief and a murderer, is set free. Jesus carries his cross to Calvary where he is crucified, while his mother, John, Mary Magdalene, and Mary and Martha of Bethany mourn at his feet. At the moment of his death, there is a spectacular storm and earthquake. Judas hangs himself. A few days later, Jesus rises from the dead and appears to his mother, Mary Magdalene, and the apostles and then ascends into the heavens.

52   THE GODLESS GIRL

Credits

Producer and Director: Cecil B. DeMille
Scenario: Jeanie Macpherson

Dialogue Sequence:	Jeanie Macpherson and Beulah Marie Dix
Photographer:	J. Peverell Marley
Editor:	Anne Bauchens
Art Director:	Mitchell Leisen
Assistant Director:	Frank Urson
Cast:	Lina Basquette (Judy Craig), George Duryea (Bob Hathaway), Eddie Quillan (Bozo Johnson), Marie Prevost (Mame), Noah Beery (Schmalz, the guard)

Released by Pathe Exchange, Incorporated, March 1929
Screening time: Depending upon the version, approximately 117 or
102 minutes
Note
    Due to the advent of sound, The Godless Girl was distributed both
as a silent film and a film with some sound sequences.

Synopsis

    Judy Craig, an atheist, and Bob Hathaway, a devout believer, are
high school students who quarrel about her activities to promote atheism
on the campus. Judy points to her First Amendment rights and holds a
meeting to explain the theory of evolution. Bob retaliates by organiz-
ing protesters who break up the session with rotten eggs and vegetables.
Fighting erupts and a girl plunges to her death when a stairway ballus-
trade collapses. Judy, Bob, and his friend, Bozo Johnson, are subsequently tried and convicted of manslaughter and sent to a reform school.

    The regimen at the reformatory is cruel and sadistic. Judy meets
a Christian girl, Mame, and though their beliefs differ, they eventually
become good friends. Judy even establishes a rapport with Bob and begins to read the Bible. Bob, on the other hand, has become so embittered by the brutality of a guard named Schmalz that he begins to lose
faith and makes an escape attempt with Judy. During their brief time
together, Bob and Judy fall in love but they are tracked down by
Schmalz and his blood hounds and punished with solitary confinement.
A fire breaks out and Bob manages to free himself and to reach Judy,
who has been trapped in her cell. Together, they even rescue Schmalz,
badly injured in the blaze, and are rewarded for this deed with parole.

53   DYNAMITE

Credits

Producer and Director:	Cecil B. DeMille
Scenario:	Jeanie Macpherson
Dialogue:	John Howard Lawson, Gladys Unger, and Jeanie Macpherson
Photographer:	J. Peverell Marley
Editor:	Anne Bauchens
Art Director:	Mitchell Leisen and Cedric Gibbons
Costumes:	Adrian
Assistant Director:	Mitchell Leisen

Production Manager: Roy Burns
Music: Herbert Stothart
Cast: Kay Johnson (Cynthia Crothers),
        Charles Bickford (Hagon Derk),
        Conrad Nagel (Roger Towne), Julia
        Faye (Marcia Towne), Muriel
        McCormick (Katie)
Released by Metro-Goldwyn-Mayer Distributing Corporation, December 1929
Screening time: Approximately 130 minutes
Note
    Dynamite was DeMille's first all-talking picture.

Synopsis

    Cynthia Crothers is a young heiress whose grandfather's will stipulates that she must be married by her twenty-third birthday in order to inherit a large fortune. Unfortunately Cynthia is in love with Roger Towne, another woman's husband. Marcia Towne is not above selling her husband, however, and sets her price at two hundred fifty thousand dollars. Cynthia counters with an offer for half that sum, but time is money and several weeks will elapse before Marcia can obtain a divorce in Reno. Cynthia's solution is to marry Hagon Derk, a condemned criminal, shortly before his hanging. Derk, a coal miner who has been unjustly convicted, is desperate about his young sister's fate and wishes to leave her some funds.

    Derk is unexpectedly released from prison when the real murderer confesses, and he proceeds to Cynthia's mansion to suggest that they attempt to honor their marriage vows. Cynthia is stunned and proposes to buy him off. All her friends comment with hilarity about her "diamond in the rough," and Roger is angered to learn not only about her strange marriage but her financial dealings involving himself. Derk reacts with disgust to the antics of the wealthy but he remains fascinated with the beautiful heiress who refuses to be his wife on any lasting basis.

    Since she must be residing with her husband on her twenty-third birthday, Cynthia has no choice but to live with Derk on his terms. She becomes a housekeeper in a coal mining town, strikes up an acquaintance with Derk's younger sister, Katie, and begins to respect the man she has married. But a misunderstanding alienates them and Cynthia decides to leave town after summoning Roger. Since Roger insists on confronting Derk in the coal mine, they are all trapped together when an explosion occurs. A possibility for escape means sacrificing the life of one of the men and both contend for the privilege. Finally, Roger resorts to a ruse and leaves Derk to escort Cynthia to safety.

54   MADAM SATAN

Credits

Producer and Director:	Cecil B. DeMille
Scenario:	Jeanie Macpherson
Dialogue:	Gladys Unger and Elsie Janis
Photographer:	Harold Rosson
Editor:	Anne Bauchens
Art Director:	Mitchell Leisen and Cedric Gibbons
Production Manager:	Roy Burns
Music and Lyrics:	Clifford Grey, Herbert Stothart, Elsie Janis, and Jack King
Choreography:	Le Roy Prinz
Assistant Director:	Mitchell Leisen
Cast:	Kay Johnson (Angela Brooks), Reginald Denny (Bob Brooks), Lillian Roth (Trixie), Roland Young (Jimmy)

Released by Metro-Goldwyn-Mayer Distributing Company, September 1930
Screening time: Approximately 120 minutes

Synopsis

Angela Brooks, a matronly socialite, is dismayed by the fact that her husband Bob seems uninterested in her and is having an affair with a showgirl named Trixie. Bob accuses Angela of having become a wife instead of a pal and complains to his friend Jimmy that what he gets at home is "frozen justice," not "warm affection." Trixie is thus decidedly a "counterirritant." An argument between husband and wife leads to a rupture. Counseled by her maid, Martha, who sings "Satan's Song," Angela decides to battle to win her husband back.

Jimmy is hosting an extravagant masquerade ball aboard a Zeppelin. The guests arrive in costume and are amused by various entertainments including a performance by the Ballet Méchanique. The highlight of the ball is an auction of masked women arrayed in spectacular costumes and headdresses. The bidding becomes especially spirited when Trixie is offered as the pièce de résistance, but a mysterious woman singing "Satan's Song" suddenly disrupts the proceedings. Flaunting herself as Madam Satan, she wears an alluring costume and proclaims that she is from hell. Bob's enthsiasm for Trixie quickly wanes and he successfully bids three thousand dollars for Madam Satan. She refuses to unmask herself, however, and flirts seductively with him throughout the evening. When she finally reveals her identity, Bob is stunned to discover that he has fallen in love with his own wife. At that moment, lightning strikes and the Zeppelin is thrown from its moorings. Guests panic as they fight for parachutes. Despite her protests, Bob forces Angela to parachute to safety while he makes a daring last minute escape. Afterwards, Bob comments about Angela's indecent and outrageous costume and her singing and dancing, but he confesses to having been a fool for having wandered from the hearth.

55   THE SQUAW MAN

Credits

Producer and Director:	Cecil B. DeMille
Scenario:	Lucien Hubbard and Lenore J. Coffee (based on the play by Edwin Milton Royle)
Dialogue:	Elsie Janis
Photographer:	Harold Rosson
Editor:	Anne Bauchens
Art Director:	Mitchell Leisen
Costumes:	Adrian§
Assistant Director:	Mitchell Leisen
Production Manager:	Roy Burns
Music:	Herbert Stothart
Cast:	Warner Baxter (James Wynnegate), Eleanor Boardman (Lady Diana), Lupe Valez (Naturich), Paul Cavanaugh (Sir Henry), Charles Bickford (Cash Hawkins), DeWitt Jennings (Sheriff)

Released by Metro-Goldwyn-Mayer Distributing Corporation, September 1931
Screening time: Approximately 115 minutes
Note
    A remake of the 1914 and 1918 silent versions, this film has a plot that is essentially the same though minor details differ. See entries 1 and 33.

56   THE SIGN OF THE CROSS

Credits

Producer and Director:	Cecil B. DeMille
Screenplay:	Waldemar Young and Sidney Buchanan (based on the play by Wilson Barrett)
Dialogue:	Dudley Nichols
Photographer:	Karl Struss
Editor:	Anne Bauchens
Art Director:	Mitchell Leisen
Costumes:	Mitchell Leisen
Assistant Director:	Mitchell Leisen
Music:	Rudolph Kopp
Cast:	Frederic March (Marcus Superbus), Elissa Landi (Mercia), Claudette Colbert (Poppaea), Charles Laughton (Nero), Ian Keith (Tigellinus), Tommy Conlon (Stephan)

Released by Paramount Publix Corporation, December 1932
Screening time: Approximately 130 minutes

Synopsis

After setting Rome ablaze, the emperor Nero finds it politically adept to blame the catastrophe on the Christians and entrusts his favorite, Marcus Superbus, with their persecution. Marcus's ambition to serve the emperor is tempered, however, by his infatuation for Mercia, a blonde Christian girl, and his predicament complicated by indifference to the attentions lavished upon him by Poppaea, Nero's strong-willed wife. Further, Marcus's rival, Tigellinus, intends to curry favor with Nero by assiduously hunting down Christians himself. Using spies, Tigellinus captures and tortures a young boy named Stephan and learns that the Christians are planning to meet in secret. Also alerted about the meeting, Marcus arrives in time to prevent a massacre and orders the imprisonment of the Christians instead. Mercia is singled out and brought to his house, but she is horrified by Roman debauchery and Marcus's lustful feelings and wishes to join the Christians. Poppaea, in the meanwhile, is determined to destroy her blonde rival and orders her and the Christians sent to the arena. Marcus pleads for Mercia's life before Nero, but the emperor will not relent unless the girl renounces her faith.

The Christians are to be fed to the lions in the Colisseum as part of a series of bloody and grotesque events staged for the pleasure of the emperor and empress. As they await their turn in the dungeon, the Christian prisoners find solace in Mercia's unshakeable conviction in God. She even gives courage to Stephan, who has betrayed them and is feeling cowardly and despicable. At the last moment, Marcus enters the dungeon with hopes that he will be able to persuade Mercia to abandon her faith and to live as his wife. Although she admits that she loves him, Mercia speaks glowingly of a greater love and chooses instead to embrace death. Transfixed by the strength of her religious beliefs, Marcus decides to die in the arena with Mercia in expectation of life hereafter.

Prologue: Added during World War II, the prologue depicts an Irish priest accompanying a crew on a mission to drop leaflets upon Rome. As they fly over the Eternal City and its famous landmarks, the men discuss the historical past while condemning "modern vandals." The transition to the original film is made by a series of quick dissolves to the scenes of Rome burning during the reign of Nero.

57   THIS DAY AND AGE

Credits

Producer and Director:	Cecil B. DeMille
Screenplay:	Bartlett Cormack (based on the story, "Boys in the Office" by Sam Mintz)
Photographer:	J. Peverell Marley
Editor:	Anne Bauchens
Art Director:	Roland Anderson
Assistant Director:	Cullen Tate

Production Manager: Roy Burns
Music: Howard Jackson, L.W. Gilbert, and
                              Abel Baer
Cast: Charles Bickford (Louis Garrett),
                              Richard Cromwell (Steve Smith),
                              Judith Allen (Gay Merrick), Lester
                              Arnold (Sam Weber), Michael Stuart
                              (Billy Anderson), Oscar Rudolph
                              (Gus Ruffo), Bradley Page (Toledo),
                              Harry Green (Herman)
Released by Paramount Productions, Incorporated, August 1933
Screening time: Approximately 86 minutes

Synopsis

Sam Weber, a high school student, witnesses the bombing of a small
business establishment by gangsters intent on terrorizing its owner, a
tailor named Herman. Although Herman calls the police and makes accusa-
tions against certain thugs, he is told that there is not enough evidence to warrant any arrests. Later that evening, Louis Garrett, the
leader of the hoodlums, murders Herman in his shop. Sam and his friends,
Steve Smith, Billy Anderson, and Gus Ruffo, assume civic office positions during Boys Week and decide to solve Herman's murder. When they
are stymied by bureaucratic procedure, Steve becomes cynical while Sam,
Billy, and Gus return to the scene of the crime and find Garrett's cuff
link. Unfortunately, Garrett surprises them when they break into his
apartment to search for the missing half of the pair. Billy is shot
and killed while Gus is arrested on theft charges.

After Billy's funeral, Steve decides to take matters into his own
hands. While his sweetheart Gay distracts a bodyguard named Toledo,
Steve and his high school chums abduct Garrett and subject him to their
own court proceedings. Bail, habeas corpus, and rules of evidence are
not allowed. Garrett is crossexamined while suspended over a rat's
nest and forced to confess his crimes. When Toledo arrives with
men and machine guns, he finds that Gay has succeeded in leading police to the scene. Feeling triumphant, the students truss up Garrett,
parade through the streets while singing songs like Oh, Susannah and
Battle Hymn of the Republic, and deliver their prisoner to the judge.

58   FOUR FRIGHTENED PEOPLE

Credits

Producer and Director: Cecil B. DeMille
Screenplay: Bartlett Cormack and Lenore J. Coffee
                              (based on the novel by E. Arnot
                              Robertson)
Photographer: Karl Struss
Editor: Anne Bauchens
Art Director: Roland Anderson
Assistant Directors: Cullen Tate and James Dugan

Production Manager:	Roy Burns
Music:	Karl Hajos, Milan Roder, Heinz Rohenheld, and John Leipold
Cast:	Claudette Colbert (Judy Cavendish), Herbert Marshall (Arnold Ainger), William Gargan (Stewart Corder), Mary Boland (Mrs. Mardick), Leo Carillo (Montague)

Released by Paramount Productions, Incorporated, January 1934
Screening time: Approximately 78 minutes

Synopsis

Stewart Corder, a famed journalist; Mrs. Mardick, a wealthy matron; Arnold Ainger, a chemist; and Judy Cavendish, a geography teacher, all become stranded on an island after they escape from a plague-infested ship. An English-speaking native named Montague volunteers to lead them to safety through a dense jungle. The foursome are none too congenial since Corder is arrogant and hot-tempered and Judy frightened and whining. As they proceed further into the jungle, they are captured by natives who demand a female hostage. Mrs. Mardick, a clubwoman who speaks native languages and carries her Pekinese dog everywhere, volunteers. She fares well as a captive and teaches the natives birth control. Unfortunately Montague is killed.

Stewart, Arnold, and Judy continue their dangerous trek and become a quarrelsome triangle when the latter loses her glasses and transforms herself from spinster teacher into voluptuous beauty. Cured of an earlier infatuation with Stewart, Judy now falls in love with Arnold but he happens to be a married man. When a ship is sighted, Judy asks Arnold to remain on the island with her but he respects his marital obligations. Back in New York, Arnold finds both his wife and mother-in-law insufferable and is relieved when they all agree upon divorce. Judy is in the middle of teaching a geography lesson when Arnold suddenly appears and leads her out of the classroom.

59   CLEOPATRA

Credits

Producer and Director:	Cecil B. DeMille
Screenplay:	Waldemar Young, Vincent Lawrence, and Bartlett Cormack
Photographer:	Victor Milner
Art Directors:	Hans Dreier and Roland Anderson
Costumes:	Travis Banton
Editor:	Anne Bauchens
Music:	Rudolph Kopp
Cast:	Claudette Colbert (Cleopatra), Warren William (Julius Caesar), Henry Wilcoxon (Marc Antony), Ian Keith (Octavian), Joseph Schildkraut

(Herod), Irving Pichel
(Appollodorus), C. Aubrey Smith
(Enobarbus)
Released by Paramount Productions, Incorporated, July 1934
Screening time: Approximately 100 minutes
Note
    Cleopatra won an Academy Award for best cinematography and nominations for best editing and sound recording.

Synopsis

    In her struggle against her brother Ptolemy for the Egyptian throne, Cleopatra allies herself with Julius Caesar by preying upon his ambitions. Despite gossip in Rome about his infidelity, Caesar returns to make a triumphant entry with the Egyptian queen arrayed in gold and carried by black footmen. The Roman conqueror's triumph is short lived, however, as he is assassinated by conspirators. The Senate decrees that Marc Antony and Octavian shall be joint rulers and that Antony's task shall be to punish the Egyptian queen. At Tarsus, Cleopatra arrives on her luxurious barge to meet Antony and stages a sumptuous banquet and entertainments to seduce him. Although he has previously declared that women should be mere "playthings," Antony is soon enchanted by the queen and dallies with her. When Octavian learns about these events, he exclaims, "Who is that poisonous snake that wrecks our men?"

    Cleopatra learns from King Herod that Antony has fallen into disfavor and is now a political liability. Appollodorus, a loyal servant and mentor, persuades her to poison Antony but her emotions now conflict with her political ambitions. Before she can execute the deed, however, news arrives that Rome has declared war on Egypt. Antony springs to life as a general and issues commands to prepare for battle. Cleopatra stands by adoringly and says, "I've seen a god come to life. I'm no longer a queen. I'm a woman." Unfortunately for the Egyptian cause, Antony's generals, including his close friend, Enobarbus, refuse to fight against Rome and depart with their legions. When it becomes apparent to Cleopatra that the struggle has been lost, she goes to Octavian to plead for Antony's life. Antony believes, however, that she has betrayed him and stabs himself. Cleopatra returns to find her lover dying and prepares for her own death to elude Roman conquest.

60   THE CRUSADES

Credits

Producer and Director:	Cecil B. DeMille
Screenplay:	Harold Lamb, Waldemar Young, and Dudley Nichols
Photographer:	Victor Milner
Editor:	Anne Bauchens
Art Directors:	Hans Dreier and Roland Anderson[§]
Costumes:	Travis Banton
Special Effects:	Gordon Jennings

The Films: Credits, Synopses, and Notes

Music: Rudolph Kopp
Lyrics: Harold Lamb
Cast: Henry Wilcoxon (Richard the Lion-
                                    Hearted), Loretta Young (Berengaria),
                                    Ian Keith (Saladin), Joseph
                                    Schildkraut (Conrad of Montferrat),
                                    C. Henry Gordon (King Philip of
                                    France), Katherine deMille (Alice),
                                    George Barbier (King of Navarre)
Released by Paramount Productions, Incorporated, August 1935
Screening time: Approximately 123 minutes
Note
     The Crusades received an Academy Award nomination for best cinema-
tography.

Synopsis

     King Richard the Lion-Hearted is betrothed to Alice, sister of the
French monarch, Philip, but he is more interested in hunting than marriage to a "surly-tempered wench." When a saintly hermit from
Jerusalem arrives with tales of Christians enslaved by Saracen infidels,
Richard embarks on a crusade in order to avoid marriage. Upon arrival
in Marseilles, however, he does not have enough provisions for his men
and agrees to marry Berengaria, daughter of the King of Navarre, in exchange for cattle and fodder. Rather thoughtlessly, he sends a minstrel
with his sword as proxy for the wedding ceremony and continues to car-
ouse with his men. Although she is angered, Berengaria reciprocates
by sending Richard her bridal veil and is insulted when she later sees
it bandaging a horse's leg. After Richard learns that Berengaria is
in fact a beautiful woman, he insists that she accompany him on board
a ship to Palestine.

     When Richard proclaims Berengaria his queen before the Council of
Kings, he arouses the enmity of Philip, who threatens to withdraw from
the Crusades and declare war on England. The saintly hermit chastises
Richard for splintering the Christian cause. Despite Berengaria's
pleas on behalf of the crusade, Richard stubbornly refuses to have their
marriage annulled. Berengaria decides to sacrifice herself and leaves
the encampment for the battlefield. She is injured, taken prisoner by
the Saracens, and falls into the hands of the infidel king, Saladin.
The Saracen ruler is himself captivated and courts Berengaria while
his men battle Christian legions.

     Conrad of Montferrat visits the Saracen stronghold and attempts to
interest Saladin in a plot to assassinate Richard. Berengaria pleads
for Richard's life and promises to marry Saladin in return. She also
appeals for peace between Christians and Saracens, and Saladin responds
by opening the gates of Jerusalem to all unarmed believers except
Richard. Finding himself excluded from the holy city, the humbled
Englishman beseeches God for his wife and his prayers are answered.
Saladin has been impressed by Berengaria's devotion to her husband
and magnanimously releases her so that she may rejoin him.

61   THE PLAINSMAN

Credits

Producer and Director:	Cecil B. DeMille
Screenplay:	Waldemar Young, Harold Lamb, and Lynn Riggs (material compiled by Jeanie Macpherson; based on writings by Courtney Riley Cooper and Frank J. Wilstach)
Photographer:	Victor Milner
Editor:	Anne Bauchens
Art Directors:	Hans Dreier and Roland Anderson
Costumes:	Natalie Visart, Dwight Franklin, and Joe DeYong
Special Effects:	Farciot Edouart and Dewey Wrigley
Music:	George Antheil
Second Unit Director:	Arthur Rosson
Executive Producer:	William LeBaron
Cast:	Gary Cooper (Wild Bill Hickok), Jean Arthur (Calamity Jane), James Ellison (Buffalo Bill Cody), Charles Bickford (John Lattimer), Helen Burgess (Louisa Cody), Paul Harvey (Yellow Hand), Porter Hall (Jack McCall)

Released by Paramount Pictures, Incorporated, January 1937
Screening time: Approximately 115 minutes

Synopsis

Buffalo Bill Cody arrives in St. Louis with his bride, Louisa, and intends to start a hotel business while his friend, Wild Bill Hickok, carries a picture of Calamity Jane in his watch but claims "women and me don't agree." Since an unscrupulous villain named Lattimer is distributing repeating rifles to the Indians, Bill Hickok is concerned about the safety of frontier settlers. The Sioux, Cayowas, and Cheyenne are all on the warpath. Despite Louisa's opposition, Bill Hickok persuades Buffalo Bill to serve with the cavalry. Calamity Jane is comforting Louisa when Indians invade the house and demand to know the whereabouts of a munitions train. The Indians take Jane captive but they are sighted by Bill Hickok. When Bill attempts to parley with their leader, Yellow Hand, he is reminded about the land stolen from the Indians and the slaughter of the buffalo. Yellow Hand is determined to drive the white man out and inquires about the route of the munitions train. Bill asks Jane to remain silent but she is unwilling to see him dead and divulges the information. Subsequently the Indians attack the train but General Custer and his men ride to the rescue.

Back in town, Bill Hickok confronts and kills three corrupt soldiers who are working for Lattimer. Although the gunfight was fair, Louisa is distraught by the killing. An Indian suddenly arrives in town with the news of General Custer's defeat. To avert Lattimer's plan to supply Sitting Bull with rifles, Buffalo Bill rides to bring General Merritt and the fifth cavalry. Meanwhile, Bill Hickok wanders into a bar and confesses to Jane that he thinks Buffalo Bill chose the right path; there is no place in the country for a man like himself. Bill even muses about Louisa's detestation of killing but he is then drawn into a gunfight with Lattimer. Determined to surrender Lattimer's men to General Merritt, Bill forces them to wait in the saloon and play cards. During a game, Jack McCall, an inconsequential man who envies Bill's reputation as a gunfighter, shoots him in the back. Bill dies as Calamity Jane mourns him.

62   THE BUCCANEER

Credits

Producer and Director:	Cecil B. DeMille
Screenplay:	Edwin Justus Mayer, Harold Lamb, and C. Gardner Sullivan (based on Jeanie Macpherson's adaptation of Lafitte the Pirate by Lyle Saxon)
Photographer:	Victor Milner
Art Directors:	Hans Dreier and Roland Anderson
Editor:	Anne Bauchens
Music:	George Antheil
Second Unit Director:	Arthur Rosson§
Associate Producer:	William H. Pine
Executive Producer:	William LeBaron
Cast:	Frederic March (Jean Lafitte), Franciska Gaal (Gretchen), Margot Grahame (Annette de Remy), Akim Tamiroff (Dominique You), Fred Kohler, Sr. (Gramby), Robert Barrett (Captain Brown), Hugh Sothern (Andrew Jackson), Louise Campbell (Marie de Remy)

Released by Paramount Pictures, Incorporated, February 1938
Screening time: Approximately 125 minutes
Note
     The Buccaneer received an Academy Award nomination for best cinematography.

Synopsis

     During the War of 1812, passengers in New Orleans board the Corinthian, a ship bound for Holland. Among them is Gretchen, a Dutch girl en route to see her father, and Marie de Remy, a young woman eloping with her lover. Before the ship's departure, Marie asks her sister Annette for a miniature that once belonged to their mother. The Corinthian's voyage is brief, however, since the New Orleans waterways are controlled by Jean Lafitte and his pirates, the Baratarians. Against Lafitte's orders, Captain Brown of the Vulcan burns the

97

Corinthian after seizing its cargo but makes the mistake of allowing a survivor, Gretchen, to live. When Lafitte condemns Brown to be hanged, Gretchen intercedes for the life of the Vulcan's second-in-command, Gramby. Assigned the duties of a scullery maid, she falls in love with Lafitte but finds him completely unresponsive.

Because the United States is at war with Great Britain, Lafitte seizes the opportunity to offer his services to the Americans. By doing so, he hopes to achieve the respectable status of a gentleman and thus win the hand of Annette de Remy, the woman whom he loves. But American ships level Barataria to the ground and Lafitte's men are imprisoned. Lafitte finds himself in a better bargaining position, however, when British troops threaten New Orleans and Andrew Jackson refuses to surrender. Jackson needs men and munitions and is willing to make a deal with the pirate. Lafitte and his colorful first lieutenant, Dominique You, inspire their men to fight for Jackson as well as their freedom and they win a great victory, but its results are short-lived. At the Victory Ball, Gretchen is determined to win Lafitte's approval and she wears Marie de Remy's finery and miniature. Annette is shocked to learn about the fate of her sister and incites the crowd against Lafitte and his men. Jackson grants the pirates one hour to escape, and Lafitte consoles himself by contemplating for the first time Gretchen's charms as a woman.

63 UNION PACIFIC

Credits

Producer and Director:	Cecil B. DeMille
Screenplay:	Walter De Leon, C. Gardner Sullivan, and Jesse L. Lasky, Jr. (based on Jack Cunningham's adaptation of the novel, Trouble Shooter, by Ernest Haycox)
Photographer:	Victor Milner
Special Photographic Effects:	Gordon Jennings
Process Photography:	Farciot Edouart and Dewey Wrigley
Editor:	Anne Bauchens
Art Directors:	Hans Dreier and Roland Anderson
Costumes:	Natalie Visart
Music:	Sigmund Krumgold and John Leipold
Second Unit Director:	Arthur Rosson
Associate Producer:	William H. Pine
Executive Producer:	William LeBaron
Cast:	Joel McCrea (Jeff Butler), Barbara Stanwyck (Mollie Monahan), Robert Preston (Dick Allen), Brian Donlevy (Sid Campeau), Lynne Overman (Leach), Akim Tamiroff (Fiesta), Henry Kolker (Asa Barrows)

Released by Paramount Pictures, Incorporated, April 1939
Screening time: Approximately 130 minutes

The Films: Credits, Synopses, and Notes

<u>Note</u>
    <u>Union Pacific</u> received an Academy Award nomination for best special effects.

<u>Synopsis</u>
    Jeff Butler is hired as a troubleshooter for the Union Pacific Railroad, which is racing to finish construction of a transcontinental line but plagued by mishaps and Indian attacks. Jeff quickly surmises that the Union Pacific's costly delays have been deliberately caused by Sid Campeau, but he has yet to learn that the real culprit is Asa Barrows, a financier backing the Union Pacific's rival, the Central. For the moment, his role as troubleshooter is complicated by the fact that Campeau's right hand man is Dick Allen, a close friend from his days of fighting in the Confederate Army. Dick has been courting Mollie Monahan, the postmistress, but without success. After she meets Jeff, Mollie finds herself attracted to him and describes him as having "the manners of a gentleman, the smile of a boy, and quick hand of a gunman."

    Barrows orders Campeau to steal the Union Pacific's payroll money and the job falls to Dick. During a wild pursuit after the robbery, Dick and his men take refuge in Mollie's mailroom. When Jeff arrives to investigate, Mollie fears for his life and drives him out of the room by revealing her engagement to Dick. Discarding "aces for queens," Dick accepts Mollie's terms for marriage, the return of the payroll money. While Dick rushes Mollie through a wedding ceremony that very night, Jeff confronts Campeau to learn about Dick's role in the robbery. Scarcely married, Mollie helps Dick escape but he rejoins her on a train shortly before it is derailed by the Sioux. Jeff is also aboard and the three fight a losing battle against marauding Indians until a train with federal troops arrives. Jeff gives Dick enough provisions to escape, and in return Dick informs him about Asa Barrows.

    The Union Pacific has made excellent progress and will soon be joining its tracks with those of the Central Pacific at Promontory Point in Utah. Jeff has had his men, Leach and Fiesta, abduct Barrows but he still has a score to settle with Campeau. While festivities are being held at Promontory Point, a gunfight takes place. Stalking Jeff, Campeau kills Dick by mistake and is in turn gunned down by Leach. Jeff returns to the scene of the celebration to inform Mollie about her husband's death.

    64   NORTH WEST MOUNTED POLICE

<u>Credits</u>

Producer and Director:	Cecil B. DeMille
Screenplay:	Alan LeMay, Jesse L. Lasky, Jr., and C. Gardner Sullivan (based on the story, "Royal Canadian Mounted Police," by R.C. Fetherstonhaugh)

Photographers: Victor Milner and W. Howard Green
Editor: Anne Bauchens
Art Directors: Hans Dreier and Roland Anderson
Costumes: Natalie Visart and Joe DeYong
Color Consultant: Natalie Kalmus
Special Photographic Effects: Gordon Jennings
Process Photography: Farciot Edouart
Music: Victor Young
Second Unit Director: Arthur Rosson
Associate Producer: William H. Pine
Executive Producer: William LeBaron
Consultants: Sergeant Major James G.E. Griffin and
                      Sergeant George A. Pringle

Cast: Gary Cooper (Dusty Rivers), Madeleine
                      Carroll (April Logan), Paulette
                      Goddard (Louvette Corbeau), Preston
                      Foster (Jim Bret), Robert Preston
                      (Ronnie Logan), George Bancroft
                      (Jacques Corbeau), Francis J.
                      McDonald (Louis Riel), Akim Tamiroff
                      (Dan Duroc), Walter Hampden (Big
                      Bear)

Released by Paramount Pictures, Incorporated, October 1940
Screening time: Approximately 125 minutes

Note

North West Mounted Police was the first DeMille film shot entirely
in technicolor. It received an Academy Award for best editing and
nominations for best color cinematography, best set design in color,
and best sound recording.

Synopsis

Louis Riel, the exiled leader of Canadian halfbreeds, is persuaded
by Dan Duroc and Jacques Corbeau, who has possession of a gattling gun,
to return to Batoche to lead an uprising which will be supported by the
Indians. Sergeant Jim Bret of the North West Mounted Police, on the
other hand, is responsible for defusing a halfbreed rebellion by making
certain that the Indians adhere to their peace treaty with Great Britain.
While he is in Batoche, Jim courts a blonde nurse named April Logan but
she thinks he is too arrogant and too wedded to duty. April's impulsive,
young brother, Ronnie, also pursues a woman but unfortunately she is
Louvette, the halfbreed daughter of Jacques Corbeau. Batoche's political and romantic landscape is further complicated by the arrival of a
Texas Ranger, Dusty Rivers, who has a warrant for Corbeau's arrest and
begins to show a decided preference for April.

At the camp of the Indian chief, Big Bear, Jim argues for the
Indians' continued loyalty to the Great White Mother, while Corbeau
demonstrates the effectiveness of the gattling gun. Since Big Bear
asks for several empty redcoats before he will declare war, Corbeau
and his men plot to ambush the mounted police at Duck Lake. April
learns about their secret plans in Batoche and pleads with Louvette

100

to send word to the Canadian forces. Louvette's only concern is for
Ronnie, however, and she entices him away from his post and holds him
captive while his friends are slaughtered. Jim is charged with bring-
ing Ronnie to justice for desertion and finds April very much distraught
about her brother's fate.

While Jim succeeds in retaining Big Bear's loyalty to the British
empire, Dusty singlehandedly destroys the gattling gun and tracks down
Ronnie's whereabouts. Louvette is fearful that Dusty will persuade
Ronnie to leave her, so she arranges for the Texan's murder. Unfortunately her plans backfire and Ronnie is killed instead. For April's
sake, Dusty returns with Ronnie's body and credits him with brave exploits, including the destruction of the gattling gun. April is grateful but decides she prefers Jim after all. Dusty is left without a
bride and returns to Texas with Corbeau as his prisoner.

65   REAP THE WILD WIND

Credits

Producer and Director:	Cecil B. DeMille
Screenplay:	Alan LeMay, Charles Bennett, and Jesse L. Lasky, Jr. (based on a story by Thelma Strabel)
Photographers:	Victor Milner and William V. Skall
Editor:	Anne Bauchens
Art Directors:	Hans Dreier and Roland Anderson
Costumes:	Natalie Visart
Technicolor Director:	Natalie Kalmus
Special Photographic Effects:	Gordon Jennings, W.L. Pereira, and Farciot Edouart
Underwater Photography:	Dewey Wrigley
Music:	Victor Young
Second Unit Director:	Arthur Rosson
Associate Producer:	William H. Pine
Executive Producer:	Buddy DeSylva
Cast:	Paulette Goddard (Loxi Claiborne), Ray Milland (Stephen Tolliver), John Wayne (Jack Stuart), Raymond Massey (King Cutler), Robert Preston (Dan Cutler), Susan Hayward (Drusilla), Lynne Overman (Captain Phil), Victor Kilian (Widgeon), Walter Hampden (Commodore Devereaux)

Released by Paramount Pictures Incorporated, March 1942
Screening time: Approximately 124 minutes
Notes
Reap the Wild Wind won an Academy Award for best special effects
and received nominations for best color cinematography and best set
design in color.

Synopsis

As the man of her family, Loxi Claiborne commands a salvage ship
that rescues men and cargo from schooners wrecked off Key West. On
one venture, she and her mate, Captain Phil, have to settle for Captain
Jack Stuart, the wounded skipper of the Jubilee, and lose cargo shares
to King Cutler. Recuperating in Loxi's room, Jack is unaware that his
ship was deliberately sunk by his mate, Widgeon, who is part of Cutler's
dishonest but lucrative salvaging business. Jack fears that the dis-
aster will affect his chances to command the Southern Cross, an impressive steamship to be launched by the Devereaux firm. While recovering from his wounds, he falls in love with Loxi and the two plan to
rendezvous in Charleston, home of the Devereaux shipping line.

Although Charleston society finds her behavior unladylike, Loxi
attracts the attention of Steve Tolliver, Commodore Devereaux's attorney.
Steve is fascinated by Loxi's headstrong and insouciant manner and decides to marry her despite her preference for Jack. Loxi is deceived
by Steve's elegant dress and manners, labels him a "lace ruffled . . .
jaybird," and becomes antagonistic when she wrongly suspects him of
scuttling Jack's career. Actually, Steve has undertaken to clear Jack
of the loss of the Jubilee and has supported his promotion to command
the Southern Cross.

Jack eventually assumes command of the Southern Cross but he is embittered by Steve's interference with his plans to marry Loxi and dismayed by the news that Commodore Devereaux has died and that Steve now
heads the shipping firm. Cutler preys upon Jack's fears and persuades
him to wreck the Southern Cross and profit from the rich cargo to be
salvaged. When Steve discovers the plot, he commandeers Loxi's vessel
and sails in pursuit. Loxi refuses to believe that Jack is capable of
conspiracy and incapacitates her ship by cutting the ropes. Adrift in
the fog, she, Steve, and Captain Phil hear the Southern Cross ignore
warnings and crash on the reef.

During the inquest which follows, Jack denies any wrongdoing but a
black stoker testifies that he heard a woman's dying scream when the
Southern Cross struck the reef. The court is adjourned so that divers
may ascertain whether or not anyone died in the crash. In fact, Loxi's
cousin, Drusilla, who had been having a secret romance with Cutler's
younger brother, Dan, had stowed away on the Southern Cross. Dan is
stricken by the possibility that Drusilla has perished and vows to turn
against his brother if the stoker is correct.

Steve and Jack both volunteer to make the perilous dive. Cutler
orders Jack to kill Steve while they are investigating the wreck. The
two men engage in an underwater struggle made spectacular by the sudden
appearance of a giant squid. Jack saves Steve from the monster only to
become entangled in its tentacles and perish himself. Steve emerges
from the water with a fragment of Drusilla's shawl, a gift from Dan
and proof that she is dead. Cutler shoots his brother to silence him
but is in turn shot by Steve. Although Loxi is anguished by the turn

of events and blames herself for being willful, she and Steve are
reconciled in the end.

66   THE STORY OF DR. WASSELL

Credits

Producer and Director:	Cecil B. DeMille
Screenplay:	Alan LeMay and Charles Bennett (based on the story of Commander Corydon Wassell and a story by James Hilton)
Photographers:	Victor Milner and William Synder
Editor:	Anne Bauchens
Art Directors:	Hans Dreier and Roland Anderson
Costumes:	Natalie Visart
Set Decorator:	George Sawley
Technicolor Director:	Natalie Kalmus
Special Photographic Effects:	Gordon Jennings
Process Photography:	Farciot Edouart and Wallace Kelley
Music:	Victor Young
Second Unit Director:	Arthur Rosson
Associate Producer:	Stanley Biddell
Executive Producer:	Buddy DeSylva
Consultants:	Corydon M. Wassell, Lieutenant Commander H.D. Smith, and Captain Fred F. Ellis
Cast:	Gary Cooper (Corydon Wassell), Laraine Day (Madeline), Signe Hasso (Bettina), Dennis O'Keefe (Hoppy), Carol Thurston (Tremartini), Philip Ahn (Ping), Lester Matthews (Dr. Ralph Wayne), Carl Esmond (Lieutenant Dirk van Daal)

Released by Paramount Pictures, Incorporated, April 1944
Screening time: Approximately 136 minutes
Note
    The Story of Dr. Wassell received an Academy Award nomination for
best special effects.

Synopsis

    During World War II in the Dutch East Indies, Dr. Corydon Wassell,
a physician from Arkansas, is supervising the care of wounded soldiers.
When he meets Hoppy, a patient from his native state, he reminisces
about his days as a country doctor and his work as a medical missionary
in China. Among the wounded is Ping, Cory's Chinese friend, who nar-
rates a flashback about the doctor's research to find the cause of a
plague blighting China. Ping dies during a Japanese air raid and his
story is unfinished. Meanwhile the wounded men are distraught when
they learn that stretcher cases will not be permitted aboard the Pecos,
the last ship to leave Java. Cory decides to stay behind with his pa-
tients, including a wounded commander, and he relates more about his

experience in China. Unhappily, a colleague named Dr. Ralph Wayne was first to discover the parasite causing the plague and was also a rival for Madeline, the nurse whom he loved.

Cory decides to transport his wounded men across Java in the company of British troops headed for Australia. During the perilous journey, Hoppy and a Javanese nurse, Tremartini, fall into the hands of the Japanese, but most of them arrive at a harbor where a British transport ship waits. Again, the wounded are refused passage but Cory sneaks them aboard. Bettina, a nurse who has accompanied them, says farewell to her fiancé, Dirk, who bravely remains behind to report on a massive Japanese invasion. When the mist clears, Japanese bombers attack the ship until they are met by American flying fortresses. While caring for the wounded on the deck, Cory meets Wayne and learns that Madeline never married. Unfortunately she was on board the <u>Pecos</u>, which has since been sunk by the Japanese. After he reaches Australia, Cory is surprised to hear President Franklin Roosevelt commend his bravery on a radio broadcast. Madeline and other survivors of the <u>Pecos</u> listen to the same broadcast as they are flown to safety. Later, Cory is decorated at a formal ceremony attended by the men he has saved.

At the end of the film, the audience is informed that Hoppy is alive and is a prisoner of war in Japan.

67   UNCONQUERED

Credits

Producer and Director:	Cecil B. DeMille
Screenplay:	Charles Bennett, Frederic M. Frank, and Jesse L. Lasky, Jr. (based on the novel by Neil H. Swanson)
Photographer:	Ray Rennahan
Editor:	Anne Bauchens
Art Directors:	Hans Dreier and Walter Tyler
Costumes:	Gwen Wakeling
Set Decorators:	Sam Comer and Stanley Jay Sawley
Color Consultant:	Natalie Kalmus
Director of Photographic Effects:	Gordon Jennings
Special Photographic Effects:	Paul Lerpae and Devereux Jennings
Process Photography:	Farciot Edouart and Wallace Kelley
Music:	Victor Young
Choreography:	Jack Crosby
Second Unit Director:	Arthur Rosson
Assistant Director:	Edward Salven
Consultants:	Captain Fred F. Ellis and Iron Eyes Cody[§]
Cast:	Gary Cooper (Captain Chris Holden), Paulette Goddard (Abby Hale), Howard DaSilva (Garth), Boris Karloff (Guyasuta), Katherine

deMille (Hannah), Virginia Grey
(Diana)

Released by Paramount Pictures, Incorporated, September 1947
Screening time: Approximately 146 minutes

Note

Unconquered received an Academy Award nomination for best special
effects.

Synopsis

On board a ship bound for the New World in the late eighteenth
century, Abigail Hale, a beautiful indentured servant, attracts the
attention of Garth, an unsavory character in league with the Indians.
Garth bids for Abby during an auction but he is outbid by Captain Chris
Holden, who has no further interest in her after he buys and frees her.
When Chris leaves the ship to meet his fiancée, Diana, Garth persuades
the agent to void Abby's sale to Chris and takes possession of her instead. Chris learns that Diana has married his brother in his absence
and recalling what he paid for an indentured servant, he says, "I think
you are overpriced."

Chris discovers evidence that Garth is encouraging the Indians, led
by Guyasuta, to go on the warpath and follows him to Pittsburgh. When
he comes across Abby in a tavern, he abducts her and introduces her to
Pittsburgh society in a beautiful gown that had been intended for his
bride-to-be. Garth enters the ballroom with a bill of sale to prove
that Abby belongs to him and repossesses her. At an Indian camp, Garth
plans the destruction of Fort Pitt but he is unable to protect Abby
from Hannah, his Indian wife and the daughter of Guyasuta. Chris bravely enters the camp alone, resorts to trickery, and escapes with Abby.
After a spectacular chase that takes them over dangerous rapids and a
waterfall, Chris and Abby find safety in an abandoned cabin. Abby
dreams about domestic life until Chris discovers the family who lived
in the cabin; they have been butchered by the Indians.

Chris decides to return to Fort Pitt to warn against an Indian attack even though Abby will be returned to Garth. When he arrives at
the fort, however, he is arrested for desertion, courtmartialed, and
sentenced to death. Abby appeals to Garth and promises to marry him
in exchange for Chris's life. Still treacherous, Garth arranges for
Chris to be killed during an escape attempt, but Hannah foils his plan
by deliberately drawing the gunman's fire. Chris resorts to trickery
against the Indians once more and cleverly manages to save a beseiged
Fort Pitt. Afterwards, he and Abby decide to marry and settle in the
West.

68 SAMSON AND DELILAH

Credits

Producer and Director:	Cecil B. DeMille
Screenplay:	Jesse L. Lasky, Jr. and Frederic M. Frank

Photographer:	George Barnes
Director of Photographic Effects:	Gordon Jennings
Editor:	Anne Bauchens
Art Directors:	Hans Dreier and Walter Tyler
Set Decorators:	Sam Comer and Ray Moyer
Costumes:	Edith Head, Gile Steele, Dorothy Jeakins, Gwen Wakeling, and Elois Jenssen
Color Consultants:	Natalie Kalmus and Robert Brower
Special Photographic Effects:	Paul Lerpae and Devereux Jennings
Process Photography:	Farciot Edouart and Wallace Kelley
Music:	Victor Young
Choreography:	Theodore Kosloff
Second Unit Directors:	Arthur Rosson and Ralph Jester
Assistant Director:	Edward Salven
Associate Producer:	Henry Wilcoxon§
Cast:	Victor Mature (Samson), Hedy Lamarr (Delilah), George Sanders (The Saran of Gaza), Henry Wilcoxon (Ahtur), Angela Lansbury (Semadar), Olive Deering (Miriam), Russ Tamblyn (Saul)

Released by Paramount Pictures, Incorporated, October 1949
Screening time: Approximately 130 minutes

Note

Samson and Delilah received Academy Awards for best art direction and set decoration and best costumes and nominations for best color cinematography, special effects, and music.

Synopsis

Samson, a Danite renowned for his strength, is infatuated with Semadar, the blonde daughter of a wealthy Philistine, and arouses the jealousy of her dark-haired sister, Delilah. When he slays a lion with his bare hands, the Saran of Gaza awards him the hunter's prize, his choice of a bride, and he selects Semadar. Delilah seeks revenge by engaging Ahtur, a warrior who also covets Semadar, in a plot to ruin Samson. As part of a wager, Samson has promised cloaks to thirty warriors if they can solve a riddle which he has posed. Ahtur tricks Semadar into revealing the answer to him, and Samson must therefore commit crimes to keep his part of the wager. When he returns with the cloaks, he finds that Ahtur has further tricked Semadar into marriage and he erupts in a great fury. During the melee which ensues, Semadar is killed by a javelin. As retaliation, Samson burns the field and lays waste the countryside.

Samson defies whole armies and cannot be subdued, but Delilah predicts that he will fall before a woman. She lures him by traveling through the country with a well-laden caravan and establishing luxurious quarters. Since the Danites are heavily taxed, Samson arrives to steal the riches but finds Delilah enchanting, spends several days

106

with her, and reveals to her the secret of his strength. Delilah becomes irresolute until Miriam and Saul arrive to inform Samson that his parents are being persecuted by the Philistines. She mistakes Samson's decision to leave her as a preference for Miriam and betrays him to Ahtur on condition that his flesh remain untouched and unharmed. When the Saran later takes her to see Samson chained to a millstone, she is horrified to discover that his eyes have been blinded. Samson ascertains shortly thereafter that his strength has returned and on an appointed day when all the people of Gaza come to mock him, he causes their temple to collapse and destroys everyone including himself and Delilah.

69   THE GREATEST SHOW ON EARTH

Credits

Producer and Director:	Cecil B. DeMille
Screenplay:	Frederic M. Frank, Barre Lyndon, and Theodore St. John
Photographer:	George Barnes
Additional Photography:	J. Peverell Marley and Wallace Kelley
Editor:	Anne Bauchens
Art Directors:	Hal Pereira and Walter Tyler
Set Decorators:	Sam Comer and Ray Moyer
Costumes:	Edith Head and Dorthy Jeakins
Color Consultant:	Robert Brower
Special Photographic Effects:	Gordon Jennings, Paul Lerpae, and Devereux Jennings
Music:	Victor Young
Choreography:	Richard Barstow
Second Unit Director:	Arthur Rosson
Assistant Director:	Edward Salven
Associate Producer:	Henry Wilcoxon
Consultant:	John Ringling North
Cast:	Charlton Heston (Brad), Betty Hutton (Holly), Cornel Wilde (Sebastian), Gloria Grahame (Angel), James Stewart (Buttons), Lyle Bettger (Klaus)

Released by Paramount Pictures, Incorporated, July 1952
Screening time: Approximately 153 minutes
Note
The Greatest Show on Earth received Academy Awards for best picture and best motion picture story and nominations for best director, editing, and costumes.

Synopsis

As circus manager, Brad hires a famous trapeze artist billed as the Great Sebastian in order to attract crowds for a full season and moves Holly, Queen of the Flying Trapeze, out of the center ring. Since Holly is in love with Brad, she wonders about his decision and whether or not he loves stardust more than he loves her. She challenges Sebastian to a duel and they attract large crowds by working without nets and competing with each other in dangerous trapeze acts. Brad is irked by Holly's recklessness and by her flirtation with Sebastian, who has a well-deserved reputation as a ladies' man. Angel, the elephant girl, has already had an affair with Sebastian and advises Holly to stick with a "one-woman guy" like Brad.

When Holly decides to become more sensible, Sebastian fuels their competition under the big top and their lapsed romance by attempting a double forward, but he falls to the ground and is seriously injured. Holly is so guilt-stricken that she decides to marry Sebastian in order to care for him. Angel mocks her as Joan of Arc and decides to take advantage of the opportunity to ingratiate herself with Brad. But she arouses the jealousy of her partner, Klaus, who is fired for subjecting her to a dangerous stunt. Subsequently, Klaus becomes involved in a hold-up scheme that leads to a spectacular derailment of the circus train. Brad is trapped beneath the wreckage and badly injured. Holly prevails upon one of the clowns, Buttons, to save his life even though she knows he will be arrested. Buttons is a former physician who is wanted for a murder and has been eluding a dogged detective. Responding to the emergency, Buttons saves Brad with a blood transfusion and even diagnoses Sebastian's old trapeze injury as one which may be cured.

Despite the massive train wreck, the show must go on. Holly takes charge and finds in a role reversal that she is now too busy to respond to Brad's romantic gestures. Buttons gives away his dog, Squeaker, to a little girl and is led away handcuffed by an apologetic police detective. And Angel and Sebastian decide to renew their former love affair and to marry.

70   THE TEN COMMANDMENTS

Credits

Producer and Director:	Cecil B. DeMille
Screenplay:	Aeneas MacKenzie, Jesse L. Lasky, Jr., Jack Gariss, and Frederic M. Frank (based on Prince of Egypt by Dorothy Clarke Wilson, Pillar of Fire by Reverend J.H. Ingraham, and On Eagle's Wings by Reverend G.E. Southon)
Photographers:	Loyal Griggs, J. Peverell Marley, John Warren, and Wallace Kelley
Editor:	Anne Bauchens
Art Directors:	Hal Pereira, Walter Tyler, and Albert Nozaki
Set Decorators:	Sam Comer and Ray Moyer
Costumes:	Edith Head, Ralph Jester, John Jensen, Dorothy Jeakins, and Arnold Friberg
Color Consultant:	Richard Mueller

Special Effects:	John P. Fulton
Optical Photography:	Paul Lerpae
Process Photography:	Farciot Edouart
Music:	Elmer Bernstein
Choreography:	Leroy Prinz and Ruth Godfrey
Second Unit Director:	Arthur Rosson
Assistant Directors:	Francisco Day, Michael Moore, Edward Salven, Daniel McCauley, and Fouard Aref
Associate Producer:	Henry Wilcoxon
Consultants:	Dr. William C. Hayes, Dr. Labib Habachi, Dr. Keith C. Seele, Dr. Ralph Marcus, Dr. George R. Hughes, and Rabbi Rudolph Lupo
Cast:	Charlton Heston (Moses), Yul Brynner (Rameses), Anne Baxter (Nefretiri), Edward G. Robinson (Dathan), Yvonne de Carlo (Sephora), Debra Paget (Lilia), John Derek (Joshua), Vincent Price (Baka), Sir Cedric Hardwicke (Pharaoh), Nina Foch (Bithiah), Martha Scott (Yochabel), Judith Anderson (Memnet)

Released by Paramount Pictures, Incorporated, October 1956
Screening time: Approximately 220 minutes

Note

A remake of the 1923 silent film prologue, this version was filmed in Vista Vision with scenes on location in Egypt. DeMille appeared in a brief introduction before the credits. The film received an Academy Award for best special effects and nominations for best picture, color cinematography, art direction and set decoration, color costumes, editing, and sound recording.

Synopsis

In ancient Egypt, Yoshabel defies the order of the Pharaoh that every manchild born to the Hebrews be put to death and places her infant son in a basket to be set adrift in the river. Bithiah, the Pharaoh's sister, discovers the child, names him Moses, and commands her slave, Memnet, to remain silent about his origin. Several years later, Moses has grown to manhood as an Egyptian and rivals the Pharaoh's son, Rameses, for the affection of the people, the Pharaoh, and the lovely Nefretiri. The Pharaoh is displeased with Rameses's inability to finish construction of the massive new city of Goshen and assigns the task to Moses. While he is supervising work at the building site, Moses rescues from death an old woman whom he does not recognize as his mother and orders more humane treatment of the Hebrew slaves.

Nefretiri learns about Moses's Hebrew origins from Memnet and throws the old woman off the balcony to keep her silent. She is unable to disguise her agitation, however, and discloses the secret to Moses.

Curious about his identity, Moses confronts Bithiah as well as
Yoshabel, goes to work among the Hebrew slaves in the brick pit, and
learns about the myth of the deliverer. Rameses is in fact determined
to discover the identity of the deliverer himself and in so doing become his father's heir. Events at Goshen play into his hands. Baka,
an architect, orders a beautiful Hebrew water bearer named Lilia to be
brought to his house. Joshua, a slave who is in love with Lilia, attempts to rescue her but is overpowered. When Moses kills Baka, Joshua
hails him as the deliverer. Dathan, an informant, has secretly observed
these events and reveals his information to Rameses in exchange for
Baka's house and Lilia. On the day of the Pharaoh's jubilee, Moses is
brought to the throne room in chains. The Pharaoh declares Rameses his
heir and orders Moses's name be stricken from his monuments.

Moses is driven into the desert but miraculously survives and begins a new life among Bedouin shepherds. As time passes, he marries
Sephora, the daughter of a sheik, and she bears him a son. But the
real transformation in his life occurs when he ascends Mount Sinai and
speaks with God. After this miraculous event, he returns to Egypt to
confront Rameses and demand the freedom of his people. Rameses is un-
yielding until a series of spectacular misfortunes, including the death
of his son and heir, afflict him and the Egyptians. On an appointed
day, Moses leads thousands of his joyous people out of Egypt. Nefretiri,
embittered by Moses's rejection of her advances and the death of her son,
goads Rameses into pursuing the Hebrews with his chariots. Rameses expects his men to engage in butchery but instead they are engulfed by
the waters of the Red Sea.

While Moses receives the ten commandments on Mount Sinai, his people are worshipping a golden calf and engaging in bacchanalian revels.
As punishment, they are forced to wander in the wilderness for forty
years. When this period draws to a close, Moses bids farewell to
Sephora and Joshua, whom he appoints as a successor, and ascends a
mountain within sight of the promised land.

IV. Writings about Cecil B. DeMille

1914

71   "The Man from Home." Motion Picture News 20, no. 20 (21
      November):42.
         A positive review of DeMille's fourth film, as well as Lasky
    productions in general.

1915

72   CARR, HARRY C. "Directors: The Men Who Make the Plays."
      Photoplay 8, no. 9 (June):80–85.
         Discussion of early film directors including DeMille; some
    material about his theatrical background.

1917

73   LINDSAY, VACHEL. "Queen of My People." New Republic 11, no.
      140 (7 July):280–81.
         A very laudatory review of Mary Pickford's performance in
    Romance of the Redwoods, one of two films the actress made under
    DeMille's direction.

1918

74   HASKINS, HARRISON. "The Big Six Directors." Motion Picture
      Classic 8, no. 1 (September):16–17, 68.
         An assessment of the work of early film directors including
    DeMille.

75   MISTLEY, MEDIA. "Why Husbands Leave Home." Motion Picture
      Classic 6, no. 5 (July):54–57.
         An account of DeMille's views about marriage and wives.

1919

76   NAYLOR, HAZEL SIMPSON. "The Master of Mastery." Motion Picture
      Magazine 18, no. 10 (November):36-37, 126.
          An interview of DeMille who discusses the beginnings of his
film career and gives his views on women and marriage.

1920

77   "DeMille Discusses New Policy." Motion Picture News 23, no. 1
      (25 December):130.
          Discussion of long-run pictures and Famous Players-Lasky's
new all-star production policy.

78   LOWREY, CAROLYN. The First One Hundred Noted Men and Women of
      the Screen. New York: Moffat, Yard & Co., pp. 46-47.
          Some interesting biographical data and anecdotes about DeMille.

79   MANTLE, BURNS. "The Shadow Stage." Photoplay 17, no. 6 (May):
      64-65.
          An amusing review of Why Change Your Wife? and comments about
the "social sex film."

80   St. JOHNS, ADELA ROGERS. "What Does Marriage Mean?" Photoplay
      19, no. 1 (December):28-31.
          DeMille's views on sex and marriage in response to criticism
about his "sex pictures."

81   NAYLOR, HAZEL SIMPSON. "Kisses According to Cecil B. DeMille."
      Motion Picture Magazine 21, no. 5 (June):28-29, 36.
          A summary of DeMille's views about marriage as occasioned
by the production of The Affairs of Anatol.

82   St. JOHNS, ADELA ROGERS. "More about Marriage." Photoplay 19,
      no. 6 (May):24-26, 105.
          DeMille's views about relationships between men and women.

1922

83   DELLUC, LOUIS. "Les cinéastes: Cecil B. DeMille." Cinéa,
      nos. 63-64, 21 July, p. 11.
          A positive assessment of DeMille's early work, especially
Joan the Woman and The Cheat.

84   MILNE, PETER. Motion Picture Directing. New York: Falk
      Publishing Co., pp. 48-56.
          A very positive assessment of DeMille's early pictures.

1923

85 GOLDWYN, SAMUEL. Behind the Screen. New York: George H. Doran Co., pp. 20-27, 53-54, 86-96.
      A recounting of the formation of the Jesse M. Lasky Feature Play Co. and DeMille's early filmmaking.

86 LANE, TAMAR. What's Wrong with the Movies? Los Angeles: Waverly Co., pp. 64-66.
      A scathing criticism of DeMille's catering to the mass audience.

87 St. JOHNS, ADELA ROGERS. "Cecil and Bill." Photoplay 24, no. 5 (October):50-51, 127-28.
      A description of the different personalities, life styles, and films of the DeMille brothers.

1925

88 "Keep Your Head in Your Feet." Photoplay 28, no. 1 (June):33.
      A description of DeMille's opinions about feminine appearance.

89 MULLETT, MARY B. "How Cecil DeMille Works and What He Knows about Us." American Magazine 100, no. 1 (July):34-35, 131-33, 138, 140-43.
      Colorful anecdotes about DeMille's beginnings in the industry and the filming of various pictures.

90 SHERWOOD, ROBERT. "The Hollywood Zeus." New Yorker 1, no. 40: 11-12.
      An intelligent assessment of DeMille's work as a director.

1926

91 BARRY, IRIS. Let's Go to the Movies. New York: Payson & Clarke, pp. 231-32.
      A very negative review of DeMille's films.

1927

92 "Christ on the Screen." Literary Digest 93, no. 8 (21 May): 31-32.
      A very laudatory review of The King of Kings with reference to the reviews of New York critics.

93 SMITH, FREDERICK. "How Christ Came to Pictures." Photoplay 32, no. 2 (July):39, 118.
      A discussion of the production of The King of Kings.

94 TALMEY, ALLENE. Doug and Mary and Others. With woodcut por-
    traits by Bernard Zadig. New York: Macy-Masius, pp. 138-46.
      Biographical sketches of silent film figures including
    DeMille.

1928

95 HOWARD, CLIFFORD. "Cecil B. DeMille." Close Up 3, no. 2
    (August):41-47.
      A summary of DeMille's early contributions to filmmaking
    (not always accurate) and his attitudes towards a mass audience.

1929

96 THORP, DUNHAM. "Shooting for the Bathtubs." Motion Picture
    Classic 29, no. 4 (June):23, 76.
      An interview with DeMille that focuses on his preaching in
    pictures.

1930

97 SHAFFER, ROSALIND. "I Never Choose Beautiful Women." Photoplay
    38, no. 4 (September):30-31, 114.
      DeMille's views about actresses with whom he has worked.

1932

98 CRUIKSHANK. "Will Russia Rival Hollywood?" Movie Classic 1,
    no. 6 (February):60, 78.
      An interview with DeMille about his travels in Russia and
    the Middle East and his views on the unit production system adopted
    by major studios.

99 SKINNER, RICHARD DANE. "The Screen." Commonweal 17, no. 8
    (21 December):215.
      A lacerating review of The Sign of the Cross for its "inten-
    tional and deliberate hypocrisy" and "profanation of a sacred
    theme."

1934

100 "DeMille's Sixtieth." Time 24, no. 9 (27 August):36.
      A review of DeMille's latest film, Cleopatra, and an assess-
    ment of his status as a director. DeMille's picture appeared on
    the cover.

101 GRANT, JACK. "Are the Movies Guilty? Cecil B. DeMille Speaks
     for the Defense." Motion Picture 48, no. 2 (September):30-31,
     84-85.
         DeMille's views about motion picture censorship.

1935

102 BARDECHE, MAURICE, and BRASILLACH, ROBERT. Histoire du cinéma.
     Paris: Denoël & Steele, pp. 120-21.
         Description of the acclaim afforded Forfaiture (French title
     for The Cheat) upon its release in France and positive assessment
     of DeMille's early films (summary of The Cheat is inaccurate).
     Also a negative discussion of DeMille's twenties films about sex
     appeal, etiquette, and the lives of the rich. (An edition trans-
     lated into English by Iris Barry was published as The History of
     Motion Pictures in 1938.)

103 BOONE, ANDREW R. "Ancient Battles in the Movies." Scientific
     American 153, no. 2 (August):61-63.
         A detailed description of the weaponry, military tactics,
     and sets for the battle scenes used in The Crusades.

104 "Cinema." Time 26, no. 10 (2 September):38.
         A negative review of The Crusades that includes production
     data.

105 St. JOHN BRENAN, AILENE. "New in the Limelight." Stage 12,
     no. 11 (August):53.
         A description of the production of The Crusades and a review
     of DeMille's theatrical and film career.

1936

106 UNITED STATES CIRCUIT COURT OF APPEALS FOR THE NINTH CIRCUIT.
     Commissioner of Internal Revenue, Petitioner, vs. Cecil B.
     DeMille Productions, Inc., Respondent. Transcript of the
     Record, 3 vols. San Francisco: Parker Printing Co.
         Court transcript of tax controversy regarding returns for
     1924-26. Records include personal and corporate tax returns;
     profit and loss sheets; lists of corporate holdings in securities
     and real estate, studio equipment, etc. DeMille's testimony in-
     cludes important business details of his early film career. (Con-
     tent reverses the title and identifies Productions as petitioner
     and Commissioner of Internal Revenue as respondent.)

1937

107 "Movie of the Week: The Plainsman." Life 2, no. 1 (4 January):
     62-68.

Several pages of stills from the film; minimal text as was
standard for this format in the magazine.

108   QUIGLEY, MARTIN. Decency in Motion Pictures. New York:
       Macmillan Co., p. 39.
          A brief description of the erotic dance scene in The Sign of
       the Cross as an example of an "objectionable . . . incident liable
       to an evil audience effect."

109   STALLINGS, LAURENCE. "Four of a Kind." Stage 14, no. 7 (April):
       53-59.
          An essay about four pictures, including The Plainsman, which
       contains perceptive remarks about DeMille's style.

1938

110   FARRAR, GERALDINE. The Autobiography of Geraldine Farrar: Such
       Sweet Compulsion. New York: Graystone Press, pp. 165-88.
          Operatic diva's recollection of starring in six of DeMille's
       early pictures, including his first spectacle, Joan the Woman.

111   "Movie of the Week: The Buccaneer." Life 4, no. 2 (10 January):
       54-57.
          Several captioned stills from the film.

112   ORME, MICHAEL. "The World of the Kinema." Illustrated London
       News 192 (19 February):300.
          A tribute to DeMille on his twenty-fifth year in the movie
       industry. Reviews his part in the organization of the Lasky Co.
       and his films.

1939

113   "Cinema." Time 33, no. 19 (3 May):66-67.
          A review of Union Pacific that includes some anecdotal mate-
       rial and production figures (e.g., DeMille shot 205,000 feet but
       used 12,158 feet in the final cut) and a description of the film's
       premiere at a jubilee celebration in Ogden, Utah.

114   DEMILLE, WILLIAM. Hollywood Saga. New York: E.P. Dutton & Co.,
       passim.
          Recollections of filmmaking during the silent era in Hollywood.
       Contains several references to his brother, Cecil, with whom he
       worked in the early days.

115   "Omaha's Union Pacific Fiesta a Rousing Taste of Old West."
       Newsweek 13, no. 18 (8 May):24-25.
          Description of the premiere of Union Pacific at a jubilee
       celebration of the completion of the transcontinental railroad
       line in Utah.

1940

116   "DeMille and the Madonna." Time 35, no. 17 (22 April):44.
       A report about the objections of the Catholic Church to
DeMille's projected film, The Queen of Queens, the story of the
mother of Christ.

117   PERCEY, HELEN GLADYS. "Union Pacific." Oregon Historical
       Quarterly 41, no. 2 (June):128-32.
       A description of the research undertaken for Union Pacific
by the head of Paramount's research department.

1942

118   "Cinema." Time 39, no. 16 (20 April):86-88.
       A negative review of Reap the Wild Wind and of DeMille's
career as the producer of spectacle films.

119   van RYN, FREDERICK. "When You See Paramount, Remember DeMille."
       Reader's Digest 41, no. 245 (September):35-38.
       An account of DeMille's early career with anecdotal material
about his filmmaking experiences.

1943

120   de ROCHEFORT, CHARLES. Le film de mes souvenirs. Edited by
       Pierre Andrieu. Paris: Société Parisienne d'Edition, pp.
       125-38, 154-57.
       The French actor's recollections of starring as the Pharaoh
in DeMille's first Ten Commandments.

1945

121   "AFRA and Mr. DeMille." New Republic 112, no. 6 (5 February):
       164-65.
       A report about DeMille's controversy with AFRA (American
Federation of Radio Artists) and its litigation in Los Angeles
Superior Court.

122   "DeMille Crusader, Gets Gold Medal." Motion Picture Herald 160,
       no. 13 (29 September):34.
       Description of DeMille's recognition by the American Legion,
which awarded him its gold medal for Americanism, his controversy
with AFRA, and his views about right-to-work laws.

123   "DeMille's Dollar." Newsweek 25, no. 6 (5 February):41-42.
       A report about DeMille's controversy with AFRA.

124   "The One Dollar Issue." Time 65, no. 6 (5 February):53.
        A report about DeMille's controversy with AFRA.

1947

125   "Cinema." Time 50, no. 7 (27 October):99-100.
        A tongue-in-cheek review of Unconquered that includes a re-
capitulation of DeMille's career.

1948

126   WOLL, ALBERT, and GLENN, JAMES A.   "DeMille Loses Again."
        American Federationist 55, no. 1 (January):10-11.
        A report on the latest California court decision regarding
DeMille's lawsuit against AFRA.

1949

127   BAINBRIDGE, JOHN. "Samson, Delilah and DeMille." Life 27, no.
        23 (5 December):138-49.
        An article about the filming of Samson and Delilah.

128   "Cinema." Time 54, no. 9 (29 August):74.
        A description of the promotion campaign for Samson and Delilah.

129   "In the Great Tradition." Newsweek 34, no. 22 (28 November):
        70-72.
        A review of DeMille's career and films with emphasis upon
Samson and Delilah.

1950

130   FELDMAN, JOSEPH, and FELDMAN, HARRY.   "Cecil B. DeMille's Vir-
        tues." Films in Review 1, no. 9 (December):1-6.
        A forceful reply to DeMille's critics. Asserts that DeMille
was a masterful filmmaker whose values and style were appreciated
by a generation maturing before World War I.

131   FOSTER, FREDERICK. "Matts, Miniatures and Meticulous Cinema-
        tography." American Cinematographer 31, no. 3 (March):82-83, 98.
        A discussion of the cinematic techniques used in certain
scenes in Samson and Delilah.

132   POSTER, WILLIAM. "Films." Nation 170, no. 7 (18 February):
        161-62.
        A negative review of Samson and Delilah but also some appre-
ciative remarks about DeMille's craftsmanship and the force of his
personality in shaping his work.

133   SMEAL, COLLIE. "Rock of Hollywood." Colliers 125, no. 8
      (25 February):13, 14, 66.
         A review of DeMille's career. Contains much anecdotal mate-
      rial about his filmmaking experiences.

134   ____. "Man in the Middle of a Spectacle." Colliers 125, no.
      9 (4 March):30-31, 49-50.
         A continuation of the above article about DeMille's filmmak-
      ing career.

135   WACHTEL, LILLIAN. "Good Features Never Die: They're Cut Apart
      and Used in Schools." Films in Review 1, no. 9 (December):28-32.
         A discussion of Land of Liberty, DeMille's composite film
      about American history, and its use in public schools.

                              1951

136   DONIOL-VALCROZE, JACQUES. "Samson, Cecil et Dalila." Cahiers
      du cinéma 1, no. 5 (September):19-30.
         An appreciative reappraisal of DeMille's work, especially
      his spectacle films, occasioned by the release of Samson and
      Delilah.

137   HARCOURT-SMITH, SIMON. "The Siegfried of Sex." Sight and Sound
      19, no. 10 (February):410-12, 424.
         An intelligent reconsideration of DeMille's career which goes
      beyond the usual debunking. Stresses the director's achievements
      (though the plot of The Cheat is incorrect) as well as his peculi-
      arities.

138   ROWAN, ARTHUR. "Filming the Circus." American Cinematographer
      32, no. 12 (December):494-95, 522.
         A discussion of the use of Technicolor's new low-level color
      film and Paramount's remote control incandescent lighting system
      in filming The Greatest Show on Earth.

139   "Stars on the Sawdust." Life 31, no. 1 (2 July):63-66.
         A photo essay about the production of The Greatest Show on
      Earth.

                              1952

140   DEMILLE, AGNES. Dance to the Piper. Boston: Little, Brown &
      Co., pp. 31-41, 141, passim.
         Choreographer's recollections of growing up in Hollywood.
      Includes very perceptive observations about her uncle Cecil's
      personality and style.

141   KORNITZER, BELA. American Fathers and Sons. Hermitage House,
      pp. 65-80.

                              119

Interviews of Cecil and William DeMille, who reminisce about
their childhood and discuss their work.

1953

142   ZUKOR, ADOLPH, with KRAMER, DALE. The Public Is Never Wrong.
       New York: G.P. Putnam's Sons, passim.
          Scattered references to DeMille and his tenure at Paramount.
       Does not refer to DeMille's break with Zukor in 1925 though it
       does to Goldwyn's ouster earlier.

1955

143   "The Big Screws." Sight and Sound 24, no. 5 (Spring):212.
          A query of Hollywood directors, including DeMille, about the
       use of the widescreen.

144   CHITI, ROBERTO, and QUARGNOLO, MARIO. "Revisione di DeMille."
       Bianco e nero 16, no. 8 (August):34-61.
          A detailed chronological and topical recapitulation of
       DeMille's filmmaking career. Includes filmography.

145   CRANE, RALPH. "DeMille Directs His Biggest Spectacle." Life
       39, no. 17 (24 October):142-49.
          A colorful photo essay of the filming of The Ten Commandments
       remake. Photograph of extras on the sets appeared on the cover.

146   "The Director and the Public." Film Culture 1, no. 2 (March-
       April):15-21.
          Report on questionaires answered by several directors includ-
       ing DeMille. DeMille's response is interesting in terms of his
       characterization of the audience.

147   JOHNSON, ALBERT. "The Tenth Muse in San Francisco." Sight and
       Sound 24, no. 3 (January-March):154-56.
          A discussion about DeMille with Mitchell Leisen, who began
       his career as costume designer for the Babylonian sequence in Male
       and Female.

148   LARDNER, JOHN. "While Tolstoy Sleeps." Newsweek 45, no. 8
       (February):66.
          Hedda Hopper's interview with DeMille about uniforms he is
       designing for the new Air Force Academy at Colorado Springs.

149   PICKFORD, MARY. Sunshine and Shadow. Garden City, N.Y.:
       Doubleday & Co., pp. 18-83.
          Autobiography of America's Sweetheart. Includes her recol-
       lections of her unhappy experience working with DeMille on Romance
       of the Redwoods and The Little American.

150   ROBINSON, DAVID. "Spectacle." <u>Sight and Sound</u> 25, no. 1
      (Summer):22-27, 55-56.
          An interesting account of nineteenth century spectacle
      theater and its audience and the screen adaptation of spectacle
      by Italian and American film directors. Includes material about
      DeMille and <u>The Sign of the Cross</u>.

151   VALENTRY, DUANE. "Movie with a Timeless Mission." <u>American
      Mercury</u> 81 (August):123-24.
          A discussion of the durability and timeliness of <u>The King
      of Kings</u> several years after its initial release.

                              <u>1956</u>

152   BAKER, PETER. "Showman for the Millions." <u>Films and Filming</u>
      3, no. 1 (October):9-14.
          A detailed biography of DeMille. Includes filmography.

153   COLE, CLAYTON. "Forget Spectacle--It's the Story That Counts."
      <u>Films and Filming</u> 3, no. 1 (October):7.
          An interview with DeMille who discusses the value of a story
      in filmmaking, technological improvements, stars, and morality.

154   "DeMille's Greatest." <u>Life</u> 41, no. 20 (12 November):115-18.
          An article about <u>The Ten Commandments</u>. Includes stills and
      photographs.

155   DRIVER, TOM. "Hollywood in the Wilderness." <u>Christian Century</u>
      73, no. 48 (28 November):1390-91.
          A scathing review of <u>The Ten Commandments</u> as a picture whose
      "conception, idiom and style" are "exactly opposite from that of
      the Bible." Author deplores the film for excessive reification
      and for its failure to communicate "anything of the internal life
      of man."

156   EVETT, ROBERT. "There Was a Young Fellow from Goshen." <u>New
      Republic</u> 135, no. 24 (10 December):20.
          A better than average review of <u>The Ten Commandments</u> with
      some discussion of the literary sources DeMille used for the pic-
      ture.

157   GRAY, MARTIN. "New Testament for the Old Testament." <u>Films
      and Filming</u> 3, no. 1 (October):8.
          A brief article on the production of <u>The Ten Commandments</u>.

158   HEARN, ARNOLD W. "Movies: Some Commandments Violated."
      <u>Christianity and Crisis</u> 16, no. 20 (26 November):163-64.
          A critical review of <u>The Ten Commandments</u> as "unbiblical",
      especially in its representation of miracles and God "as a cosmic
      combination of Thomas Jefferson and King Kong." Author criticizes

"the way the American churches conceive the central realities of faith and their communication" and finds endorsement of the film by the religious community to be embarassing.

159   HILL, GLADWIN. "Most Colossal of All." New York Times Magazine, 12 August, pp. 16, 18, 20.
       An interview with DeMille who discusses his career as well as his other business interests and his politics.

160   Journal of the Screen Producers Guild 4, no. 1 (February):1-2, 5-9, 20-23.
       Reprints of speeches by DeMille and his colleagues upon his acceptance of the Screen Producers Guild's Milestone Award. See entries 282 and 284.

161   "Mount Sinai to Main Street." Time 68, no. 21 (19 November): 82, 85.
       A report of DeMille's soliciting the endorsement of churchmen for The Ten Commandments.

162   "Mr. DeMille and Moses." Look 20, no. 24 (27 November):77-79.
       A photo essay about the production of The Ten Commandments. Stills from the silent version are compared with those of the remake.

163   NOERDLINGER, HENRY S. Moses and Egypt: The Documentation to the Motion Picture "The Ten Commandments." Los Angeles: University of Southern California Press, 202 pp.
       Research volume compiled during the pre-production phase of the film. Covers topics such as transportation, buildings, sculpture and paintings, costumes, sports and games, etc. Includes bibliography and list of institutions consulted. See entry 283.

164   ROWAN, ARTHUR. "Cinematography Unsurpassed." American Cinematographer 37, no. 11 (November):558-60, 680-83.
       Detailed discussion of the technicalities involved in filming The Ten Commandments.

165   "The Ten Commandments." Time 68, no. 29 (12 November):120, 122, 124.
       A negative review of "the most vulgar movie ever made" describes the Exodus as Sexodus. Gives data about production details.

                                    1957

166   "Cinema." Time 60, no. 21 (18 November):112.
       A report of the total sum grossed by The Ten Commandments upon the first anniversary of its release.

167   GRIFFITH, RICHARD, and MAYER, ARTHUR. The Movies. New York:
       Simon & Schuster, pp. 123-27, passim.
           A well-illustrated discussion of the excesses of DeMille's
       twenties films.

168   HILL, GLADWIN. "C.B. DeMille. Mr. Hollywood." U.S.
       Information Service Feature (December):1-6.
           A brief and sketchy account of DeMille's career.

169   KITCHIN, LAURENCE. "The Ten Commandments." Sight and Sound
       27, no. 3 (Winter):148-49.
           A brief but intelligent review of The Ten Commandments which
       goes beyond the usual debunking.

170   KNIGHT, ARTHUR. The Liveliest Art. New York: Macmillan Co.,
       pp. 117-20, passim.
           A discussion of DeMille's twenties films in terms of the
       moral climate of the era.

171   LASKY, JESSE L., with WELDER, DON. I Blow My Own Horn. Garden
       City, N.Y.: Doubleday & Co., pp. 88-120, 168-70, 228, 250.
           Film entrepreneur's recollections of going into the filmmak-
       ing business with DeMille, Samuel Goldwyn, and Adolph Zukor.

172   "Through Different Eyes." Christian Century 74, no. 1 (2
       January):20-21.
           Responses to a scathing review of The Ten Commandments pub-
       lished earlier, including a letter from a Methodist bishop praising
       the film. See entry 155.

173   BOYD, MALCOLM. Christ and Celebrity Gods: The Church and Mass
       Media. Greenwich, Conn.: Seabury Press, pp. 51-79.
           A thoroughgoing critique of The Ten Commandments, especially
       its reification of the religious spirit, as well as the hoopla in-
       volved in its distribution, by a clergyman who pays especial atten-
       tion to the film's reception among members of the religious com-
       munity.

                                1958

174   "DeMille on DeMille." Newsweek 51, no. 4 (27 January):92.
           An interview with DeMille who discusses The Ten Commandments
       as part of a trilogy and predicts profits.

175   NOLLI, GIANFRANCO. "La Sacra Bibbia secondo Cecil B. DeMille."
       Bianco e nero 19, no. 7 (July):13-19.
           An interesting discussion of factual errors and logical fal-
       lacies in the plot of The Ten Commandments.

176   "The Ten Commandments." <u>Films and Filming</u> 4, no. 4 (January):
        23-24.
            An intelligent review of <u>The Ten Commandments</u>.

                                    <u>1959</u>

177   BOYD, MALCOLM. "God and DeMille in Hollywood." <u>Christian</u>
        <u>Century</u> 76, no. 8 (25 February):230-31.
            A critical and negative view of the popular image of the
        "religious" movie established by DeMille.

178   "C.B." <u>Newsweek</u> 53, no. 5 (2 February):84.
            An obituary column that reviews the highlights of DeMille's
        "Bible and bathtub" career.

179   "Cecil DeMille, 77, Pioneer of Movies, Dead in Hollywood."
        <u>New York Times</u>, 22 January, pp. 1, 31.
            An article reviewing DeMille's career upon his death.

180   "DeMille's Legacy of Epics: His Work and His Life." <u>Life</u> 46,
        no. 5 (2 February):26-30.
            A photo essay of DeMille's career published shortly after
        his death.

181   "Epic-Maker." <u>Time</u> 73, no. 5 (2 February):54.
            An obituary column that reviews DeMille's career as a showman.

182   <u>Homenaje a Cecil B. DeMille</u>. Filmoteca Nacional de España. Para
        la IV Semana Internacional de Cine Religioso en Valladolid.
        April, 34 pp.
            An interesting and perceptive discussion of the visual style
        of DeMille's films, a brief biography, material about the produc-
        tion of <u>The Ten Commandments</u>, and a filmography.

183   KOURY, PHIL A. <u>Yes, Mr. DeMille</u>. New York: G.P. Putnam's Sons,
        319 pp.
            An irreverent and entertaining account of DeMille's career
        by a former staff member. Contains interesting perceptions about
        DeMille's perscnality.

184   QUARGNOLO, MARIO. "DeMille: dopo di noi (forse) il diluvio."
        <u>Bianco e nero</u> 20, no. 4 (April):v-viii.
            A concise review of DeMille's career which stresses the di-
        rector's use of spectacle for didactic purposes.

185   WEALES, GERALD. "The Gospel according to DeMille." <u>Reporter</u>
        21, no. 11 (24 December):38-40.
            A review of DeMille's posthumously published autobiography.

1960

186   ROBINSON, DAVID. "The Autobiography of Cecil B. DeMille."
      Sight and Sound 29, no. 4 (Autumn):203-4.
         A very perceptive review of DeMille's posthumously published
      autobiography. See entry 286.

1961

187   GOODMAN, EZRA. The Fifty Year Decline and Fall of Hollywood.
      New York: Simon & Schuster, pp. 199-201.
         A brief summary of DeMille's career as a director who gained
      more prominence than the stars.

1962

188   WAGENKNECHT, EDWARD. The Movies in the Age of Innocence.
      Norman, Okla.: University of Oklahoma Press, pp. 207-19, passim.
         A brief discussion of DeMille's silent comedies and melo-
      dramas about domestic life and consumption.

1963

189   MYERS, HORTENSE, and BURNETT, RUTH. Cecil B. DeMille, Young
      Dramatist. Indianapolis and New York: Bobbs-Merrill Co., 200
      pp.
         A very interesting biography of DeMille designed for ele-
      mentary school children. Emphasis is upon the director's childhood.

190   SARRIS, ANDREW. "The American Cinema." Film Culture, no. 28
      (Spring), pp. 18-19.
         Sarris's famous article about auteurism as the basis for
      classifying the work of film directors; brief consideration of
      DeMille under the category, "Third Line." (An expanded version of
      this article under the same title was published as a book in 1968.)
      See entry 206.

1964

191   DEMILLE, AGNES. "Goodnight, C.B." Esquire 61, no. 1 (January):
      119-32.
         Choreographer's perceptive essay about her uncle's personal-
      ity and career.

192   MILLER, DON. "Films on TV." Films in Review 15, no. 2 (February):
      110-12.
         A negative review of "The World's Greatest Showman," a ninety-
      minute tribute to DeMille televised by NBC on 1 December 1963.

193   RIEUPEYROUT, JEAN-LOUIS. La grande aventure du western. Paris: Les Editions du Cerf, pp. 101-3.
     A positive evaluation of DeMille's contribution to the western genre with emphasis upon The Squaw Man, The Virginian, The Plainsman, and Union Pacific.

194   SCHICKEL, RICHARD. Movies. New York: Basic Books, pp. 46, 93-94, 101, 106, 167, 169.
     A discussion of DeMille as a commercial director sensitive to shifts in the public mood.

1965

195   BICKFORD, CHARLES. Bulls, Balls, Bicycles and Actors. New York: P.S. Eriksson, pp. 157-78, 190-216.
     Actor's recollections of working with DeMille in the director's early sound films.

196   von STERNBERG, JOSEF. Fun in a Chinese Laundry. New York: Macmillan Co., pp. 37-38.
     A brief but interesting observation of DeMille's style as a director.

1966

197   WALKER, ALEXANDER. The Celluloid Sacrifice: Aspects of Sex in the Movies. London: Michael Joseph, pp. 27-32.
     A useful summary of moviemaking trends established by DeMille during the teens and twenties, especially his treatment of sex and morality. (A paperback version of this work titled Sex in the Movies was published by Penguin Books in 1968.)

1967

198   ARTHUR, ART. "C.B. DeMille's Human Side." Films in Review 18, no. 4 (April):221-25.
     A recounting of the author's experience as a member of DeMille's publicity and advertising staff in the fifties.

199   Présence du cinéma. Cecil B. DeMille: Journal de 1966, nos. 24-25 (Autumn):77 pp.
     Issue devoted to DeMille contains a foreword by Jacques Lourcelles, a biography and production credits which are not always accurate, a synopsis of films by Pierre Guinle, and the director's opinions about various subjects (e.g. censorship, stars) in an appendix. A few movie and production stills are included.

1968

200 BAXTER, JOHN. Hollikood in the Thirties. New York: A.S.
     Barnes & Co., pp. 34-38.
          Generally, a positive evaluation of DeMille's thirties films,
     especially the spectacles.

201 BROWNLOW, KEVIN. The Parades Gone By. New York: Alfred A.
     Knopf, pp. 179-88.
          A discussion of DeMille's career in terms of his lapse from
     the artistry of the early silents, a point attributed to Agnes
     deMille, and his gaudy films of the twenties.

202 FORD, CHARLES. "Cecil B. DeMille." Anthologie du cinéma. Paris:
     L'Avant-Scene-C.I.B., pp. 1-56.
          A detailed, chronological reconsideration of DeMille's entire
     work. Stresses both his strengths and weaknesses as a director.
     Includes filmography with English and French titles.

203 JACOBS, LEWIS. The Rise of the American Film. New York:
     Teachers College Press, pp. 335-42, passim.
          A useful discussion of DeMille's film career up to the late
     thirties in terms of the director's responsiveness to the public
     and his significance in American social history. Devalues DeMille's
     work in any aesthetic sense. Contains some inaccuracies, espe-
     cially regarding The Cheat. (First edition of this work was pub-
     lished by Harcourt, Brace & Co. in 1939.)

204 MOURLET, MICHEL, with MARMIN, MICHEL. Cecil B. DeMille. Paris:
     Editions Seghers, 188 pp.
          Work includes a biography and a discussion of DeMille's ca-
     reer; a critical essay by Marmin; and DeMille's observations about
     various subjects (e.g., acting, spectacles and historical films,
     adaptations, etc); a translation of part of the script of The
     Greatest Show on Earth; statements made about DeMille by French
     critics, colleagues, and acquaintances; a filmography including
     some production credits and cast lists; a bibliography.

205 ROBINSON, DAVID. Hollywood in the Twenties. New York: A.S.
     Barnes & Co., pp. 86-90, passim.
          A discussion of DeMille's cycle of "socio-sexual" films and
     spectacles of the twenties. (A later version edited by Peter Cowie
     was published under the same title by Paperback Library in 1970.)

206 SARRIS, ANDREW. American Cinema. New York: E.P. Dutton & Co.,
     pp. 90-91.
          A brief discussion of DeMille's ranking "On the Far Side of
     Paradise" as an auteur. Expanded version of article with the same
     title published in Film Culture in 1963. See entry 190.

1969

207   BOND, KIRK. "Eastman House Journal." Film Culture, no. 47
      (Summer), pp. 42-48.
          A thoughtful reconsideration of DeMille's silent films,
      especially Carmen and The Cheat, praised for lighting, composition,
      and editing.

208   EVERSON, WILLIAM K. A Pictorial History of the Western Film.
      New York: Citadel Press, pp. 59, 161-66.
          A brief discussion of DeMille's blockbuster, sound westerns,
      The Plainsman and Union Pacific; the latter especially is praised
      as a film superior to John Ford's silent, The Iron Horse.

209   FRENCH, PHILIP. The Movie Moguls. Chicago: Henry Regnery Co.,
      passim.
          Several references to DeMille with emphasis upon his silent
      period.

210   RINGGOLD, GENE, and BODEEN, DeWITT. The Films of Cecil B. DeMille.
      Secaucus, N.J.: Citadel Press, 373 pp.
          Production credits, casts, plot synopses, and selected reviews
      of DeMille's films; movie and production stills. Contains a few in-
      accuracies but proves very useful. Includes a list of the Lux Radio
      Theater broadcasts hosted by DeMille from 1 June 1936 to 22 January
      1945.

211   "A Tribute to--and from Hollywood's Greatest Showman." American
      Cinematographer 50, no. 1 (January):58-60, 123-25, 136-37, 140.
          A summary of DeMille's career with emphasis upon his contri-
      bution to technical developments. Also a reprint of DeMille's
      speech on the occasion of the American Society of Cinematographer's
      twenty-fifth birthday party in 1946. See entry 288.

212   ZIEROLD, NORMAN. The Moguls. New York: Coward-McCann, pp.
      131-33, 166-80.
          A recounting of DeMille's career that includes some amusing
      anecdotal material.

1970

213   ESSOE, GABE, and LEE, RAYMOND. DeMille: The Man and His
      Pictures. New York: A.S. Barnes & Co., 311 pp.
          A lightweight treatment of DeMille's career which is most
      useful for its numerous stills and photographs. Appendix contain
      essays about the director by various persons who worked with him.

214   HAMPTON, BENJAMIN B. A History of the American Film Industry.
      New York: Dover Publications, passim.
          An excellent discussion, though scattered throughout the book,
      of the significance of DeMille's role in the history of silent films.

(Work was first published as A History of the Movies by Covici Friede in 1931.)

1971

215   SPEARS, JACK. Hollywood: The Golden Era. South Brunswick and
      New York: A.S. Barnes & Co., pp. 22-23, 174-76.
      A brief discussion of two of DeMille's World War I films,
Joan the Woman and The Little American, and the director's uneasy
relationship with superstar, Mary Pickford, who starred in the
latter film.

1972

216   KAUFFMANN, STANLEY, with HENSTELL, BRUCE. American Film
      Criticism. New York: Liveright, pp. 74-77, 149-50, passim.
         Reprints of a positive review of DeMille's first Squaw Man
in Moving Picture World and Robert Sherwood's appreciative consideration of the first Ten Commandments.

217   MANVELL, ROGER, ed. The International Encyclopedia of Film.
      New York: Crown Publishers, p. 157.
      A brief but useful review of DeMille's career.

1973

218   CHIERICHETTI, DAVID. Hollywood Director: The Career of Mitchell
      Leisen. New York: Curtis Books, pp. 22-28.
         Leisen's interesting recollections of his experience as
DeMille's costume designer and art director during the twenties.

219   DEMILLE, AGNES. Speak to Me, Dance with Me. Boston: Little,
      Brown & Co., passim.
         Choreographer's recounting of her unpleasant experience while
working for her uncle on Cleopatra and observations about his personality and career.

220   FLEMING, ALICE. "Cecil B. DeMille." The Moviemakers. New York:
      St. Martin's Press, pp. 52-68.
      A breezy summary of DeMille's film career.

221   GAULIER, PATRICK. "Une aventure de Buffalo Bill." La revue du
      cinéma, no. 269, pp. 149-51.
         An interesting analysis of The Plainsman as an unconventional
work of demystification.

222   HASKELL, MOLLY. From Reverence to Rape. New York: Holt,
      Rinehart & Winston, pp. 76-77, passim.

A brief discussion of DeMille's contribution to the "woman's film" genre.

223   HIGHAM, CHARLES. The Art of the American Film. Garden City, N.Y.: Doubleday & Co., pp. 49–52, 114–19.
A brief summary of DeMille's silent film career with emphasis on The Cheat, Joan the Woman, the Biblical spectacles, and the sex comedies.

224   _____. Cecil B. DeMille. New York: Charles Scribner's Sons, 335 pp.
To date, the best available biography of DeMille but hurriedly written and not always accurate. Based upon DeMille papers now housed at Brigham Young University.

225   LASKY, JESSE L., Jr. Whatever Happened to Hollywood? New York: Funk & Wagnalls, passim.
An entertaining and frequently hilarious account of the author's experience as one of DeMille's scriptwriters for the sound epics.

226   MAIRAL, JEAN-CLAUDE. "Notes sur deux films hollywoodiens." La revue du cinéma, no. 269, pp. 111–22.
A Cahiers du cinéma-style reading of The Plainsman and Young Mr. Lincoln with emphasis on the socioeconomic conditions prevailing in the industry and country during the thirties, as well as on the film itself.

227   PRATT, GEORGE. Spellbound in Darkness. Greenwich, Conn.: New York Graphic Society, pp. 238–46.
Excerpts from selected articles and reviews about DeMille's work that first appeared in film magazines and newspapers during the teens and twenties. (A first edition was published under the same title by the University of Rochester in two volumes in 1966.)

228   ROSEN, MARJORIE. Popcorn Venus. New York: Coward, McCann & Geoghegan, pp. 63–67, passim.
An inaccurate discussion of DeMille's attitude towards women; also discusses his Jazz Age films.

229   SADOUL, GEORGES. Dictionary of Film Makers. Translated and edited by Peter Morris. Berkeley and Los Angeles: University of California Press, pp. 59–60.
An appreciative account of DeMille's work with reference to Louis Delluc's essay about the director. See entry 83.

1974

230   BEYLIE, CLAUDE. "Le signe de la croix et Samson et Dalila." Ecran, no. 29 (October), pp. 75–76.

A reconsideration of The Sign of the Cross and Samson and Delilah as the works of "un très grand cinéaste."

231   CARY, JOHN. Spectacular: The Story of Epic Films. Edited by
      John Kobal. London: Hamlyn, pp. 24-43.
          An oversized book with large, color foldout illustrations
      from DeMille's spectacles and a brief text.

232   DORR, JOHN. "The Griffith Tradition." Film Comment 10, no. 2
      (March-April):48-52.
          An intelligent analysis of the work of various directors in-
      cluding DeMille, who continued Griffith's narrative tradition in
      American film.

233   HOCHMAN, STANLEY, ed. A Library of Film Criticism: American
      Film Directors. New York: Frederick Ungar, pp. 80-89.
          An excellent selection of excerpts from various film reviews
      and articles printed about DeMille through the decades.

                                1975

234   SECOND, JACQUES. "Les Livres." Positif, no. 167 (March), pp.
      86-87.
          An intelligent review of three works about DeMille (Charles
      Higham's Cecil B. DeMille, Jesse L. Lasky, Jr.,'s Whatever Happened
      to Hollywood?, and David Chierchietti's Hollywood Director: The
      Career of Mitchell Leisen) by a French critic who regards DeMille
      as one of "les plus grand metteurs en scène américains." See en-
      tries 223-25.

235   SKLAR, ROBERT. Movie Made America. New York: Random House,
      pp. 91-97, passim.
          An assessment of DeMille's significance as a director during
      the silent and early sound period.

236   WOOD, MICHAEL. America in the Movies. New York: Basic Books,
      pp. 165-68.
          An interesting and insightful analysis of the ideological
      significance of fifties spectacle films. Contains a section on
      DeMille and The Ten Commandments.

                                1976

237   KOSZARSKI, RICHARD, ed. The Rivals of D.W. Griffith: Alternate
      Auteurs 1913-1918. Minneapolis: Walter Art Center, pp. 43-46.
          Catalog for a film series that included The Cheat. Contains
      a brief discussion of the film by Marshall Deutelbaum and two
      lengthy excerpts from very positive reviews printed at the time
      of the film's release.

238   MARX, ARTHUR. <u>Goldwyn: A Biography of the Man behind the Myth</u>.
      New York: W.W. Norton & Co., pp. 29-67, passim.
           An account of Goldwyn's professional relationship with DeMille,
      especially in the early days of the Lasky Company.

239   MAST, GERALD. <u>A Short History of the Movies</u>. Indianapolis:
      Bobbs-Merrill Co., pp. 129-32.
           A discussion contrasting the films of DeMille with those of
      Erich von Stroheim. Includes an extended and negative analysis of
      <u>Male and Female</u>.

240   McCREARY, EUGENE. "Louis Delluc, Film Theorist, Critic, and
      Prophet." <u>Cinema Journal</u> 16, no. 1 (Fall):14-35.
           Reference to the significance of DeMille's silent films,
      especially <u>The Cheat</u>, for Delluc as a film theorist.

241   PARRISH, ROBERT. <u>Growing Up in Hollywood</u>. New York: Harcourt,
      Brace, Jovanovich, pp. 89-92, 201-10.
           A recollection of the author's experience as an extra and
      actor in DeMille's films; also an account of DeMille's attempt to
      oust Joseph Mankiewicz from the presidency of the Screen Directors
      Guild in the fifties.

242   PERLMUTTER, RUTH. "For God, Country and Whoppee: DeMille and
      the Floss." <u>Film Comment</u> 12, no. 1 (January-February):24-27.
           A perceptive analysis of the themes and visual style of
      DeMille's silent films.

                                    1977

243   D'AMICO, JAMES. "Beasts and Angels: The Forbears of Dirty
      Harry and Clean Billy." <u>Journal of Popular Film</u> 6, no. 2,
      pp. 141-55.
           A study of <u>This Day and Age</u> as a thirties film with fascist
      overtones.

                                    1978

244   ECKERT, CHARLES. "The Carole Lombard in Macy's Window."
      <u>Quarterly Review of Film Studies</u> 3, no. 1 (Winter):1-23.
           An interesting and detailed account of the role of films in
      promoting consumption during the thirties; some consideration of
      the significance of DeMille's pictures in pioneering "a cinematic
      style . . . perfectly tailored to the audience's desire to see the
      rich detail of furnishings and clothes."

245   HIGASHI, SUMIKO. <u>Virgins, Vamps and Flappers: The American
      Silent Movie Heroine</u>. Montreal: Eden Press, pp. 132-42.
           A study of DeMille's heroines within the context of the
      socioeconomic changes of the Jazz Age.

                                    132

246   SCORSESE, MARTIN. "Martin Scorsese's Guilty Pleasures." <u>Film
      Comment</u> 14, no. 5 (September–October):63.
          Director's brief discussion of <u>The Ten Commandments</u>, a film
      viewed "forty or fifty times," as one of his favorite spectacles.

247   SOLOMON, JON. <u>The Ancient World in the Cinema</u>. South Brunswick,
      N.J.: A.S. Barnes & Co., pp. 42–44, 85–101, 112–13.
          An illustrated discussion of DeMille's spectacles, especially
      <u>Cleopatra</u>, both <u>Ten Commandments</u>, <u>The King of Kings</u>, and <u>Samson and
      Delilah</u> with emphasis upon the achievement of certain visual effects.

1979

248   "The Approach to Create: James Wong Howe." In <u>"Image" on the
      Art and Evolution of the Film</u>. Edited by Marshall Deutelbaum.
      New York: Dover Publications, pp. 225–27.
          Interview by George C. Pratt. Interesting anecdotal material
      about the cinematographer's early days as an assistant to Alvin
      Wyckoff, DeMille's cameraman.

249   CARD, JAMES. "The Silent Films of Cecil B. DeMille." In <u>"Image
      on the Art and Evolution of the Film</u>. Edited by Marshall
      Deutelbaum. New York: Dover Publications, pp. 118–19.
          A positive reappraisal of DeMille's silent films by the former
      film curator of George Eastman House.

250   COCTEAU, JEAN. <u>Mes monstres sacrés</u>. Edited by Edouart Dermit
      and Bertrand Meyer. Paris: Encre Editions, p. 76.
          A tribute to DeMille that focuses on <u>The Cheat</u> as does most
      French criticism about the director.

1980

251   CLARENS, CARLO. "Cecil B. DeMille." In <u>Cinema: A Critical
      Dictionary</u>. <u>The Major Film Makers</u>. Vol. 1. Edited by Richard
      Roud. Norwich: Fletcher & Sons, pp. 265–71.
          An intelligent and appreciative reassessment of DeMille's
      work.

252   EDMONDS, I.G., and MIMURA, REIKO. <u>Paramount Pictures and the
      People Who Made Them</u>. San Diego and New York: A.S. Barnes &
      Co., passim.
          A lightweight discussion of DeMille's career in relation to
      the growth of Paramount studios and its history.

253   MAY, LARY. <u>Screening Out the Past</u>. New York: Oxford University
      Press, pp. 200–236.
          An interesting analysis of the significance of DeMille's films
      in relation to post–World War I consumerism. Several inaccuracies
      about film plots and a few about DeMille.

254 SWANSON, GLORIA. Swanson on Swanson. New York: Random House,
     passim.
          Actress's recounting of her silent film career under the
     tutelage of "Mr. DeMille," to whom she owed her status as a super-
     star. Contains interesting anecdotal material.

                                  1981

255 BODEEN, DeWITT. "Cecil B. DeMille." Films in Review 32, no. 7
     (August-September):385-97.
          A recapitulation of DeMille's career, mostly via plot synopses
     of random films, on the occasion of the hundredth anniversary of the
     director's birth. Contains factual errors (e.g., Jeanie Macpherson
     is not credited in the text for her work on the scenarios of The
     Cheat and The Heart of Nora Flynn) and oversimplifications about
     DeMille's status as a director in various studios and companies.
     Includes a filmography.

256 CAMPBELL, RICHARD, and PITTS, MICHAEL R. The Bible in Film:
     A Checklist 1897-1980. Metuchen, N.J.: Scarecrow Press, pp.
     17-18, 27-30, 37-41, 105-8.
          A reference work about Biblical pictures that lists produc-
     tion credits and cast and contains a plot summary and critique for
     the following DeMille films: The Ten Commandments (1923), Samson
     and Delilah, The Ten Commandments (1956), and The King of Kings.
     Contains inaccuracies and typographical errors.

257 THOMSON, DAVID. A Biographic Dictionary of Film. 2d ed. New
     York: William Morrow & Co., pp. 142-43.
          A review of DeMille's career which downplays his spectacles
     (Cleopatra is confused with The Sign of the Cross) but praises his
     frontier epics.

                                  1982

258 CANBY, VINCENT. "Cecil B. DeMille's 'Madam Satan.'" New York
     Times, 26 September, p. 55.
          A review of DeMille's only musical, selected for a retrospec-
     tive screening at the New York Film Festival. Critic agrees with
     the original Times review by Mordaunt Hall who panned the film.

259 EWEN, STUART, and EWEN, ELIZABETH. Channels of Desire: Mass
     Images and the Shaping of American Consciousness. New York:
     McGraw-Hill, pp. 99-102.
          A discussion of DeMille's sex comedies and melodramas in
     terms of the impact of these films upon immigrant women adjusting
     to "the new logic of consumption."

260   RICKEY, CARRIE. "Retro Spectives." <u>Village Voice</u>, 5 October,
        p. 48.
          A positive review of a retrospective screening of <u>Madam Satan</u>
at the New York Film Festival. Critic discusses film as "an ambitious boudoir drama," a "casebook of 30's sexuality and class structure," and a work that is "aesthetically avant-garde and socio-
logically status quo."

261   STEIN, ELLIOTT. "The Twentieth New York Film Festival." <u>Film
        Comment</u> 18, no. 6 (November-December):69.
          A negative review of the retrospective showing of <u>Madam Satan</u>
at the film festival. Critic describes musical as "talky and dull"
but containing "one of the great nut sequences in American cinema"
(a reference to the finale in which the cast parachutes off a doomed
dirigible).

1983

262   HEAD, EDITH, and CALISTRO, PADDY. <u>Edith Head's Hollywood</u>. New
        York: E.P. Dutton, pp. 80-88.
          Academy Award-winning designer, who won one of her Oscars for
the costumes in <u>Samson and Delilah</u>, recalls with acerbity her unhappy experience as a DeMille employee.

263   MANDELL, P.R. "Parting the Red Sea." <u>American Cinematographer</u>
        64, no. 4 (April):46-52, 124.
          An interesting and technically detailed discussion of <u>The Ten
Commandments</u> as a fifties, "state of the art," special effects film.

264   SAID, EDWARD W. "Egyptian Rites." <u>Village Voice</u>, 30 August,
        pp. 43-44, 46.
          A discussion about the negative portrayal of Egypt in the
United States; some consideration of DeMille's <u>Ten Commandments</u>,
especially its ideological implications.

265   WOLFE, CHARLES. "Cecil B. DeMille." In <u>American Directors</u>.
        Vol. 1. Edited by Jean Pierre Coursodon. With Pierre Sauvage.
        New York: McGraw-Hill, pp. 91-99.
          An interesting and perceptive discussion of DeMille's career
in terms of the director's penchant for spectacle and self-theatricalization and his interest in the Biblical and historical past.

1984

266   CANBY, VINCENT. "For DeMille, Moses' Egypt Was Really America."
        <u>New York Times</u>, 25 March, Arts and Leisure, pp. 19, 22.
          A positive review of <u>The Ten Commandments</u> projected for re-
release during the Easter season. Critic describes film as "American
as apple pie and the striptease" and attributes to the director a
"basic if primitive storytelling genius."

267   D'ARC, JAMES V. "The Squaw Man." <u>Magill's Cinema Annual 1984</u>.
       Englewood Cliffs, N.J.: Salem Press.
            A reconsideration of DeMille's first film in terms of the
       many conflicting accounts about its plot and production details.
       (Not yet published at time of this writing.)

268   GUSSOW, MEL. "A Look at 'The deMille Dynasty.'" <u>New York Times</u>,
       27 April, p. C11.
            A review of an exhibit about three generations of deMilles on
       display at the New York Public Library at Lincoln Center. Guest
       curator Louise Kerz organized the exhibit which focused upon the
       careers of Cecil and Agnes.

                                <u>1985-86</u>

269   KOBAL, JOHN. <u>DeMille and His Artists</u>. New York: Alfred A.
       Knopf, Inc.
            A biography that reconsiders the director in terms of his
       association with artists, especially those who worked on the set
       and costume designs of his productions. Includes photos and re-
       productions of sketches, paintings, etc. (Not yet published at
       the time of this writing; publication date and title as well as
       content are projections.)

V . Writings by Cecil B. DeMille

Although the material below was attributed to DeMille, most likely it was written by members of his staff. As was his custom in supervising the details of any phase of a film production, DeMille probably reviewed and approved the final version.

1926

270 "Motion Pictures of Tomorrow." Motion Picture Director, July, pp. 22-23.
DeMille's views about the role of movie stars, the international dimension of film, and future technological improvements in filmmaking.

1927

271 "Building a Photoplay." In The Story of Films. Edited by Joseph P. Kennedy. Chicago and New York: A.W. Shaw Co., pp. 123-50.
DeMille's address before the Harvard Graduate School of Business about the myriad aspects of filmmaking.

1934

272 "How I Make a Spectacle." Photoplay 46, no. 5 (October):43, 99-100.
A description of the preproduction phase of Cleopatra.

1945

273 "Must Union Members Give Up Their American Rights?" Reader's Digest 47, no. 279 (July):93-94.
A political tirade against AFRA (American Federation of Radio

Artists) with whom DeMille quarreled about its stand on right to work laws in California.

274   "My Favorite Tree." <u>American Forests</u> 51, no. 3 (March):99.
A discussion of the oak trees on the director's famed ranch, Paradise, in San Fernando Valley.

275   "Stand Up and Be Counted: Control of Right to Work Un-American." <u>Vital Speeches</u> 12, no. 2 (1 November):48-51.
A condemnation of union members lobbying against right to work laws. Delivered on the steps of Federal Hall in New York City at the invitation of the American Legion and The Bill of Rights Commemorative Society on 25 September 1945.

1946

276   "Cecil B. DeMille Writes about the Movies." <u>Film Review</u>. Edited by Maurice Speed. London: MacDonald & Co., pp. 25-26.
DeMille's thoughts about the responsibility of the motion picture industry to produce pictures that are inspirational and meaningful for the audience.

277   "A House United." <u>Vital Speeches</u> 13, no. 5 (15 December):151-52.
A political speech about DeMille's dispute with AFRA, his views about right to work laws, and the purpose of the DeMille Foundation. Delivered at the annual meeting of the Western Growers Association in Los Angeles, California on 20 November 1946.

278   "Le sex-appeal au cinéma." In <u>Anthologie du cinéma</u>. Edited by Marcel Lapierre. Paris: La Nouvelle Edition, pp. 117-21.
A defense of the portrayal of sexual attraction on the screen, though sexual attractiveness is described in terms of stereotyped, feminine attributes.

1948

279   "While Rome Burns: The Right to Work." <u>Vital Speeches</u> 14, no. 16 (1 June):495-97.
A political speech about right to work laws. Delivered before The Economic Club in Detroit, Michigan, on 19 April 1948.

1950

280   "Cecil B. DeMille Speaking."
A weekly, syndicated column for General Features Corporation that appeared in newspapers across the country during 1950-51. DeMille's filmmaking experience was the source of various topics.

1955

281   Foreword to <u>Sunshine and Shadow</u>, by Mary Pickford. Garden City,
      N.Y.: Doubleday & Co., pp. 9–13.
          A gracious remembrance of the director's professional and
      personal relationship with Pickford though the actress indicates
      later in the autobiography that she was unhappy about their col-
      laboration on two films.

1956

282   "After Seventy Pictures." <u>Films in Review</u> 8, no. 3 (March):
      97–102.
          DeMille's acceptance speech upon receiving the Milestone Award
      of the Screen Producers Guild. See entry 160.

283   Introduction to <u>Moses and Egypt: The Documentation to the
      Motion Picture "The Ten Commandments,"</u> by Henry S. Noerdlinger.
      Los Angeles: University of Southern California Press, pp. 1–3.
          DeMille's remarks about the massive research required for the
      filming of <u>The Ten Commandments</u>. See entry 163.

284   "A Man Is No Better Than What He Leaves behind Him." <u>Journal of
      the Screen Producers Guild</u> 4, no. 1 (February):5–7, 20–21.
          DeMille's acceptance speech upon receiving the Milestone
      Award of the Screen Producers Guild. See entry 160.

1958

285   "How to Be a Critic." <u>Films and Filming</u> 4, no. 6 (March):11.
          DeMille's response to critics who ridicule his pictures and
      a plea for more critical awareness of film's mass audience.

1959

286   <u>The Autobiography of Cecil B. DeMille</u>. Edited by Donald Hayne.
      Englewood Cliffs, N.J.: Prentice-Hall, 440 pp.
          DeMille's weighty, posthumously published autobiography ren-
      dered in patriarchal tones. Contains useful information about his
      career but is only indirectly revealing about his personality and
      private life. See entries 185 and 186.

287   "DeMille's Epic Story of Film's First Epic." <u>Life</u> 47, no. 16
      (19 October):152–68.
          An excerpt from DeMille's autobiography. Focuses on his be-
      ginnings in the film industry.

1969

288   "A Tribute to--and from Hollywood's Greatest Showman." <u>American</u>
      <u>Cinematographer</u> 50, no. 1 (January):125, 136-37, 140.
           A reprint of DeMille's speech at the twenty-fifth birthday
      party of the American Society of Cinematographers. See entry 211.

1976

289   "The Public Is Always Right." In <u>Hollywood Directors 1914-1940</u>.
      Edited by Richard Koszarski. New York: Oxford University Press,
      pp. 161-70.
           A reprint of an article that initially appeared in <u>The Ladies'</u>
      <u>Home Journal</u> in September 1927. DeMille recollects advances in
      filmmaking techniques in relation to audience response.

1985

290   <u>The Autobiography of Cecil B. DeMille</u>. New York: Garland.
           A reprint of the director's posthumously published auto-
      biography first published by Prentice-Hall in 1959. (Not yet pub-
      lished at the time of this writing.) See entry 286.

VI. Miscellaneous Career Data

291 <u>THEATRICAL CAREER</u>.
      Details about DeMille's theatrical career are few. The following chronology was compiled on the basis of material at the New York Public Library and in the William deMille Collection at the University of Southern California. Also helpful were DeMille's autobiography and research done by George C. Pratt, whose source was <u>The New York Dramatic Mirror</u>. Plays were not necessarily produced in New York and in fact were mostly performed in one night stands on the road.

1899   <u>The Fan</u>. Actor.
       <u>Put to the Test</u>. Actor
1900   <u>La père prodigue</u>. Actor.
       <u>Mas'r Van</u>. Actor.
       <u>A Repentance</u>. Actor.
       <u>The Coxcomb</u>. Actor.
       <u>Hearts Are Trump</u>. Actor
1901   <u>To Have and to Hold</u>. Actor.
       <u>Are You a Mason?</u> Actor.
       <u>Alice of Old Vincennes</u>. Actor.
1902- <u>His Grace the Janitor</u>. Actor.
1903   <u>Mistakes Will Happen</u>. Actor.
       <u>Nell Gwynne</u>. Actor.
       <u>Lord Chumley</u>. Actor.
       <u>If I Were King</u>. Actor.
       <u>Hamlet</u>. Actor.
1903- <u>A Gentleman of France</u>. Actor.
1904
1904   <u>The Genius</u>. Writer (with William deMille).
1904- <u>The Missourians</u>. Actor.
1905
1905   Lord Chumley. Actor.
       <u>My Wife's Husbands</u>. Actor.
       Summer stock in Elitch Gardens, Denver. Actor.
          <u>A Japanese Nightingale</u>
          <u>The Maneuvers of Jane</u>
          <u>Hearts Courageous</u>
          <u>As You Like It</u>
          <u>Mice and Men</u>

Dorothy Vernon of Haddon Hall
Tess of the D'Urbervilles
The Taming of the Shrew
Ingomar
Madame Sans Gene
When Knighthood Was in Flower
Under Two Flags

1905– The Prince Chap. Actor.
1906 The Genius and the Model. Writer (with William deMille).
1906 Standard Opera Company. Stage manager and director.

The Bohemian Girl
Martha
The Chimes of Normandy
The Mikado

Son of the Winds. Writer (with William deMille).
1907 The Warrens of Virginia. Actor.
Kit. Writer.
The Man's the King. Writer.
1908 The Royal Mounted. Writer (with William deMille).
The Duelist. Writer.
DeMille Players. Organized company that toured Argentina.
1909 Church Play. Writer (with William deMille).
The Wishing Ring. Actor
1910 The Land of the Free. Producer.
The Stampede. Producer. Also writer (with Lillian Buckingham).
The Return of Peter Grimm. Writer (with David Belasco).
1911 Speed. Producer.
California. Writer of book.
1912 After Five. Writer (with William deMille).
The Antique Girl. Writer of book and lyrics (with William
Le Baron).
The Marriage-Not. Director.
In the Barracks. Writer of book and lyrics (with William
Le Baron).
Cheer Up. Producer.
1913 An Unfinished Play. Writer (with William deMille).
The Reckless Age. Writer.
After Five. Writer (with William deMille).
The Water Cure. Writer of dialogue (with Mary Roberts
Rinehart).

292 LASKY FILM PRODUCTIONS
    As director-general of the Jesse L. Lasky Feature Play
Company and then Famous Players-Lasky (later Paramount) during the
beginning of his film career, DeMille supervised a number of productions but soon became too busy with his own films. The following is an incomplete list of films which he supervised, partially
directed, or assisted in some capacity.

1914 Brewster's Millions
Cameo Kirby
The Circus Man

```
        The Ghost Breaker
        The Making of Bobby Burnet
        The Man on the Box
        The Master Mind
        The Only Son
        Ready Money
        Where the Trail Divides
1915    After Five
        Armstrong's Wife
        The Clue
        The Country Boy
        The Fighting Hope
        A Gentleman of Leisure
        The Goose Girl
        The Governor's Lady
        The Marriage of Kitty
        Mr. Grex of Monte Carlo
        The Puppet Crown
        The Secret Orchard
        Snobs
        Stolen Gods
        The Woman
        Young Romance
1916    Betty to the Rescue
        Each Pearl a Tear
        Evil Eye
        Lost and Won
        The Love Mask
        Tennessee's Pardner
        Victoria Cross
        Victory of Conscience
1917    Golden Fetter
        Mormon Maid
        Nan of Music Mountain
1918    Less Than Kin
1921    Don't Tell Everything
1924    Changing Husbands
1925    The Night Club
```

293   DEMILLE STUDIO PRODUCTIONS
        The following is a list of films produced by the DeMille
Studio during its brief existence. As indicated, the distributor
was either Producers Distributing Corporation or Pathe.

```
1925    The Coming of Amos. Dir. Paul Sloane. PDC.
        Hell's Highroad. Dir. Rupert Julian. PDC.
1926    Braveheart. Dir. Alan Hale. PDC.
        The Clinging Vine. Dir. Paul Sloane. PDC.
        The Cruise of the Jasper B. Dir. James W. Horne. PDC.
        Eve's Leaves. Dir. Paul Sloane. PDC.
        For Alimony Only. Dir. William deMille. PDC.
```

Gigolo. Dir. William K. Howard. PDC.
Her Man O'War. Dir. Frank Urson. PDC.
Made for Love. Dir. Paul Sloane. PDC.
Red Dice. Dir. William K. Howard. PDC.
Risky Business. Dir. Alan Hale. PDC.
Silence. Dir. Rupert Julian. PDC.
Sunny Side Up. Dir. Donald Crisp. PDC.
The Wedding Song. Dir. Alan Hale. PDC.
Young April. Dir. Donald Crisp. PDC.
1927 The Angel of Broadway. Dir. Lois Weber. Pathe.
Combat. Dir. Albert Hiatt. Pathe.
Corporal Kate. Dir. Paul Sloane. PDC.
The Country Doctor. Dir. Rupert Julian. PDC.
Dress Parade. Dir. Donald Crisp. Pathe.
The Fighting Eagle. Dir. Donald Crisp. PDC.
Fighting Love. Dir. Nils Olaf Crisander. PDC.
The Forbidden Woman. Dir. Paul L. Stein. Pathe.
Getting Gertie's Garter. Dir. E. Mason Hooper. PDC.
A Harp in the Hock. Dir. Renaud Hoffman. Pathe.
His Dog. Dir. Karl Brown, Pathe.
Jim the Conqueror. Dir. George Brackett Seitz. PDC.
The Little Adventuress. Dir. William deMille. Pathe.
The Main Event. Dir. William K. Howard. Pathe.
Nobody's Widow. Dir. Donald Crisp. PDC.
On to Reno. Dir. James Cruze. Pathe.
A Perfect Gentleman. Dir. Clyde Bruckman. PDC.
The Rejuvenation of Aunt Mary. Dir. Erle. C. Kenton. Pathe.
Rubber Tires. Dir. Alan Hale. PDC.
The Rush Hour. Dir. E. Mason Hooper. Pathe.
Vanity. Dir. Donald Crisp. PDC.
White Gold. Dir. William K. Howard. PDC.
The Yankee Clipper. Dir. Rupert Julian. PDC.
1928 Almost Human. Dir. Frank Urson. Pathe.
A Blonde for a Night. Dir. E. Mason Hooper. Pathe.
The Blue Danube. Dir. Paul Sloane. Pathe.
The Bride of the Colorado. Dir. Elmer Clifton. Pathe.
The Cop. Dir. Donald Crisp. Pathe.
The Girl in the Pullman. Dir. Erle C. Kenton. Pathe.
His Country. Dir. William K. Howard. Pathe.
Hold 'Em Yale. Dir. Edward H. Griffith. Pathe.
The Leopard Lady. Dir. Rupert Julian. Pathe.
Let'er Go Gallagher. Dir. Elmer Clifton. Pathe.
Man-Made Women. Dir. Paul L. Stein. Pathe.
Midnight Madness. Dir. F. Harmon Weight. Pathe.
My Friend from India. Dir. E. Mason Hooper. Pathe.
The Night Flyer. Dir. Walter Lang. Pathe.
Sin Town. Dir. J. Gordon Cooper. Pathe.
Sky Scraper. Dir. Howard Higgin. Pathe.
Stand and Deliver. Dir. Donald Crisp. Pathe.
Tenth Avenue. Dir. William deMille. Pathe.
Walking Back. Dir. Rupert Julian. Pathe.
The Wise Wife. Dir. E. Mason Hooper. Pathe.
The Wreck of the Hesperus. Dir. Elmer Clifton. Pathe.

294   MISCELLANEOUS PARAMOUNT PRODUCTIONS
          Upon his return to Paramount in 1932, DeMille was involved
     in the following projects in addition to his own pictures.

     1941   Land of Liberty. A history of America composed of scenes
               from selected short subjects and feature films. Narration
               written by Jeanie Macpherson and Jesse L. Lasky, Jr.
     1958   The Buccaneer. A remake of DeMille's earlier film directed
               by actor Anthony Quinn.

295   FILM APPEARANCES
          DeMille played himself in the following films.

     1923   Hollywood. MGM. Dir. James Cruze.
     1930   Free and Easy. MGM. Dir. Edward Sedgwick.
     1942   Star Spangled Banner. Paramount. Dir. George Marshall.
     1947   Variety Girl. Paramount. Dir. George Marshall.
     1950   Sunset Boulevard. Paramount. Dir. Billy Wilder.
     1952   Son of Paleface. Paramount. Dir. Frank Tashlin.
     1956   The Buster Keaton Story. Paramount. Dir. Sidney Sheldon.

296   MISCELLANEOUS FILM FOOTAGE
          DeMille appears in the following miscellaneous film footage.

     1934   The Hollywood You Never See. DeMille directing scenes in
               Cleopatra.
     1935   Hollywood Extra Girl. DeMille directing a crowd scene in
               The Crusades (from the Paramount series, Paramount
               Varieties).
     1948   The Right to Work. DeMille testifying before House Committee
               on Education and Labor in 1947.
     1948   Aid to Nation. DeMille testifying before House Committee on
               Education and Labor in 1947.
     1948   History Brought to Life. DeMille comments on clips from his
               films (from the Paramount series, The Movies Are Better
               Than Ever).

297   LUX RADIO THEATER
          From 1 June 1936 to 22 January 1945, DeMille hosted and di-
     rected a weekly broadcast of radio programs based upon the plots
     of films previously released. A complete list of programs and
     titles is in The Films of Cecil B. DeMille by Gene Ringgold and
     DeWitt Bodeen. All the scripts for the radio programs are avail-
     able at the Margaret Herrick Library at the Academy of Motion
     Picture Arts and Sciences and in the DeMille Collection at Brigham
     Young University.

298   TELEVISION PROGRAMS
          The following television programs are about DeMille.

     1963   "The World's Greatest Showman." Introduction by Walt
               Disney. Written by Stanley Roberts and directed by Boris
               Segal. Televised on NBC.

1964 "Hollywood and the Stars: The Great Directors." Televised on NBC.

1981 "Ready When You Are, Mr. DeMille." Written and presented by Barry Norman. Televised on BBC and PBS.

299   TRIBUTES

1981 A Tribute to DeMille. Academy of Motion Picture Arts and Sciences, Beverly Hills, 24 August. Film clips, a screening of The Little American, and a panel featuring Jetta Goudal, Evelyn Keyes, Henry Wilcoxon, and Ron Haver to commemorate the hundredth anniversary of DeMille's birth.

1981 Cecil B. DeMille. Los Angeles County Museum of Art, 7 August-30 September. Retrospective screening of DeMille films to commemorate the hundredth anniversary of the director's birth.

1984 The deMille Dynasty. Library and Museum of the Performing Arts at Lincoln Center, April-October. Exhibit organized by Louise Kerz focuses on three generations of deMilles, especially Cecil and Agnes.

VII. Archives and Libraries

300   British Film Institute, 127 Charing Cross Road, London   WC2H OEA.
       01 437 4355
          Cecil B. DeMille
          Card catalog lists articles in periodicals, several of
          them British and a few French and Italian, from the teens
          to the eighties but with emphasis upon the fifties. Also
          listed are several books in English and French.

LOS ANGELES

301   Academy of Motion Picture Arts and Sciences, Margaret Herrick
       Library, 8949 Wilshire Boulevard, Beverly Hills, CA   90211.
       (213) 278-8990
          Clipping Files
              Clipping files under Cecil B. DeMille and the individual
          titles of his films consist of clippings from newspapers,
          magazines, and trade journals. Although material from the
          twenties and thirties is scarce, there is slightly more
          material from the forties and quite a bit more from the
          fifties, especially from Los Angeles newspapers.
              Clipping files exist for practically all of DeMille's
          pictures though content varies. As would be expected,
          there are more reviews and materials for the later films.
          Cecil B. DeMille Trust Collection of Still Photograph Books
          and Loose Still Photographs. Compiled by Robert Cushman.
              A list of films in alphabetical order specifies the number
          of 8" x 10" stills from each picture and whether the stills
          are loose or bound in volumes. Stills in other than 8" x
          10" size are specified as such. Collection totals more
          than 40,000 stills from all of DeMille's pictures as well
          as from some films not directed by DeMille.
          Paramount Collection
              An inventory compiled by Samuel Gill lists in alphabetical
          order for each picture, the release title and date and the
          type and quantity of material available. If no material
          was found in the folder for a particular film, this is

147

indicated as well. Depending upon the film, material for
DeMille's pictures include still books, loose stills in
folders, pressbooks, and script materials. Again, depending upon the film, the type and quantity of script material
varies and may include synopses, treatments, script drafts,
continuities, and like documents from the story department.
Some material is available for most DeMille Paramount films,
more for the sound than silent productions.

Pathe Collection 1927-31
   Financial statements include some production cost figures
   for Cecil B. DeMille Pictures Corporation, e.g., salaries
   of staff members; daily and weekly cost statements for
   pictures that are further broken down into figures for
   staff, continuity, camera, cutting, extras, and so forth;
   and royalty statements.

Scripts
   Films: The Buccaneer
           Cleopatra
           The Crusades
           North West Mounted Police
           The Sign of the Cross
           Union Pacific
   Lux Radio Theater
           All the scripts for the weekly broadcasts hosted
           by DeMille from 1 June 1936 to 22 January 1945 are
           available in bound volumes.

Stills
   Loose production and movie stills for practically all of
   DeMille's films are available and filed according to title
   of picture. Stills filed under Cecil B. DeMille are also
   available.

Note: Arrangements to examine material from the Paramount, Pathe,
and DeMille Still Collection should be made in advance. All other
materials are readily available.

302   University of California at Los Angeles, 405 Hilgard Avenue,
Los Angeles, CA 90024.

Film Archive, Melnitz Hall. (213) 206-8013
Appointments should be made well in advance. Safety film may
be viewed on 16mm or 35mm flatbeds. Nitrate prints must be viewed
on a flatbed in a separate facility located several miles away
from the campus at 1015 North Cahuenga Boulevard, (213) 462-4931.
   Films:
      The Affairs of Anatol
      The Captive
      The Cheat
      Cleopatra
      The Crusades
      Forbidden Fruit
      Four Frightened People

2

North West Mounted Police
The Plainsman
Reap the Wild Wind
Right to Work (DeMille's testimony before a House
    Committee on right to work laws)
The Sign of the Cross (one print contains the World War
    II prologue)
The Story of Dr. Wassell
The Ten Commandments prologue (1923)
This Day and Age
Unconquered (black and white print)
Union Pacific
The Whispering Chorus

303   University Research Library
          Special Collections
             Cecil B. DeMille 100, Box 92
                Contains undated notes from DeMille to Phil A. Koury,
                miscellaneous photos of DeMille and his colleagues,
                some production stills, typescript and galleys of
                Koury's Yes, Mr. DeMille.

304   Theater Arts Library
          Cecil B. DeMille Pamphlet File
          Contains clippings from newspapers and magazines.

305   University of Southern California, University Library, Archives
       of Performing Arts, Los Angeles, CA 90007. (213) 734-6058
       Appointments should be made in advance.
          Cecil B. DeMille Script Collection
             A gift from the Cecil B. DeMille Estate, this collection
             consists of bound volumes of scripts for all of DeMille's
             films. Several of the scripts for the sound films have
             frames from a print or negative of the film pasted to the
             pages. In addition to the scripts, the collection contains
             the following: research bibliographies for Samson and
             Delilah and Union Pacific; musical scores for The Greatest
             Show on Earth, Joan the Woman, Madam Satan, North West
             Mounted Police, Reap the Wild Wind, The Story of Dr.
             Wassell, Unconquered, The Ten Commandments (1956); the
             script for Land of Liberty; and one bound volume of letters
             regarding The King of Kings.
          William deMille Collection
             Collection includes playbills from the years 1896-1923 and
             materials pertaining to the theatrical career of Henry,
             William, and Cecil.

306   Museum of Modern Art, 11 West 53rd Street, New York, NY 10019.
       (212) 708-9613
       Appointments should be made well in advance to screen films.

Screening equipment includes 16mm projector and flatbed and 35mm projector in recently renovated facilities. A fee is charged for each film.
    Cecil B. DeMille Clipping File
    Films:
        Carmen (incomplete)
        Forbidden Fruit
        Male and Female
        Manslaughter
        The Sign of the Cross
        The Squaw Man (1914)
        The Ten Commandments (1923)
    Film Materials
        A card file indicates whether or not there is material about individual films either in folders or on microfiche, e.g. program notes, reviews, clippings, and the like.

307   New York Public Library, Manuscripts and Archives Division, Annex Section, 521 West 43rd Street, New York, NY 10018. (212) 930-0804
Researchers must first present two forms of identification at the Office of Special Collections in Room 319 to receive an admission card. Admission is restricted to qualified researchers and graduate students. Pencils must be used in taking notes.
    William deMille Papers
        Collection includes letters to Cecil about his decision to become a filmmaker, notes for articles about the motion picture industry, and copies of plays written jointly with Cecil: After Five, Church Play, The Royal Mounted, and Son of the Winds.

308   New York Public Library, Library and Museum of the Performing Arts at Lincoln Center, 111 Amsterdam Avenue, New York, NY 10023. (212) 870-1639
    Cecil B. DeMille Cage File
        Collection includes the director's 1916 contract with Famous Players-Lasky Corporation; correspondence regarding litigation about the motion picture rights of various plays after the sale of the DeMille Play Company; and a few miscellaneous letters.
    Cecil B. DeMille Clipping File
        Files include extensive clippings from newspapers and magazines, especially during the fifties.
    Cecil B. DeMille Scrapbook in Robinson Locke Collection
        Scrapbooks under Cecil's name as well as those of other members of his family contain clippings about his theatrical and early film career.
    William deMille Cage File
        Written permission to examine the file must first be obtained from Agnes deMille Prude. Address is available at library upon request. Collection includes eight letters

written by William to his wife upon his arrival in Los
Angeles in 1914. Letters contain information about Cecil's
filmmaking and the Los Angeles environs. Additionally
there are notes, lectures, and articles about the film
industry.
Film Materials
According to card catalog entries for individual films,
an assortment of material is listed. These include clipping files, loose and bound stills and photographs, press
sheets and pressbooks, reviews, programs, posters, and
references to material in various scrapbooks.

PARIS

309 Bibliothèque de l'Arsenal, 1 rue de Sully, 75004 Paris. 272-19-09
Researchers may apply for a day pass at the library but if ex-
tended research is necessary, applications for an admissions card
must be made at the Bibliothèque Nationale, 58 Rue de Richelieu.
Depending upon the length of time the card is valid, a fee is
charged. Researchers are limited to a certain number of call
slips per day.
Collection Rondel
Cecil B. DeMille Scrapbooks. Volume 1 (1920-1939) and
Volume 2 (1945-1959). Scrapbooks contain clippings from
French newspapers and magazines.
Film Materials
Clippings for individual films are available, but the films
are listed according to the French title. Conveniently,
Michel Mourlet's Cecil B. DeMille is in the library col-
lection and has a filmography with French titles.

310 Institut des Hautes Etudes Cinématographiques, Palais de Chaillot,
9 Avenue Albert de Mun, 75016 Paris. 627-06-32
Researchers are limited to a certain number of call slips per
day.
Cecil B. DeMille
The card catalog lists a number of articles and books
about the director in French and English.
Film Materials
Under individual film titles (in English), the card catalog lists articles that are mostly in French film journals
and popular magazines. A few are in Italian and English
publications. Except for the Biblical films, there is
little or no material for silent pictures. Sound films
fare better.

PROVO, UTAH

311 Brigham Young University, Harold B. Lee Library, Arts and
Communications Archives, Provo, UT 84602. (801) 378-3514
Cecil B. DeMille Collection
Donated by the Cecil B. DeMille Estate to BYU in 1977,
this mammoth collection consists of more than 1,100

archival boxes and more than 6,000 pieces of artwork. An exhaustive inventory has been compiled by James V. D'Arc and will be published in the future. Although several items do not necessarily belong under specified subject or date headings, the original sequential order of the documents and memorabilia has been preserved. Further, the filing of personal and business papers was not kept separate and these overlap. The final inventory will be cross-referenced to overcome these difficulties.

The following description is mostly based upon the classification system devised by DeMille's staff and retained by BYU. Some minor categories have either been omitted or compressed for the sake of convenience. The descriptions are by no means exhaustive and specify only those items which may be of interest to film researchers. The collection gives an indication not only of the range of DeMille's filmmaking activities but also his business and political interests. Additions may be made to the collection in the future.

Miscellaneous and Memorabilia

Contains such miscellany as clippings, reviews, interviews, stills, speeches, stockholders' reports, personal bank statements, political material, the diary of Henry C. deMille, form letters, shooting schedules, budgets and research for pictures, advertising and publicity materials. Memorabilia include stereoscopic viewers, rubber stamps, and photographs.

Family Memorabilia

Contains material about Henry C. deMille's theatrical career, including his plays.

Personal Files ca. 1926-58

Contains tax information; monthly receipts and disbursements; monthly and annual profit and loss statements; items about personal loans made to colleagues, friends, and relatives; personal and business correspondence and memos; life insurance policies; bonds; theater information programs; family genealogies; political correspondence; cost, gross, and profit for films made during 1924-38; papers regarding financial transactions; stock market quotes; receipts; birthday and anniversary cards; stock certificates; theater programs; papers about Paradise Ranch.

Autobiography Research Files

Contains research material accumulated for the writing of DeMille's posthumously published autobiography.

Death of DeMille

Several obituaries.

Early Scripts, Contracts, Clippings

Contains material relating to Henry C. deMille's theatrical career and Beatrice deMille's agency, the DeMille Play Company, e.g. revisions, plays, contracts, clippings, reviews, and publicity material.

Play Scripts
>   Contains story outlines, treatments, synopses, adaptations,
>   continuities, and scenarios of films or proposed films, as
>   well as plays and books.

Famous Players-Lasky ca. 1915-25
>   Contains material from the period when DeMille was under
>   contract to Famous Players-Lasky, e.g. contracts, produc-
>   tion memos, personal financial statements, film rental
>   statements, correspondence and telegrams, production and
>   theater receipts, salary schedules. There are miscellane-
>   ous items about the following films: The Captive, The
>   Golden Chance, Joan the Woman, Saturday Night, The Ten
>   Commandments (1923), Feet of Clay, and The Golden Bed.

DeMille Studio ca. 1925-28
>   Items are filed chronologically and within each year, in
>   alphabetical order. Contains miscellany such as exploita-
>   tion and publicity material; shooting schedules; production
>   memos; censorship statements; production budget and weekly
>   cost statements for pictures made at the studio but not
>   directed by DeMille; papers regarding business dealings
>   with Orpheum-Keith, RKO, and Pathe; board meeting minutes;
>   material about Famous Players-Lasky; bookings; contracts
>   with exhibitors; theater receipts; audience preview cards;
>   exhibition reports; foreign distribution materials; tele-
>   graphic files. Separate files exist for The King of Kings
>   and The Godless Girl.

MGM 1931
>   Items are filed alphabetically. Contains material about
>   Dynamite, Madam Satan, and The Squaw Man.

Paramount 1935-59
>   Items are filed chronologically and within each year, by
>   alphabetical order. Contains miscellany such as corre-
>   spondence, notes and memos; telegrams and nightwires; pub-
>   licity and censorship material; studio policies, bulletins
>   and operations memos; bills; story department items; Lux
>   Radio Theater material; clippings and film reviews, includ-
>   ing those of spectacles not made by DeMille; speeches;
>   production schedules; appointments; syndicated weekly
>   columns for General Features Corporation; tax information;
>   personal financial papers; production reports for various
>   spectacle films.

Miscellaneous Scripts
>   Scripts in various stages of revision and completion and
>   related materials are available for the following films:
>   The Buccaneer
>   Cleopatra
>   The Crusades
>   Four Frightened People
>   The Greatest Show on Earth
>   Land of Liberty
>   The Plainsman

Madam Satan
North West Mounted Police
Reap the Wild Wind
Samson and Delilah
The Sign of the Cross
The Story of Dr. Wassell
Paramount Sound Films
    For the films listed below, there are various miscellane-
    ous items though the same items do not recur uniformly
    for each film. The bulk of material for The Ten Commandments
    (1956) alone almost equals the holdings for all the other
    films. Items include miscellany such as scripts in differ-
    ent versions; production correspondence; research, adver-
    tising, and publicity material; shooting schedules; pro-
    duction notes and reports; materials about sound dubbing,
    sets and props, casting, extras, location shooting, special
    effects, budget and production costs, trailers, premiers
    and previews; reviews.
The Buccaneer
Cleopatra
The Crusades
Four Frightened People
The Greatest Show on Earth
Land of Liberty
The Plainsman
North West Mounted Police
Reap the Wild Wind
Samson and Delilah
The Sign of the Cross
The Story of Dr. Wassell
The Ten Comandments
This Day and Age
Unconquered
Union Pacific
Financial
    Contains check stubs, statements and cancelled checks,
    paid bills, ledgers, and tax returns.
Political
    Contains material about the DeMille Foundation, speeches,
    miscellaneous political literature.
DeMille Productions 1933-53
    Items are filed chronologically and within each year or
    two, in alphabetical order. Contains mostly material
    dealing with financial operations of Productions. Included
    are lists of holdings in real estate, oil, mines, stocks
    and bonds, individual companies; papers involving business
    investments and transactions, dealings with Paramount, in-
    surance, and taxes; monthly receipts and disbursements,
    profit and loss statements, bank statements, and minutes
    for Productions; material involving DeMille's estate in
    Laughlin Park, his yacht, The Seaward, and his ranch; led-
    gers and cash books.

General Correspondence 1946-48
    Items are listed alphabetically.
General Files 1933-34, 1943, 1949-51, 1941
    Items are listed alphabetically. Contains diverse miscel-
    laneous material, especially for Four Frightened People,
    This Day and Age, The Sign of the Cross, Cleopatra, The
    Crusades, and Samson and Delilah.
Unproduced Subjects
    Contains items regarding pictures which were planned but
    never produced, especially Rurales, Queen of Queens, and
    On My Honor.
Scrapbooks
    Approximately 495 volumes contain reviews for all of
    DeMille's films from American and foreign publications;
    some items are about DeMille's career.
Lux Radio Theater
    Contains correspondence, story suggestions, programs, cast
    lists, and tapes of the various broadcasts. Scripts for
    all the programs are also available.
Tapes
    Contains DeMille's speeches, interviews, and various pub-
    lic appearances. Some have been transcribed.
Photographs
    Collection includes more than 10,000 photographs that are
    movie or production stills or research photos.
Videotapes
    Videotapes of the following silent films are available:
    Adam's Rib
    The Call of the North
    Carmen
    The Cheat
    Chimmie Fadden Out West
    Don't Change Your Husband
    For Better, For Worse
    Forbidden Fruit
    Girl of the Golden West
    The Golden Bed
    The Golden Chance
    The Heart of Nora Flynn
    Joan the Woman
    Kindling
    The King of Kings
    Male and Female
    Maria Rosa
    Old Wives for New
    Road to Yesterday
    Romance of the Redwoods
    Rose of the Rancho
    Saturday Night
    Something to Think About
    The Squaw Man (1914)

The Ten Commandments (1923)
Till I Come Back to You
The Trail of the Lonesome Pine
Triumph
The Unafraid
The Virginian
The Volga Boatman
The Whispering Chorus
Why Change Your Wife?
The Woman God Forgot

Videotapes of the following miscellaneous items are available:
Location footage for Rurales.
Silent footage of the exodus scene from The Ten Commandments
(1956) being filmed on location.
Promotional trailer for The Ten Commandments (1956).
DeMille's testimony before a House subcommittee on right-
to-work laws.
Miscellaneous footage of Mercury Aviation Company's land-
ing strip.
Interview with Sheila Graham (1955).
Interview with Donald Hayne (1958)
DeMille's appearance on "This Is Your Life" starring Bebe
Daniels.
Clips from television newsreel footage about DeMille's
death.
"The World's Greatest Showman" televised on NBC (1963).
"Ready When You Are, Mr. DeMille" televised on BBC (1981).

ROCHESTER, NEW YORK

312   George Eastman House, 900 East Avenue, Rochester, NY 14607.
(716) 271-3361
Appointments for screenings must be made well in advance as 35mm
films are screened in the Dryden Theater. Separate facilities
exist for 16mm projection.
Films:
Adam's Rib
The Affairs of Anatol (Czech titles)
The Call of the North
Carmen
Chimmie Fadden Out West
Don't Change Your Husband
Fool's Paradise
For Better, For Worse
Forbidden Fruit
The Godless Girl
The Golden Bed
The Golden Chance
The Heart of Nora Flynn
Joan the Woman
Kindling
The King of Kings (silent version)

Male and Female
Manslaughter
Maria Rosa
Old Wives for New
The Road to Yesterday
Romance of the Redwoods
Rose of the Rancho
Saturday Night
Something to Think About
The Ten Commandments (1923)
Till I Come Back to You
The Trail of the Lonesome Pine
Triumph
The Unafraid
The Virginian
The Volga Boatman
The Warrens of Virginia
What's His Name
The Whispering Chorus
Why Change Your Wife?
The Woman God Forgot

WASHINGTON, D.C.

313 Library of Congress, Motion Picture, Broadcasting and Recorded
     Sound Division, The James Madison Memorial Building, Washington,
     D.C. 20540. (202) 287-5840
     Appointments should be made well in advance, especially if the
     viewing list contains several films. Graduate and undergraduate
     students must have letters from their professors. Facilities
     include both 35mm and 16mm flatbeds.
         Films:
             The Affairs of Anatol
             The Captive
             Cleopatra
             The Devil Stone (incomplete)
             Fool's Paradise
             Forbidden Fruit
             Girl of the Golden West
             The Greatest Show on Earth
             The Little American
             The Man from Home
             Manslaughter
             The Squaw Man (1914)
             The Ten Commandments (1923)
             The Ten Commandments (1956)
             The Trail of the Lonesome Pine
             Unconquered
             The Virginian
     Additionally, the Library of Congress has a number of films for
     which DeMille was credited as director general in 1915-17.

157

VIII. Film Distributors

314   Audio Brandon Films, 34 MacQuestin Parkway North, Mt. Vernon,
NY 10550. (914) 664-5051 and (800) 742-1889 (in New York) and
(800) 431-1994 (outside New York)
The Greatest Show on Earth
Manslaughter
Samson and Delilah
The Sign of the Cross
The Ten Commandments (1923)
The Ten Commandments (1956)

315   Budget Films, 4590 Santa Monica Boulevard, Los Angeles, CA 90029.
(213) 660-0187 and 0800
The King of Kings

316   Brigham Young University, Ed. Media Services, 290 Herald R.
Clark Building, Provo, UT 84601. (801) 374-1211 ext. 2713
The King of Kings

317   Cine-Craft Co., 1720 West Marshall, Portland, OR 79209.
(503) 228-7484 and (800) 547-4785
The King of Kings

318   Clem Williams Films, 2240 Noblestown Road, Pittsburgh, PA 15205.
(412) 921-5810
The Plainsman
Reap the Wild Wind
Unconquered
Union Pacific

319   Don Bosco Films, 48 Main Street, Box T, New Rochelle, NY 10802.
(914) 632-6562
The King of Kings

320   Em Gee Film Library, 6924 Canby Avenue, Suite 103, Reseda, CA
91335.
The Cheat
The King of Kings
The Road to Yesterday

321   Films Inc., 733 Green Bay Road, Wilmette, IL   60091.
       (312) 256-6600 and (800) 323-1406
           Dynamite
           The King of Kings
           Madam Satan

322   Images Film Archive, 300 Phillips Park Road, Mamaroneck, NY
       10543.   (914) 381-2993
           The King of Kings

323   Ivy Films, 165 West 46th Street, New York, NY   10036.
       (212) 765-3940
           The King of Kings

324   Kerr Film Exchange, 3034 Canon Street, San Diego, CA   92106.
       (714) 224-2406
           The King of Kings

325   Kit Parker Films, 1245 10th Street, Monterey, CA   93940.
       (403) 649-5573
           The King of Kings
           The Road to Yesterday

326   Lewis Film Service, 1425 East Central, Wichita, KS   67214.
       (316) 263-6991
           The King of Kings

327   MGM/United Artists, 1350 Avenue of the Americas, New York, NY
       10019, or 10202 West Washington Boulevard, Culver City, CA   90203.
       (800) 223-0933
           Dynamite
           Madam Satan
           The Squaw Man (1931)

328   Modern Sound Pictures, 1402 Howard Street, Omaha, NE   68102.
       (402) 341-8476
           The Greatest Show on Earth
           The King of Kings
           Samson and Delilah
           The Ten Commandments (1956)

329   Museum of Modern Art, Department of Film, 11 West 53rd Street,
       New York, NY   10019.   (212) 956-4204 and 4205
           Male and Female

330   National Film Service, 14 Glenwood Avenue, Raleigh, NC   27602.
       (919) 832-3901
           The King of Kings

331 Newman Film Library, 1444 Michigan Avenue, Grand Rapids, MI
49503. (616) 454-8157
The King of Kings

332 Paramount Non-Theatrical, 5451 Marathon, Hollywood, CA 90038.
(213) 462-0700 and (800) 421-4432
The Greatest Show on Earth
Manslaughter
Samson and Delilah
The Ten Commandments (1923)
The Ten Commandments (1956)

333 Roa's Films, 1696 North Astor Street, Milwaukee, WI 53202.
(414) 271-0861 and (800) 558-9015
The King of Kings

334 Select Film/Video, 115 West 31st Street, New York, NY 10001.
(212) 594-4450
The King of Kings
The Road to Yesterday

335 Swank
New York: 60 Bethpage Road, P.O. Box 280, Hicksville, NY
11801. (800) 645-7501 or call collect (516) 931-
7500
Washington, D.C.: 7926 Jones Branch Drive, McLean, VA 22102.
(300) 336-1100 or call collect (703) 821-1040
Chicago: 2777 Finley Road, Downers Grove, IL 60515.
(800) 232-2292 or call collect (312) 629-9004
St. Louis: 201 South Jefferson Avenue, P.O. Box 23, St. Louis,
MO 63166. (800) 325-3344 or call collect (314)
534-6300
Houston: 4111 Directors Row, Houston, TX 77092. (800)
231-2070 or call collect (713) 638-8222
Los Angeles: 6767 Forest Lawn Drive, Hollywood, CA 90068.
(800) 421-4590 or call collect (213) 851-6300
Cleopatra
The Crusades
Four Frightened People
North West Mounted Police
The Sign of the Cross
The Story of Dr. Wassell
This Day and Age

336 The Film Center, 983 K Street, NW, Washington, DC 20001.
(202) 393-1205
The King of Kings
Unconquered

337   Twyman Films, 4700 Wadsworth Road, Dayton, OH 45414. (513) 222-4014 and (800) 543-9594
         The King of Kings

338   Video Communications Inc., 6555 East Skelly Drive, Tulsa, OK 74145. (618) 583-2681
         The King of Kings

339   Welling Motion Pictures, 454 Meacham Avenue, Elmont, NY 11003. (516) 354-1066, 1067, and 1068
         The King of Kings

340   Wholesome Film Center, 20 Melrose Street, Boston, MA 02116. (617) 426-0155
         The King of Kings

341   Willoughby-Peerless, 115 West 31st Street, New York, NY 10001. (212) 594-4450
         The King of Kings
         The Road to Yesterday

Name Index

New York Public Library, 299,
  308
Nichols, Dudley, 56, 60
Noerdlinger, Henry S., 163
Nolli, Gianfranco, 175

Orme, Michael, 112

Paget, Debra, 70
Paramount Pictures Corporation,
  3-28
Paramount Pictures, Incorporated,
  61-70, 311
Paramount Productions,
  Incorporated, 57-60, 311
Paramount Publix Corporation,
  56, 311
Parrish, Robert, 241
Pathe Exchange, Incorporated,
  51-52, 293, 301, 311
Percey, Helen G., 117
Pereira, Hal, 69-70
Perlmutter, Ruth, 242
Peters, House, 7-10
Pickford, Mary, 25-26, 73, 149,
  215, 281
Pine, William H., 62-65
Pitts, Michael R., 256
Pomeroy, Roy, 45, 47
Poster, William, 132
Pratt, George, 227, 248, 291
Preston, Robert, 63-65
Producers Distributing
  Corporation, 50, 292

Quargnolo, Mario. 144, 184
Quigley, Martin, 108

Reid, Wallace, 15, 18, 22, 24,
  27-28, 40
Rennahan, Ray, 45, 67
Reynolds, Vera, 47-49
Rickey, Carrie, 260
Riesenfeld, Hugo, 51
Rieupeyrout, Jean-Louis, 193
Ringgold, Gene, 210, 297
Roberts, Theodore, 2, 5, 7, 12,
  19-20, 23-24, 30, 33, 36,
  38, 40, 45
Robinson, David, 150, 186, 205
Robinson, Edward G., 70
de Rochefort, Charles, 45, 120
Rosen, Marjorie, 228

Rosher, Charles, 32
Rosson, Arthur, 63-70
Rosson, Harold, 54-55
Roth, Lillian, 54
Rowan, Arthur, 138, 164

Sadoul, Georges, 229
Said, Edward, 264
St. Johns, Adela Rogers, 80, 82,
  87
Salven, Edward, 67-70
Sanders, George, 68
Sarris, Andrew, 190, 206
Schickel, Richard, 194
Schildkraut, Joseph, 49, 51, 59-60
Scorsese, Martin, 246
Second, Jacques, 234
Selwyn, Edgar, 12, 35
Shaffer, Rosalind, 97
Sherwood, Robert, 90, 216
Skinner, Richard D., 99
Sklar, Robert, 235
Smeal, Collie, 133-34
Smith, Frederick, 193
Solomon, Jon, 247
Spears, Jack, 215
Stallings, Laurence, 109
Stanwyck, Barbara, 63
Stein, Elliott, 261
Stewart, James, 69
Stothart, Herbert, 53-55
Stout, Archibald J., 45, 47
Struss, Karl, 38-41, 56, 58
Sullivan, C. Gardner, 62-64
Swanson, Gloria, 34-38, 40, 254
Sweet, Blanche, 8, 10

Talmey, Allene, 94
Tate, Cullen, 45, 57-58
Thomson, David, 257
Thorp, Dunham, 96
Turnbull, Hector, 17, 19, 21
Tyler, Walter, 67-70

Unger, Gladys, 53-54
United States Circuit Court of
  Appeals for the Ninth Circuit,
  106
University of California at Los
  Angeles, 302-4
University of Southern California,
  305

Film-Title Index